Fuzzy and Neuro-Fuzzy Intelligent Systems

Studies in Fuzziness and Soft Computing

Editor-in-chief
Prof. Janusz Kacprzyk
Systems Research Institute
Polish Academy of Sciences
ul. Newelska 6
01-447 Warsaw, Poland
E-mail: kacprzyk@ibspan.waw.pl
http://www.springer.de/cgi-bin/search_book.pl?series=2941

continued on page 195

Ernest Czogała† · Jacek Łęski

Fuzzy and Neuro-Fuzzy Intelligent Systems

With 66 Figures
and 16 Tables

Physica-Verlag

A Springer-Verlag Company

Professor Ernest Czogała†, Ph.D., D.Sc.
Professor Jacek Łęski, Ph.D., D.Sc.
Institute of Electronics
Silesian University of Technology
Akademicka 16
44-101 Gliwice
Poland
E-mail: jl@biomed.iele.polsl.gliwice.pl

ISSN 1434-9922
ISBN 978-3-662-00389-3

Cataloging-in-Publication Data applied for
Die Deutsche Bibliothek – CIP-Einheitsaufnahme
Czogala, Ernest: Fuzzy and neuro-fuzzy intelligent systems: with 16 tables / Ernest Czogala; Jacek
Leski. – Heidelberg; New York: Physica-Verl., 2000
   (Studies in fuzziness and soft computing; Vol. 47)
   ISBN 978-3-662-00389-3   ISBN 978-3-7908-1853-6 (eBook)
   DOI 10.1007/978-3-7908-1853-6

Physica-Verlag is a company in the specialist publishing group BertelsmannSpringer.
© Physica-Verlag Heidelberg 2000
Softcover reprint of the hardcover 1st edition 2000

Hardcover Design: Erich Kirchner, Heidelberg

SPIN 10762719   88/2202-5 4 3 2 1 0 – Printed on acid-free paper

To all who fought
for democratic transformations
in Poland after World War II

Preface

Intelligence systems. We perform routine tasks on a daily basis, as for example:

- recognition of faces of persons (also faces not seen for many years),
- identification of dangerous situations during car driving,
- deciding to buy or sell stock,
- reading hand-written symbols,
- discriminating between vines made from Sauvignon Blanc, Syrah or Merlot grapes, and others.

Human experts carry out the following:

- diagnosing diseases,
- localizing faults in electronic circuits,
- optimal moves in chess games.

It is possible to design artificial systems to replace or "duplicate" the human expert. There are many possible definitions of intelligence systems. One of them is that: an intelligence system is a system able to make decisions that would be regarded as intelligent if they were observed in humans. Intelligence systems adapt themselves using some example situations (inputs of a system) and their correct decisions (system's output). The system after this learning phase can make decisions automatically for future situations. This system can also perform tasks difficult or impossible to do for humans, as for example: compression of signals and digital channel equalization.

Fuzzy sets and systems. Before Prof. L.A.Zadeh introduced fuzzy sets, he worked on linear systems theory, and his papers and books are still the basis for modern control theory. In the early 60s, he concluded that classical theories had put too much emphasis on precision and could not describe complex systems. This can be formulated in the so-called principle of incompatibility: "...as the complexity of a system increases, our ability to make precision and yet significant statements about its behavior diminishes until a threshold is reached beyond which precise and significance (or relevance) become almost mutually exclusive characteristics." Succinctly this principle may be written as: "The closer one looks at a real-world problem, the fuzzier becomes its solution."

The real world is too complex and complicated to be described precisely. A reasonable model can be obtained using "fuzzy approximation". This alternative to classical approach is based on the observation that humans think using linguistic terms such as "small" or "very large" and others rather than numbers. To describe this concept in a natural language, Zadeh used fuzzy sets introduced by himself in 1965. The essence of fuzzy systems are conditional if-then statements, which use fuzzy sets as linguistic terms in premise and conclusion parts. A collection of these fuzzy if-then statements formulates the rulebase. This rulebase can be determined from human expert knowledge or alternatively generated from observed data (examples) automatically. The main advantage of such fuzzy systems is the easiness to interpret knowledge in the rulebase.

Artificial neural networks. Since humans can perform many tasks presented at the beginning of this preface better than the best machines, human brain has been of great interest for engineers. This led to perceptron in the late 50s and to artificial neural networks (ANNs) in mid 80s. ANNs were originally developed with a view to modeling learning and processing information in the brain. For the purpose of this book, the ANNs is an important tool in the arsenal of machine-learning techniques, rather than model of the brain. Prof. S. Haykin proposed the following definition of ANNs: "A neural network is a massively parallel distributed processor made up of simple processing units, which has a natural propensity for storing experiential knowledge and making it available for use. It resembles the brain in two respects: 1). Knowledge is acquired by the network from its environment through a learning process,
2). Interneuron connection strengths, known as synaptic weights, are used to store the acquired knowledge." In practice the majority of ANNs works on single-processor computers.

The most common mode of learning for both humans and ANNs is supervised. In this case we have some situations (examples) and correct decisions, which formulate a training set. If we have only situations without correct decisions, then ANNs can perform unsupervised learning, which is often called clustering. In this mode ANNs search for structures of data. Both types of learning will be used in this book for the construction of neuro-fuzzy systems.

Neuro-fuzzy systems. In most fuzzy systems fuzzy if-then rules were obtained from the human expert. However, this method of knowledge acquisition has great disadvantages: not every expert can and/or wants to share his knowledge. Artificial neural networks were incorporated into fuzzy systems forming the so-called neuro-fuzzy systems, which can acquire knowledge automatically by learning algorithms of neural networks. The neuro-fuzzy systems have advantages over fuzzy systems, i.e. acquired knowledge is easy to understand (are more meaningful) to humans. Like in neural networks knowledge is saved in connection weights, but can be easily interpreted as fuzzy if-then rules.

The most frequently used neural networks in neuro-fuzzy systems are radial basis function networks. Their popularity is due to the simplicity of structure, well-established theoretical basis and faster learning than in other types of artificial neural networks.

If the number of input variables is large then it is very difficult to apply neuro-fuzzy systems, because the input space is divided into a very large number of fuzzy regions in which one if-then rule operates dominantly (Bellman's course of dimensionality). The neuro-fuzzy system can be viewed as a mixture of local experts (rules operate dominantly in each region). To determine these regions clustering method (unsupervised networks) for input or input-output space is often used. Clustering has been employed for initialization of unknown values of neuro-fuzzy system parameters such as: a number of fuzzy if-then rules and membership function of linguistic terms from premise parts of these rules. In the next step these parameters are updated using gradient and least squares optimization methods. Recently global optimization methods are frequently used to update neuro-fuzzy system parameters. Connection of fuzzy systems, artificial neural networks, clustering and optimization methods is usually called soft computing systems.

Prerequisites and audience. The prerequisites for the book are basic calculus and algebra, at the level of an undergraduate course. Any prior knowledge of the human nervous system and nervous cells is of course helpful, but not required. It is assumed that the reader has a background in Matlab® system (produced and distributed by MathWorks, Inc.). The neuro-fuzzy system presented in this book was implemented as Matlab m-files in Appendix A included by the end of Chapter 6. Databases used in book for neuro-fuzzy system tests can be easy obtained via Internet. URLs are available in Chapter 7.

The book is aimed for use by the researcher who wants to learn basics and advanced concepts of neuro-fuzzy systems. It is also suitable for students of Computer Sciences, Electronics and Automatic Control. This book is also intended for use by biologists, economists and physicians. It is sufficiently simple for the reader to be able to implement the algorithms described in the book, or adapt them to solve particular problems.

Generals outline of the book. The book is divided into seven chapters. Chapter 1 provides an overview of fuzzy sets theory. The basic notions and terminology of this theory is presented: definition of fuzzy sets, basic types of membership functions, operations on fuzzy sets, fuzzy relations, cylindrical extension, projection of fuzzy sets and linguistic variable.

Chapter 2 is the most important theoretical chapter, since it lays the foundations for approximate reasoning principles. Different interpretations and an axiomatic definition of fuzzy implication are shown. In this chapter we also present the following: basic fuzzy rule of inference, composition and individual rule- based inference and approximate reasoning with singletons. The most important outcome of Chapter 2 is the presentation of specific equivalence of inference results using logical and conjunctive interpretations of if-then rules.

Chapter 3 focuses on an overview of basic topologies of artificial neural networks, main methods of learning in ANNs including back-propagation and its modifications. Gradient based and global optimization methods are also shown as well as optimization of the parameters which linearly depend on ANNs output.

In Chapter 4 unsupervised neural networks and clustering methods are recalled. Self-organizing feature map, vector quantization and its connection with clustering is presented. Moreover, this chapter contains the basic classical (non-fuzzy) algorithms for clustering, foundations for fuzzy clustering, possibilistic and conditional as well as cluster validity methods.

Chapter 5 is a warm-up chapter, to illustrate fuzzy systems. It presents the basic structure of fuzzy systems, Mamdani's, Takagi-Sugeno-Kang's fuzzy systems, and a system with parameterized consequents in fuzzy if-then rules. This chapter together with Chapter 6 forms the core of the book.

Chapter 6 contains an overview of neuro-fuzzy systems known from literature and Artificial Neural Network Based on Fuzzy Inference System (ANNBFIS) with parameterized consequents. A hybrid method of learning ANNBFIS, which is a connection of clustering, gradient and least squares methods, a proposal of classifier based on ANNBFIS and Matlab® m-files implementation of ANNBFIS are also shown.

Chapter 7 contains a selected list of applications of ANNBFIS to: chaotic time series prediction, classification, system identification, compression of signals, control and communication.

What is new and what is omitted in this book. In various sections of the book new, unpublished material was introduced or published (accepted to publish) but presented from a somewhat new point of view. In Chapter 2 a specific type of equivalence of inference results based on conjunctive (minimum, product) and fuzzy implication interpretations of fuzzy if-then rules is presented. This equivalence is based on new defuzzification methods. In Chapter 4 a new generalized weighted conditional fuzzy c-means clustering method is introduced. In the same chapter a new cluster validity index is presented. In Chapter 5 fuzzy inference system with parameterized fuzzy sets in consequence of fuzzy if-then rules is introduced. A special case where localization of fuzzy sets in consequence is determined as a linear combination of input singletons is described for selected fuzzy implications. This fuzzy inference system is used in Chapter 6 to construct Artificial neural network based on fuzzy inference system (ANNBFIS). The learning method which is a connection of clustering, gradient, least squares and some heuristic methods is used. A proposal of the application of ANNBFIS to classification with proof of convergence is also presented. At the end of this chapter deterministic annealing to ANNBFIS learning is proposed.

The material for the book had to be selected on the basis on our individual choice. Many important topics had to be omitted in order to stay within the assumed number of pages. We focused on algorithms for fuzzy if-then rule extraction from numerical data, so a fuzzy system with singletons as inputs was presented with special attention to detail. At the end of each chapter references with complementary interpretations can be found.

Acknowledgments. I am grateful to Prof. J. Kacprzyk from the Polish Academy of Science for his help and inspiration to write this book. This book has been supported by the Polish National Research Foundation and research of the Institute of Electronics, Silesian University of Technology. I would like to thank all the people who have provided feedback on early versions of the manuscript, especially Prof. J. Drewniak and Dr N. Henzel. T. Czogała was irreplaceable during the preparation of the English version of the manuscript. Dr N. Henzel and Prof. Czogała's children offered me moral support to finish the book after Prof. Czogała's death. My deep gratitude goes to my wife Iwona and daughters Izabela and Agata who showed patience and love during my work on this book, especially at weekends and holidays.

Jacek Łęski
Gliwice, December 1999

Contents

3 Artificial neural networks 65

(by J.Łęski)

4 Unsupervised learning
Clustering methods 93

(by J.Łęski)

1   Classical sets and fuzzy sets
Basic definitions and terminology

1.1
Classical sets

Classical sets are sets with crisp boundaries. Usually an ordinary set (a classical or crisp set) is called a collection of objects which have some properties distinguishing them from other objects which do not possess these properties. The individual objects in the collection called elements or members of the set (A), belong to (or are contained in) the set ($x \in A$). Note that all considered sets are subsets of the superset called a space or a universe of discourse X. Let $P(X)$ be a family or class of all subsets of the universe of discourse, i.e.

$$P(X) = \{A \mid A \subseteq X\}, \tag{1.1}$$

where symbol $\subseteq$ stands for the notion of containment.
Empty set $\varnothing = \{\}$ and the universe of discourse X belong to the family as well, i.e.

$$\varnothing, X \in P(X). \tag{1.2}$$

Class $P(\mathbf{X})$ creates the Boolean algebra with respect to the following operations:

$$A \cup B = \{x \in X \mid x \in A \text{ or } x \in B\}, \tag{1.3}$$

$$A \cap B = \{x \in X \mid x \in A \text{ and } x \in B\}, \tag{1.4}$$

$$\overline{A} = \{x \in X \mid x \notin A\}, \tag{1.5}$$

where $A, B \in P(X)$.
   Taking into account the above given operations, the following properties hold true:

1. $A \cup B = B \cup A$, $A \cap B = B \cap A$ (commutativity),
2. $(A \cup B) \cup C = A \cup (B \cup C)$, $(A \cap B) \cap C = A \cap (B \cap C)$ (associativity),

3. $A \cup A = A$, $A \cap A = A$ (idempotency),

4. $A \cup (A \cap B) = A$, $A \cap (A \cup B) = A$ (absorption),

5. $A \cup (B \cap C) = (A \cup B) \cap (A \cup C)$ (distributivity),

   $A \cap (B \cup C) = (A \cap B) \cup (A \cap C)$

6. $A \cup \varnothing = A$, $A \cap \varnothing = \varnothing$, $A \cup X = X$, $A \cap X = A$ (identity),

7. $\overline{(\overline{A})} = A$, $\overline{\varnothing} = X$, $\overline{X} = \varnothing$ (involution),

8. $A \cup \overline{A} = X$ (law of the excluded middle),

   $A \cap \overline{A} = \varnothing$ (law of contradiction).

Additionally, de Morgan laws hold:

$$\overline{A \cup B} = \overline{A} \cap \overline{B}, \qquad \overline{A \cap B} = \overline{A} \cup \overline{B}. \tag{1.6}$$

The characteristic function of set A can be written as

$$\chi_A : X \rightarrow \{0, 1\}, \tag{1.7}$$

so that

$$\chi_A(x) = \begin{cases} 1, & \text{for } x \in A, \\ 0, & \text{for } x \notin A. \end{cases} \tag{1.8}$$

Let as denote the set of all characteristic functions in X by $Ch(X)$ and

$$Ch(X) = \{\chi \mid \chi : X \rightarrow \{0, 1\}\}. \tag{1.9}$$

The class $Ch(X)$ creates the Boolean algebra with respect to the following operations:

$$\left(\chi_A \wedge \chi_B\right)(x) = \max\left(\chi_A(x), \chi_B(x)\right), \tag{1.10}$$

$$\left(\chi_A \vee \chi_B\right)(x) = \min\left(\chi_A(x), \chi_B(x)\right), \tag{1.11}$$

$$\overline{\chi_A(x)} = 1 - \chi_A(x), \tag{1.12}$$

where $\chi_A, \chi_B \in Ch(X)$.

It can be proved that the structures ($P(X)$, $\cup$, $\cap$, $^-$) and ($Ch(X)$, $\vee$, $\wedge$, $^-$) are isomorphic as Boolean algebras. It means that we may equivalently describe sets using intuitive model $P(X)$ operating with elements of the sets or mathematical model $Ch(X)$ operating with characteristic functions.

1.2
Fuzzy sets

In many situations the assumption of crisp membership or nonmembership of an object or element x to set A is too restrictive. For example, we can express the set of young persons as a collection of persons not exceeding 20 years of age (x = "age", A = "young person"). The dichotomous nature of the classical set classifies a person 19.99 old as a young person but not a person 20.01 year old. This classification coming from a sharp transition between inclusion and exclusion in a set, is intuitively inconsistent.

Contrary to a classical set a fuzzy set is a model of such a collection of objects in which an object needs not necessarily belong or not belong to this collection. It means that the transition from "belong to a set" ($x \in A$) to "not belong to a set" ($x \notin A$) is gradual rather than crisp. Such a transition is usually characterized by membership functions ranging from zero to one. The above mentioned membership functions enable modeling commonly used linguistic expressions such as "the person is young" or "the pressure is high".

Fuzzy sets proposed by Zadeh (1965) are uniquely described by their membership functions. Using membership function we can specify a fuzzy set as follows:

$$\mu_A\colon X \to [0, 1], \quad \text{or} \quad A\colon X \to [0, 1]. \tag{1.13}$$

A fuzzy set A in X is directly specified by the function $\mu_A(x)$ (or $A(x)$) or indirectly by a set of ordered pairs $(x, \mu_A(x))$ or $(x, A(x))$ where $\mu_A(x)$ (or $A(x)$) represent the value of the "grade of membership" of x in A:

$$A = \{(x, \mu_A(x)) \mid x \in X \}. \tag{1.14}$$

Zadeh (1973) proposed another notation for fuzzy sets:

$$A = \sum_{x \in X} \mu_A(x) / x, \tag{1.15}$$

for countable universe X (may consist of ordered or nonordered objects), and:

$$A = \int_X \mu_A(x) / x, \tag{1.16}$$

for uncountable X. The $\sum$, $\int$ signs denotes idempotent summation. For countable universe case this summation satisfies: $a / x + b / x = \max(a, b) / x$.

If the value of membership function is restricted to either 0 or 1 then A is reduced to a classical set and $\mu_A(x)$ is the characteristic function $\chi_A(x)$. Because fuzzy sets correspond to the classical sets both fuzzy and classical sets have the corresponding basic operations of union, intersection and complement.

Let $F(X)$ denote a family (a class) of all fuzzy subsets of the universe of discourse X, i.e.

$$F(X) = \{ \mu \mid \mu : X \rightarrow [0,1] \}. \tag{1.17}$$

It can be easily proved that the laws of the excluded middle and contradiction (complementation) are not fulfilled. Therefore the structure ($F(X)$, $\vee$, $\wedge$, $^-$) forms the so called de Morgan (or soft) algebra rather than Boolean algebra.

The support of fuzzy set A is a crisp set that contains all elements with positive membership degree:

$$\text{Supp}(A) = \{ x \in X \mid \mu_A(x) > 0 \}. \tag{1.18}$$

Another crisp set connected with fuzzy set is the core of set A:

$$\text{Core}(A) = \{ x \in X \mid \mu_A(x) = 1 \}. \tag{1.19}$$

A more general notion is α-level set (α-cut set) A_α. The α-level set is a crisp set that contains all elements with membership greater than or equal to α, i.e.

$$A_\alpha = \{ x \in X \mid \mu_A(x) \geq \alpha \}. \tag{1.20}$$

By putting strong inequality in (1.20) we obtain a strong α-level (strong α-cut) set. Hence the support is a strong 0-cut and the core is 1-cut sets.

A fuzzy set is convex if and only if (iff):

$$\underset{x,y \in X}{\forall} \ \underset{\lambda \in [0,1]}{\forall} \ \mu_A(\lambda x + (1 - \lambda) y) \geq \min \left[\mu_A(x), \mu_A(y) \right]. \tag{1.21}$$

Fuzzy sets (A and B) are equal iff:

$$\underset{x \in X}{\forall} \ \mu_A(x) = \mu_B(x). \tag{1.22}$$

Fuzzy set A is a subset from B ($A \subseteq B$) iff:

$$\underset{x \in X}{\forall} \ \mu_A(x) \leq \mu_B(x). \tag{1.23}$$

A fuzzy set is completely characterized by its membership function. We define usually used classes of membership functions:

1. Triangular with a, b, c parameters:

$$\mu_A(x) = \begin{cases} 0, & x \le a, \\ \dfrac{x-a}{b-a}, & a < x \le b, \\ \dfrac{c-x}{c-b}, & b < x \le c, \\ 0, & c \le x. \end{cases} \tag{1.24}$$

2. Trapezoidal with a, b, c, d parameters:

$$\mu_A(x) = \begin{cases} 0, & x \le a, \\ \dfrac{x-a}{b-a}, & a < x \le b, \\ 1, & b < x \le c \\ \dfrac{d-x}{d-c}, & c < x \le d, \\ 0, & d \le x. \end{cases} \tag{1.25}$$

3. Gaussian with m and σ parameters:

$$\mu_A(x) = e^{-\frac{(x-m)^2}{2\sigma^2}}. \tag{1.26}$$

4. Fuzzy singleton with x_0 parameter:

$$\mu_A(x) = \begin{cases} 1, & x = x_0, \\ 0, & x \ne x_0. \end{cases} \tag{1.27}$$

1.3
Operations on fuzzy sets

Although the set-theoretic operations (union, intersection and complement) possess some rigorous axiomatic properties, they are not the only possible ones to interpret the respective connectives of fuzzy subsets of a given set X. There are also other reasonable and consistent operations on fuzzy sets representing disjunctions (unions) conjunctions (intersections) and negations (complements).

By the below outlined approach to conjunctions, disjunctions and strong negations we can define the intersection ($\cap$), the union ($\cup$) and the complement ($^-$) of fuzzy subset A, B of X as follows:

$$\left(A \cap_T B \right)(x) = T\left(A(x), B(x) \right) \qquad \text{for all } x \in X, \tag{1.28}$$

$$\left(A \cup_S B \right)(x) = S\left(A(x), B(x) \right) \qquad \text{for all } x \in X, \tag{1.29}$$

where T (S) is any t-norm (s-norm), sometimes denoted as $\star_T$ $(\star_S)$;

$$\overline{A(x)} = n\left(A(x) \right) \qquad \text{for all } x \in X, \tag{1.30}$$

where n denotes a negation.

We will consider the class of intersection-union operators known as the triangular norms, i.e. t-norm T and t-conorm (s-norm) S operators considered as functions: $T: [0, 1]^2 \rightarrow [0, 1]$, $S: [0, 1]^2 \rightarrow [0, 1]$. The T serves as a basis for defining intersections of fuzzy sets while S serves as a basis for defining unions of fuzzy sets. Taking into account the properties of classical sets the following axioms may be accepted:

1. $T(x, 1) = x$, $T(x, 0) = 0$ for all $x \in [0, 1]$,   (boundary conditions),
   $S(x, 0) = x$, $S(x, 1) = 1$ for all $x \in [0, 1]$.

2. $T(x, y) = T(y, x)$ for all $x \in [0, 1]$,   (commutativity),
   $S(x, y) = S(y, x)$ for all $x \in [0, 1]$.

3. If $x \leq u$ and $y \leq r$ then
   $T(x, y) \leq T(u, y)$ for any $x, y, u \in [0, 1]$,   (monotonicity),
   $T(x, y) \leq T(x, r)$ for any $x, y, r \in [0, 1]$,
   $S(x, y) \leq S(u, y)$ for any $x, y, u \in [0, 1]$,
   $S(x, y) \leq S(x, r)$ for any $x, y, r \in [0, 1]$.

4. $T(x, T(y, z)) = T(T(x, y), z)$ for all $x, y, z \in [0, 1]$,   (associativity),
   $S(x, S(y, z)) = S(S(x, y), z)$ for all $x, y, z \in [0, 1]$.

More precisely a function $T: [0, 1]^2 \rightarrow [0, 1]$ is a triangular norm (t-norm) if and only if (iff) it satisfies the above written conditions 1. - 4. concerning T and a function $S: [0, 1]^2 \rightarrow [0, 1]$ is a t-conorm (s-norm) iff it satisfies conditions 1. - 4. concerning S. From the algebraic point of view T is a semigroup operation in $[0, 1]$ with identity 1, and, S is a semigroup operation in $[0, 1]$ with identity 0. The most important examples of corresponding t-norms and t-conorms are given in Table1.1. Graphically, these t-norms and t-conorms are presented in Figs. 1.1 to 1.12.

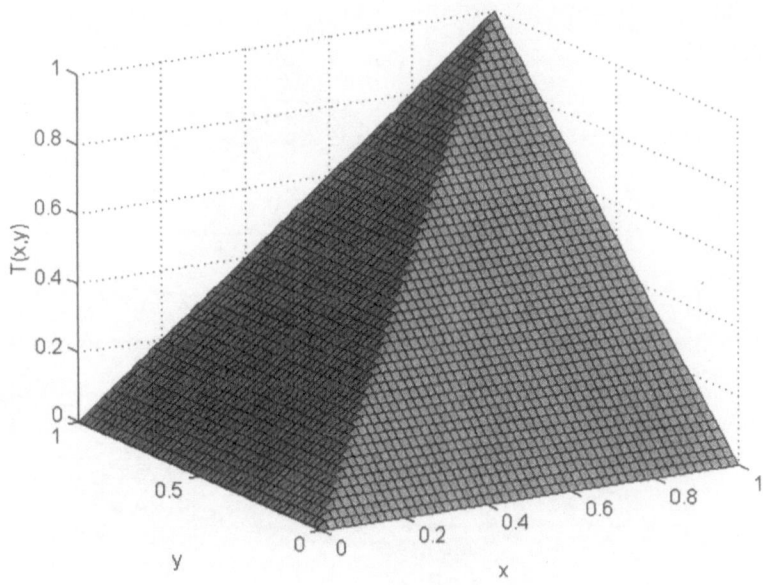

Fig. 1.1. Graphical illustration of Zadeh t-norm (minimum).

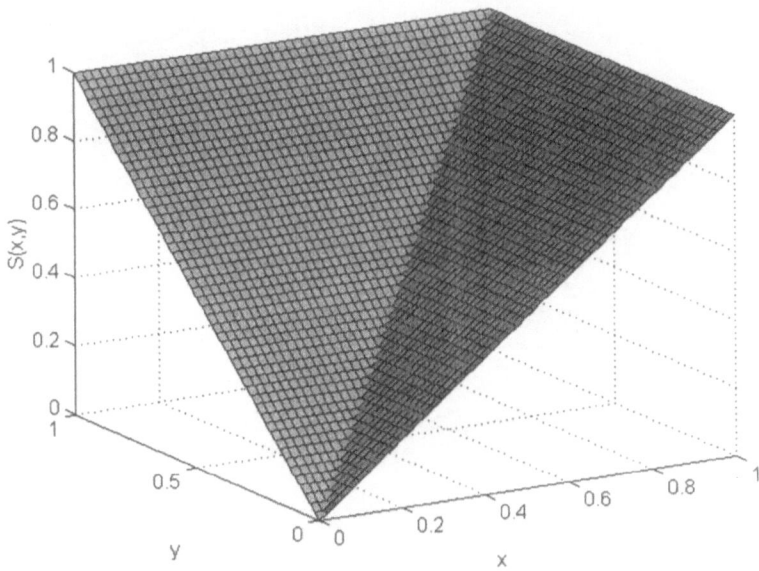

Fig. 1.2. Graphical illustration of Zadeh t-conorm (maximum).

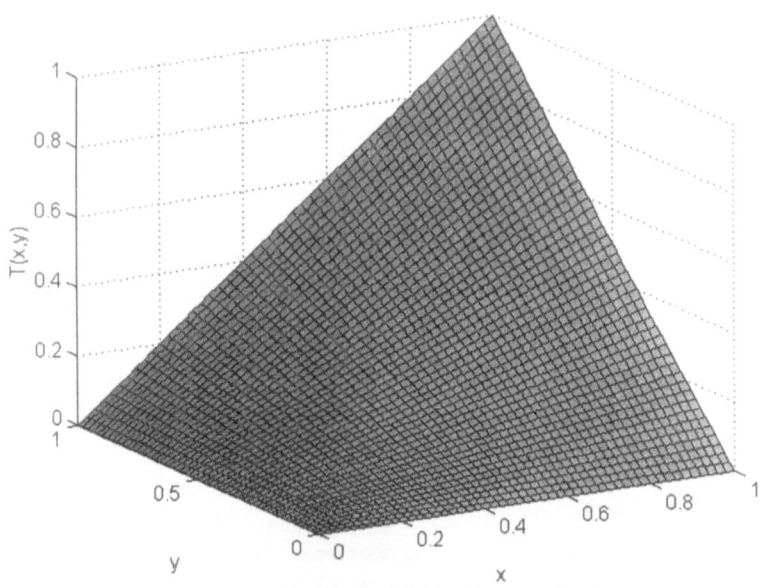

Fig. 1.3. Graphical illustration of algebraic t-norm.

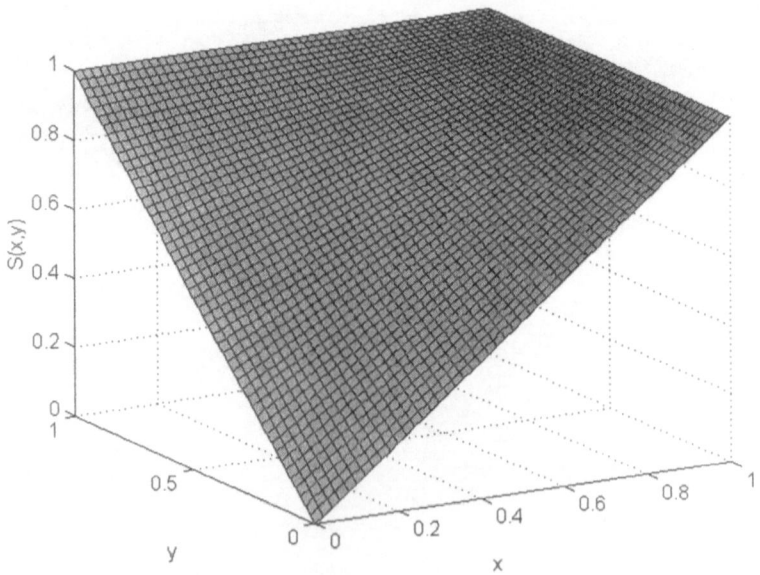

Fig. 1.4. Graphical illustration of algebraic t-conorm.

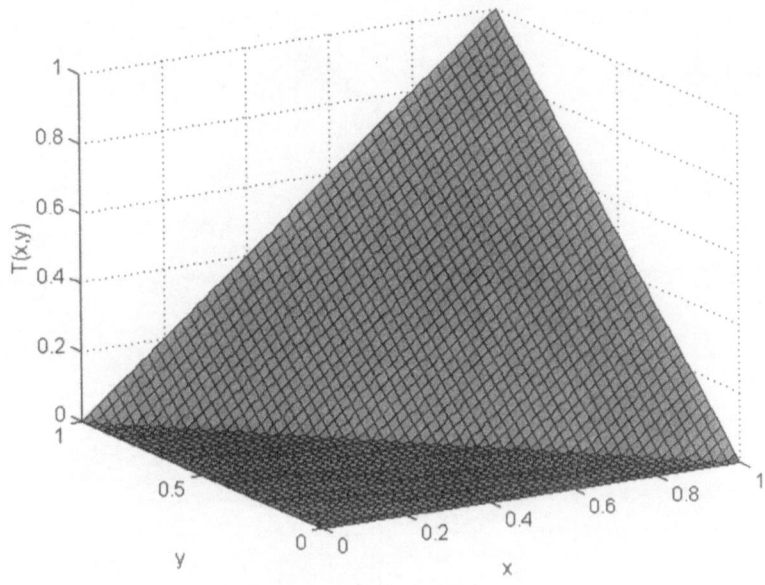

Fig. 1.5. Graphical illustration of bounded t-norm.

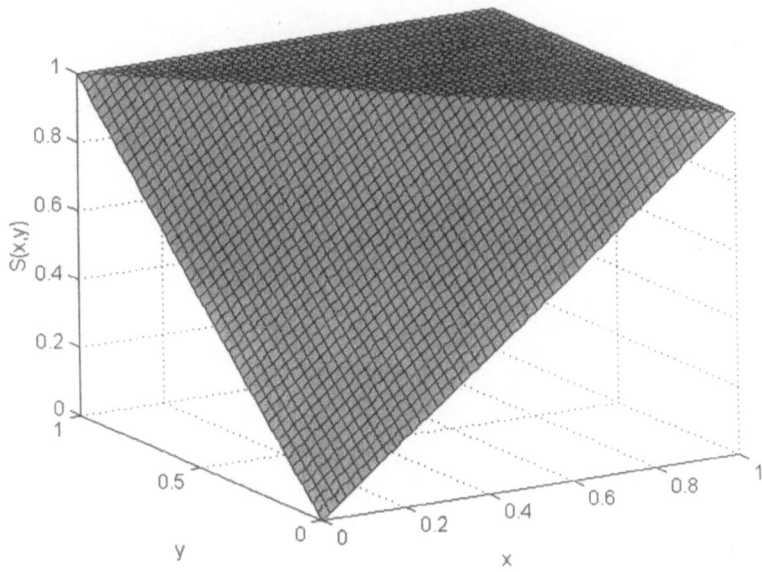

Fig. 1.6. Graphical illustration of bounded t-conorm.

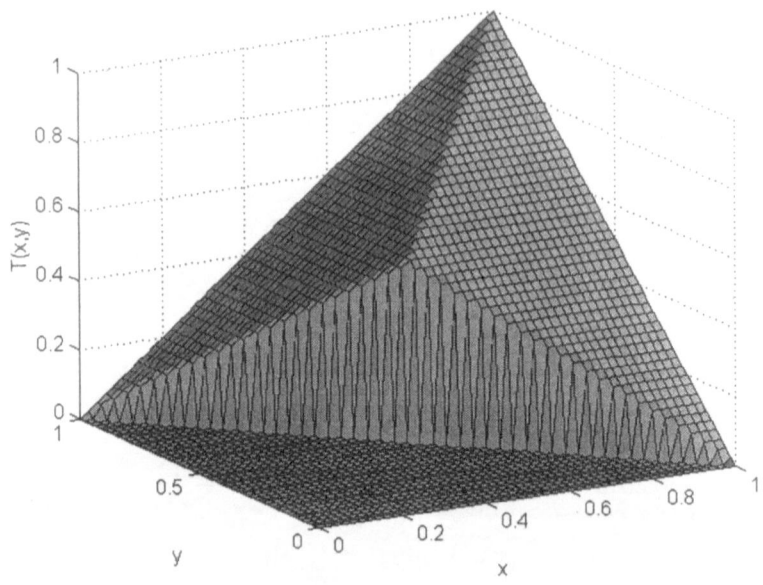

Fig. 1.7. Graphical illustration of Fodor t-norm.

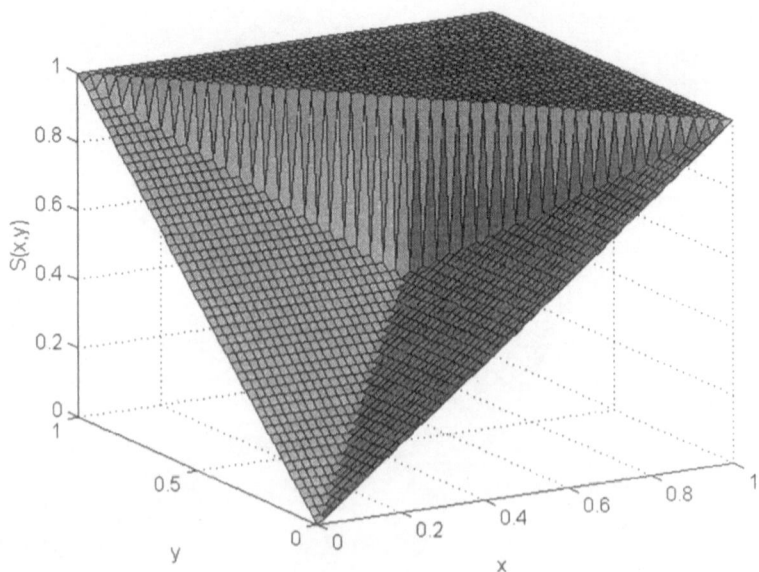

Fig. 1.8. Graphical illustration of Fodor t-conorm.

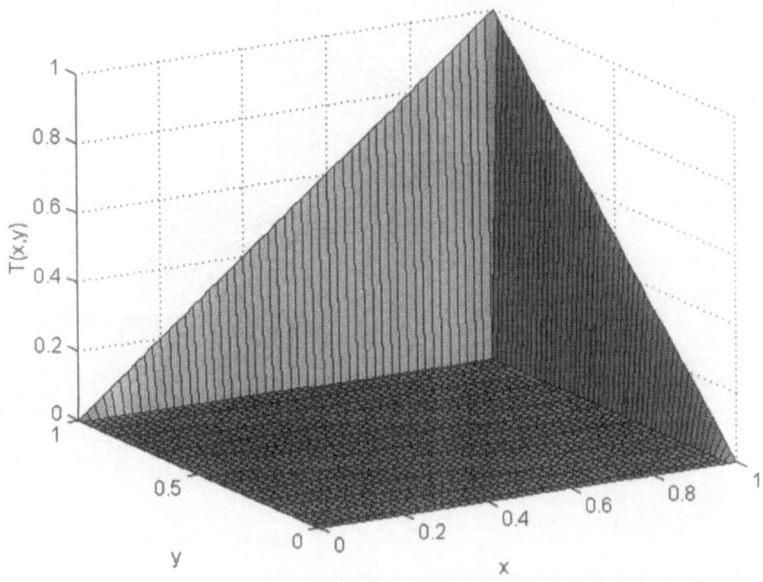

Fig. 1.9. Graphical illustration of drastic t-norm.

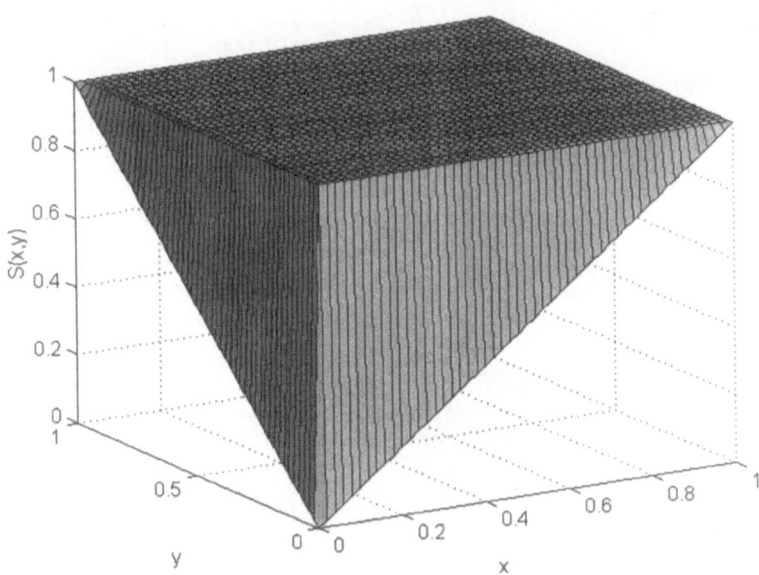

Fig. 1.10. Graphical illustration of drastic t-conorm.

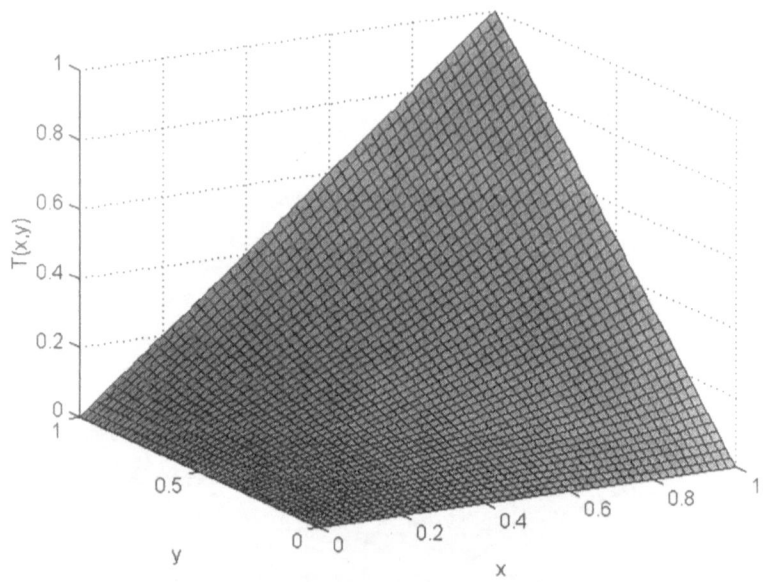

Fig. 1.11. Graphical illustration of Einstein t-norm.

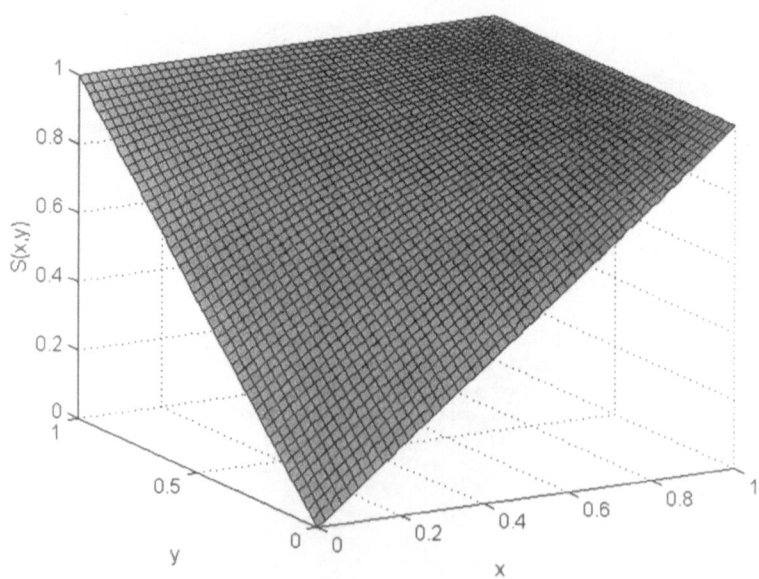

Fig. 1.12. Graphical illustration of Einstein t-conorm.

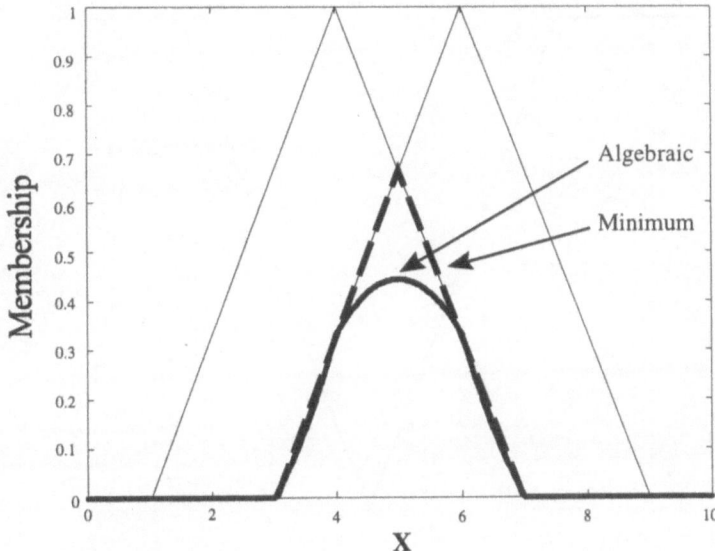

Fig. 1.13. Intersection operation between two fuzzy sets using minimum and algebraic
t-norm.

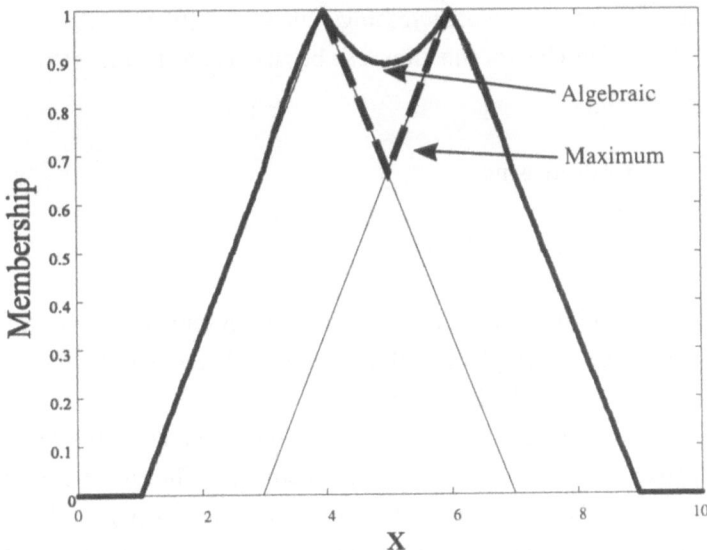

Fig. 1.14. Union operation between two fuzzy sets using maximum and algebraic
t-conorm.

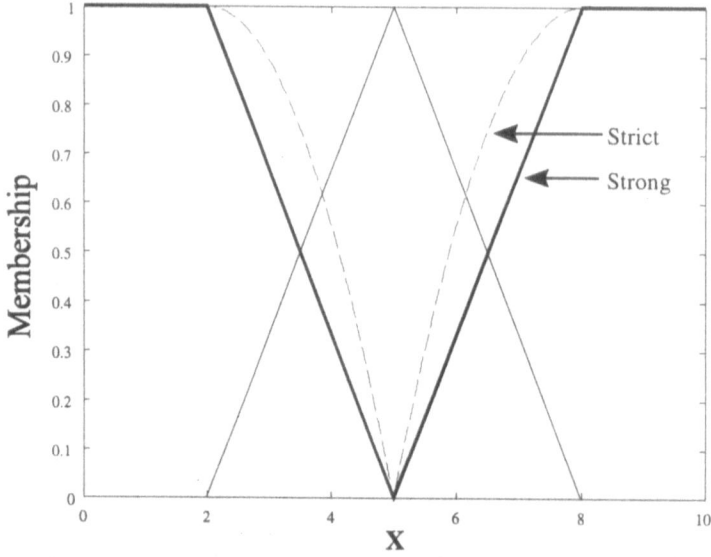

Fig. 1.15. Complement operation of fuzzy set using strict $(1-x^2)$ and strong $(1-x)$
negations.

Now we will discuss the complement of fuzzy sets. According to the minimal
requirements which are necessary to identify an operation called negation we can
postulate the existence of a nonincreasing function n: $[0, 1] \rightarrow [0, 1]$ such that
$n(0) = 1, n(1) = 0$. This class of functions can be clarified by taking into account the
following conditions:

(i). n is strictly decreasing,
(ii). n is continuous,
(iii). $n(n(x)) = x$ for all $x \in [0, 1]$.

We can define the following. A negation is strict if it satisfies (i) and (ii). A strict
negation is called strong if (iii) additionally holds. The specific strong negation
$N(x) = 1 - x$ is called a standard negation.

Since a strict negation is a strictly decreasing and continuous function its inverse
n^{-1} is also a strict negation (generally different from n). The equality $n^{-1}(x) = n(x)$
holds for all $x \in [0, 1]$ if and only if n is involutive, i.e. $n(n(x)) = x$ holds for all
$x \in [0, 1]$. This means the symmetry of the graph of the function n with respect to the
line $y = x$. Another property of a strict negation n is that there exists a unique value
$x_0 \in [0, 1]$ such that $n(x_0) = x_0$. Obviously, the equality $n^{-1}(x_0) = x_0$ holds as well.

The examples of set-theorethic operations using Zadeh and products t-norm for AND, t-conorm for OR and strong negation for NOT are presented in Figs. 1.13 to 1.15.

Table 1.1. Selected t-norms and corresponding t-conorms.

Name	t-norm	t-conorm
Zadeh	$M(x, y) = \min(x, y)$	$M'(x, y) = \max(x, y)$
Algebraic	$\Pi(x, y) = x \cdot y$	$\Pi'(x, y) = x + y - x \cdot y$
Bounded	$W(x, y) = \max(x + y - 1, 0)$	$W'(x, y) = \min(x + y, 1)$
Fodor	$\min_0(x,y) = \begin{cases} \min(x,y) & \text{if } (x+y)>1, \\ 0 & \text{otherwise.} \end{cases}$	$\max_1(x,y) = \begin{cases} \max(x,y) & \text{if } (x+y)<1, \\ 1 & \text{otherwise.} \end{cases}$
Drastic	$Z(x,y) = \begin{cases} \min(x,y) & \text{if } \max(x,y)=1, \\ 0 & \text{otherwise.} \end{cases}$	$Z'(x,y) = \begin{cases} \max(x,y) & \text{if } \min(x,y)=0, \\ 1 & \text{otherwise.} \end{cases}$
Einstein	$E(x,y) = \dfrac{x\,y}{2-(x+y-xy)}$	$E'(x,y) = \dfrac{x+y}{1+xy}$

1.4
Classification of t-norms and t-conorms

A t-norm T is

a). continuous if T as a function is continuous on $[0, 1]$ and

b). Archimedian if $T(x, x) < x$ for all $x \in [0, 1]$.

The t-norm M (see Table 1.1) is continuous but not Archimedian, Π and W are continuous and Archimedian, $\min_0$ is left-continuous and not Archimedian. The Z is not continuous but Archimedian.

A t-conorm S is

a). continuous if S as a function is continuous on $[0, 1]^2$ interval and

b). Archimedian if $S(x, x) > x$ for all $x \in [0, 1]$.

The t-conorm M' is continuous but not Archimedian, Π' and W' are continuous and Archimedian. The max_1 is right-continuous and not Archimedian. The Z' is not continuous but Archimedian.

Obviously, for any t-norm T and any t-conorm S the following inequalities hold:

- $Z \leq T \leq M,$
- $M' \leq S \leq Z'.$

Moreover, $W \leq \Pi$ and $W \leq min_0$ but Π and min_0 are not comparable in this sense. Also $\Pi' \leq W'$ and $max_1 \leq W'$ but Π' and max_1 are not comparable in the sense mentioned above. Better illustration of the above written inequalities can be obtained by means of an integrated index introducing a distance measure between the arbitrary operations $\star_1$, $\star_2$ in the interval $[0, 1]$.

Let $\star_1$, $\star_2$: $[0, 1] \times [0, 1] \rightarrow [0, 1]$ be measurable functions treated as two-argument operations in $[0, 1]$. The distance between the operations $\star_1$ and $\star_2$ with respect to their values of their argument is calculated as follows:

$$d(\star_1, \star_2) = \int_0^1 \int_0^1 |x \star_1 y - x \star_2 y| \, dx \, dy \qquad (1.31)$$

where $d(\bullet, \bullet)$ is pseudometric distance. For constant operations, i.e. $x \star_1 y = 0$, $x \star_2 y = 1$ for all $x, y \in [0, 1]$ we get $d(\star_1, \star_2) = 1$. Since constant operations differ from drastic operations Z, Z' only by boundary conditions, we also obtain the distance for drastic operations: $d(Z, Z') = 1$, where Z and Z' denote a drastic product and drastic sum, respectively.

Taking into account the min (M-norm) and max (M'-conorm) operations we can divide the $[0, 1]$ interval into three basic classes as follows:

- products $(Z \leq T \leq M),$
- averages $(M \leq \star_A \leq M'),$
- sums $(M' \leq S \leq Z').$

Note that the known averages belonging to the class of averages i.e.:

- arithmetic mean $x \star_a y = (x + y) / 2$ for $x, y \in [0, 1],$
- geometric mean $x \star_g y = (x \cdot y)^{1/2}$ for $x, y \in [0, 1],$
- harmonic mean $x \star_h y = (2 \cdot x \cdot y) / (x + y)$ for $x, y \in [0, 1].$

We calculate the distance between the following operations using (1.31), i.e.:

$d(Z, M) = d(M, M') = d(M', Z) = 1/3,$

$d(Z, \Pi) = d(\Pi', Z') = 1/4,$

$d(Z, W) = d(W, M) = d(M, \star_a) = d(\star_a, M') = d(M', W') = d(W', Z') = 1/6,$

$d(W, \Pi) = d(\Pi, M) = d(M', \Pi') = d(\Pi', W') = 1/12,$

$d(Z, E) = d(Z', E') = 3 - 4\ln(2),$

$d(M, \star_g) = 1/9,$

$d(M, \star_h) = 1 - 4\ln(2)/3.$

These and some additional known results are illustrated in Fig. 1.16. It should be also noted that the operations $\min_0$ and $\max_1$ are located within the interval [0, 1] as well.

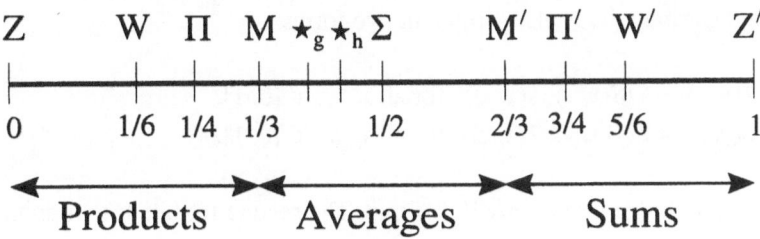

Fig. 1.16. Location of t- and s-norms within the [0, 1] interval.

1.5
De Morgan triple and other properties of t- and s-norms

As in the classical set theory, de Morgan laws establish a link between the union and intersection via the complementation. If a t-norm T, a t-conorm S and a strong negation n satisfy de Morgan laws as:

$$T(x, y) = n^{-1}\left[S(n(x), n(y)) \right] \quad \text{for all } x \in [0, 1],$$
$$S(x, y) = n^{-1}\left[T(n(x), n(y)) \right] \quad \text{for all } x \in [0, 1]. \tag{1.32}$$

then the triple (T, S, n) is called a de Morgan triple and T, S are called n-duals of each other. The t-norms and t-conorms introduced above are dual when considered with the standard negation $N(x) = 1 - x$.

Now let us make some remarks on the validity of classical properties such as idempotency, absorption, distributivity, the laws of excluded middle and contradiction in the case of triangular norms. Idempotency for T and S means that:

$T(x, x) = x$ for all $x \in [0, 1]$,
$S(x, x) = x$ for all $x \in [0, 1]$.

It can be proved (see Fodor and Roubens 1994) that T is idempotent if and only if $T = \min$, and S is idempotent if and only if $S = \max$. Absorption can be expressed as:

$T(S(x, y), x) = x$ for all $x \in [0, 1]$, and
$S(T(x, y), x) = x$ for all $x \in [0, 1]$.

The first form is proved if and only if $T = \min$ and the second form is true iff $S = \max$. Distributivity is also written in two forms:

$S(x, T(y, z)) = T(S(x, y), S(x, z))$ for all $x, y, z \in [0, 1]$,
$T(x, S(y, z)) = S(T(x, y), T(x, z))$ for all $x, y, z \in [0, 1]$.

The first form holds if and only if $T = \min$. The second form is true if and only if $S = \max$. The law of contradiction in a fuzzy case can be expressed in the following form:

$T(x, N(x)) = 0$ for all $x \in [0, 1]$,

where N is a standard negation. Examples of t-norms possessing this property are W, $\min_0$ and Z. The law of excluded middle in fuzzy case is expressed by:

$S(x, N(x)) = 1$ for all $x \in [0, 1]$,

where N is a standard negation. Examples of t-conorms satisfying the last conditions are W', $\max_1$ and Z'. The fulfilment of identity properties by t-norms and t-conorms is obvious.

1.6
Parameterized t-, s-norms and negations

In order to cover various types of set operations in fuzzy case the parameterized families of t-norms and t-conorms have been suggested. Let us recall some of such families (see Fodor and Roubens 1994):

1. The Frank family:

$$T_s(x, y) = \log_s\left(1 + \frac{(s^x - 1)(s^y - 1)}{s-1} \right),$$ (1.33)

$$S_s(x, y) = 1 - \log_s\left(1 + \frac{(s^{1-x} - 1)(s^{1-y} - 1)}{s - 1} \right)$$ (1.34)

for $s > 0$, $s \neq 1$ being a real number.
Specific t-norms can be obtained by taking limits for $s \to 0$, $s \to 1$, $s \to \infty$:

$$T_0(x, y) = \lim_{s \to 0} T_s(x, y) = \min(x, y),$$ (1.35)

$$T_1(x, y) = \lim_{s \to 1} T_s(x, y) = x \cdot y = \Pi(x, y),$$ (1.36)

$$T_\infty(x, y) = \lim_{s \to \infty} T_s(x, y) = \max(x + y - 1, 0) = W(x, y),$$ (1.37)

and t-conorm similarly:

$$S_0(x, y) = \lim_{s \to 0} S_s(x, y) = \max(x, y),$$ (1.38)

$$S_1(x, y) = \lim_{s \to 1} S_s(x, y) = x + y - x \cdot y = \Pi'(x, y),$$ (1.39)

$$S_\infty(x, y) = \lim_{s \to \infty} S_s(x, y) = \min(1, x + y) = W'(x, y).$$ (1.40)

2. The Schweizer and Sklar family:

$$T_p(x, y) = 1 - \left[(1 - x)^p + (1 - y)^p - (1 - x)^p (1 - y)^p \right]^{\frac{1}{p}}, \tag{1.41}$$

$$S_p(x, y) = \left[x^p + y^p - x^p y^p \right]^{\frac{1}{p}} \tag{1.42}$$

for $p > 0$.

3. The Yager family:

$$T_q(x, y) = 1 - \min\left(1, \left((1 - x)^q + (1 - y)^q \right)^{\frac{1}{q}} \right), \tag{1.43}$$

$$S_q(x, y) = \min\left(1, (x^q + y^q)^{\frac{1}{q}} \right) \tag{1.44}$$

for $q > 0$.

4. The Hamacher family:

$$T_r(x, y) = \frac{x \cdot y}{(1 - r)(x + y - x \cdot y)}, \tag{1.45}$$

$$S_r(x, y) = \frac{(r - 2) \cdot x \cdot y + x + y}{(r - 1) \cdot x \cdot y + 1} \tag{1.46}$$

for $r \geq 0$.

5. The Dubois and Prade family:

$$T_\alpha(x, y) = \frac{x y}{\max(x, y, \alpha)}, \tag{1.47}$$

$$S_\alpha(x, y) = \frac{x + y - x y - \min(x, y, 1 - \alpha)}{\max(1 - x, 1 - y, \alpha)} \tag{1.48}$$

for $\alpha \in [0, 1]$.

We can also order the above written families of operations with respect to the pseudometric distance mentioned earlier.

Let us recall some parameterized families of negations:

1. The Sugeno family:

$$N_\lambda(x) = \frac{1-x}{1+\lambda x},$$ (1.49)

for $\lambda > -1$.

2. The Yager family:

$$N_s(x) = (1 - x^s)^{1/s}$$ (1.50)

for $s > 0$.

1.7
Fuzzy relations

An important generalization of the fuzzy set notion is the notion of a fuzzy relation. We will consider binary relations because a generalization to multi-dimensional relations is straightforward.

Let X, Y be sets, then a fuzzy relation between X and Y is a fuzzy subset of Cartesian product $X \times Y$, i.e.:

$$R \in F(X \times Y),$$ (1.51)

or

$$R: X \times Y \rightarrow [0, 1],$$ (1.52)

or indirectly by a set of ordered pairs:

$$\{ (x, y), \mu_R(x, y) \}.$$ (1.53)

In general, a fuzzy relation is a set of ordered n-tuples:

$$R = \{ (x_1, x_2, ...x_n, \mu_R(x_1, x_2, ...x_n)) \mid x_1 \in X_1, x_2 \in X_2, ...x_n \in X_n \},$$ (1.54)

where $\mu_R: X_1 \times X_2 \times ... \times X_n \rightarrow [0, 1]$ is a membership function of relation. In Zadeh notation relation would have been denoted by:

$$R = \int_{X_1} \int_{X_2} \cdots \int_{X_n} \mu_R(x_1, x_2, \ldots x_n) / (x_1, x_2, \ldots x_n). \tag{1.55}$$

Fuzzy relations are obviously fuzzy sets in product spaces. Therefore set-theoretic and algebraic operations can be defined for them in analogy to the definitions introduced above.

Fuzzy relations defined in product spaces can be combined through a supremum-T-norm (sup-T-norm) composition operation. Let R_1 and R_2 be two fuzzy relations defined on $X \times Y$ and $Y \times Z$. The sup-T-norm composition of R_1 and R_2 is relation $R_1 \circ R_2$ defined on $X \times Z$:

$$R_1 \circ R_2 = \{ \, [\, (x, z), \sup_{y \in Y} T(\mu_{R_1}(x, y), \mu_{R_2}(y, z)) \,] \mid x \in X, y \in Y, z \in Z \, \}, \tag{1.56}$$

or, directly:

$$\mu_{R_1 \circ R_2}(x, z) = \sup_{y \in Y} T(\mu_{R_1}(x, y), \mu_{R_2}(y, z)). \tag{1.57}$$

For finite spaces a supremum operator can be changed by a maximum operator and the relation can be expressed as a matrix. In this case composition (1.56) can be described as matrix multiplication with •, + operations replaced by t-norm and max, respectively. Usually the min or product as t-norm T are used.

Let R_3 be a fuzzy relation on $Z \times U$, additionally to previous definition. We can easily proved (see Fodor and Roubens 1994) the associativity:

$$R_1 \circ (R_2 \circ R_3) = (R_1 \circ R_2) \circ R_3, \tag{1.58}$$

and monotonicity:

$$\text{if } R_1 \subseteq R_1' \text{ then } R_1 \circ R_2 \subseteq R_1' \circ R_2. \tag{1.59}$$

In his paper Zadeh (1971) introduced and investigated fuzzy similarity and fuzzy orderings relations.

1.8
Cylindrical extension and projection of fuzzy sets

Cylindrical extension and projection are the two notions important for considering future operations on fuzzy sets (and relations). Let A be a fuzzy set defined on X, then its cylindrical extension in $X \times Y$ is a fuzzy set $Ce(A)$ defined by:

$$Ce(A) = \int_{X \times Y} \mu_A(x) / (x, y). \tag{1.60}$$

In a multi-dimensional case we have set A defined on $\underline{X} = X_1 \times X_2 \times ... \times X_n$ and cylindrical extension in $\underline{X} \times \underline{Y}$ ($\underline{Y} = Y_1 \times Y_2 \times ... \times Y_m$) defined by:

$$Ce(A) = \int_{\underline{X} \times \underline{Y}} \mu_A(x_1, x_2, ... x_n) / (x_1, x_2, ... x_n, y_1, y_2, ... y_m). \tag{1.61}$$

Cylindrical extension is a method of extending an n-dimensional fuzzy set to $(n+m)$-dimensional ones.

Projection operation is in some sense opposite to the above mentioned operation. Let B be a $(n+m)$-dimensional fuzzy set defined on $\underline{X} \times \underline{Y}$, then the projection of B onto $\underline{X}$ is defined by:

$$\text{Proj}_{\underline{X}}(B) = \int_{\underline{X}} \sup_{y_1, y_2, ..., y_m} \mu_B(x_1, x_2, ..., x_n, y_1, y_2, ..., y_m) / (x_1, x_2, ..., x_n). \tag{1.62}$$

In a two-dimensional case we have set B defined on $X \times Y$ and projection of B on X described as:

$$\text{Proj}_{\mathbf{X}}(B) = \int_X \sup_y \mu_B(x, y) / x. \tag{1.63}$$

1.9
Extension principle

The basic concept of fuzzy set theory is the extension principle that allows the extension of the function domain from crisp points to fuzzy set. Mapping from point-to-point is extended to mapping between sets. Let $A_1, A_2, ..., A_n$ be fuzzy sets, defined on $X_1, X_2, ..., X_n$ and g be a function from $X_1 \times X_2 \times ... \times X_n$ to Y. Hence, $y = g(x_1, x_2, ..., x_n)$. The extension of g such that it operates on $A_1, A_2, ..., A_n$ and returns a fuzzy set B on Y is:

$$\mu_B(y) = \bigstar_S \atop \{(x_1, ... x_n) | g(x_1, ... x_n) = y\} \quad [\mu_{A_1}(x_1) \star_T ... \star_T \mu_{A_n}(x_n)], \tag{1.64}$$

if $g^{-1}(y)$ exists, and $\mu_B(y) = 0$ otherwise.

The $\bigstar_S$, $\star_T$ are s-norm S and t-norm T, respectively.

1.10
Linguistic variable

At the end of this chapter let us recall two important notions, i.e. the notion of a linguistic variable and the notion of a fuzzy rule. Formally, a linguistic variable can be considered as quintuple (see Zadeh 1973):

$$L = (N, \; L(G), \; X, \; G, \; M), \tag{1.65}$$

where N stands for the name of the variable, $L(G)$ denotes the family of labels of fuzzy sets in a given universe of discourse (the language generated by grammar G), X is a universe of discourse, G means syntactic rules defined by a grammar that defines all propositions in $L(G)$. M stands for semantics of the variable which is represented in the form of the mapping $M: L(G) \rightarrow F(X)$, that assigns to each string in $L(G)$ the corresponding fuzzy set in X ($F(X)$ denotes a family of fuzzy sets in X). If we denote a finite collection of basic (generic) linguistic terms (e.g. small, medium, big and so on) by $T = \{t_1, t_2, ..., t_l\}$ we can also construct linguistic modifiers (hedges) which may be applied to the elements of T (e.g. very small, more or less big etc.). We may consider a finite set of such modifiers $H = \{h_1, h_2, ..., h_j\}$. The task of the modifiers is to modify the original membership functions in a mathematical way.

Two main methods of building modifiers are exploited:

1. the modifiers affect the membership functions by using their exponents, i.e.

$$h(A) \, (x) = \left[A(x) \right]^p \quad \text{for } p > 0, \tag{1.66}$$

where h denotes the linguistic modifier (header). Depending on the exponent value, the modifier gives rise to a concentration ($p > 1$) or dilution ($p < 1$). In particular, we get:
- "very" $h(A)(x) = A^2(x)$,
- "more or less" $h(A)(x) = A^{0.5}(x)$.

2. the modifier shifts the original membership function to the left or right along the universe of discourse:

$$h(A)(x) = A(x \pm \tau). \tag{1.67}$$

These two constructions can be combined into a two-parametric class, i.e.:

$$h(A)(x) = [A(x \pm \tau)]^p. \tag{1.68}$$

The syntax of the linguistic variable is given by a context-free grammar G defined as the quadruple:

$$G = (V, \Sigma, P, \sigma), \tag{1.69}$$

where V and Σ are sets of terminal and nonterminal symbols, respectively. P stands for the set of productions (production rules) and σ denotes an initial symbol. The set of terminal symbols V consists of primary terms t_i and modifiers h_i, i.e.: $V = \{t_1, t_2, ..., t_I, h_1, h_2,..., h_J\}$.

The set of nonterminal symbols Σ contains all symbols used in the productions:

$$\Sigma = \{\sigma, \langle \text{expression} \rangle, \langle \text{simple\_expresion} \rangle\}. \tag{1.70}$$

The set of productions P represented in the BNF notation is written in the form:

$$\begin{aligned}
&\sigma ::= \langle \text{expression} \rangle, \\
&\langle \text{expression} \rangle ::= \langle \text{simple\_expression} \rangle \mid \langle \text{expression} \rangle, \\
&\langle \text{simple\_expression} \rangle ::= t_i \mid h_j\, t_i, \qquad i = 1, 2, ..., I; \quad j = 1, 2, ..., J.
\end{aligned} \tag{1.71}$$

Now let us consider the last notion of this chapter, i.e. a fuzzy conditional rule. In general, a fuzzy conditional rule is made up of a premise and conclusion. It can be written in the following form:

$$\textbf{IF } \underline{\text{premise}} \textbf{ THEN } \underline{\text{conclusion}}. \tag{1.72}$$

The premise is made up of a number of fuzzy propositions P_i (henceforth also called antecedents) of the general form (e.g. Tom is young) that may be negated or combined by different operators such as "AND" or "OR", computed with t-norms or t-conorms. In the example "Tom is young" Tom is the value of the linguistic variable defined in the universe of discourse of men and young is one of the names of the term set of the linguistic variable (e.g. {young, middle_aged, old}). The following is an example of a fuzzy conditional rule using such operators:

$$\text{IF } P_1 \text{ and } P_2 \text{ or } P_3 \text{ THEN } P_4,$$

where: $P_1 = (\text{error is small})$,
   $P_2 = (\text{change\_in\_error is average})$,
   $P_3 = (\text{change\_in\_error is high})$,
   $P_4 = (\text{control\_action is medium})$.

1.11
Summary

In this chapter we have recalled the following:

- the definition of classical set, its characteristic function and basic operations, such as: union, intersection and complement,
- the definition of a fuzzy set, meaning of membership functions and basic concepts associated with a fuzzy set, such as: support, core, α-cut, convexity, equality and inclusion of fuzzy sets,
- basic types of membership functions, operations on fuzzy sets (union, intersection and complement),
- fuzzy sets operations as t-norms, s-norms, its classification and some important properties,
- parameterized t-norms, s-norms and negations,
- fuzzy relations, cylindrical extension and projection of fuzzy sets; extension principle,
- linguistic variable at the end of the chapter.

Bibliographical notes

The best source material to learn fuzzy sets concepts is Zadeh's original paper (Zadeh 1965). There are many good books devoted to fuzzy sets. Examples include Pedrycz (1993), Zimmermann (1985), Wang (1998), Berkan and Trubatch (1997).

Some other creative and inspiring papers on multi-value and fuzzy logic are: Łukasiewicz (1963), Zadeh (1968), Zadeh (1971), Zadeh (1978), Zadeh (1996), Zadeh (1997), Dubois and Prade (1991), Dubois et al. (1991), Giles (1976), Kacprzyk and Iwański (1992), Rasiowa (1992).

For an exposition of fuzzy connectives the reader may consult Fodor (1993), Fodor and Roubens (1994), Fodor (1993a), Jeneri and Fodor (1998).

The Zadeh (1978a) paper was introduced fuzzy sets as a basis for a theory of possibility. For sisterly rough set theory see Pawlak (1991), Pawlak (1992). As an example of the association of fuzzy and rough set theories the reader may see Czogała et al. (1995). For interesting concept of shadowed sets see Pedrycz (1998b).

Applications of fuzzy logic were collected in Hirota (1993), Chen (1996), Kartalopoulos (1996), Kosko (1997).

2 Approximate reasoning

2.1
Interpretation of fuzzy conditional statement

A fuzzy conditional statement (or conditional rule, or fuzzy if-then rule) assumes the form:

$$\text{IF } X \text{ is } A \text{ THEN } Y \text{ is } B, \qquad (2.1)$$

where A and B are linguistic values of linguistic variables X and Y, defined by fuzzy sets A and B, respectively. Proposition "X is A" is called the premise or antecedent, and "Y is B" is called conclusion or consequence. In classical logic the statement "if P then Q" is written with implication $P \Rightarrow Q$. Implication is a connective defined by Table 2.1.

Table 2.1. Truth table for $P \rightarrow Q$

P	Q	$P \Rightarrow Q$
0	0	1
0	1	1
1	0	0
1	1	1

where "0" denotes false and "1" truth for propositions from the above table. From this table we see that $P \Rightarrow Q$ is equivalent to:

$$\neg P \lor Q, \quad (\text{not } (P) \text{ or } Q), \qquad (2.2)$$

and

$$(P \land Q) \lor \neg(P), \quad ((P \text{ and } Q) \text{ or not}(P)) \qquad (2.3)$$

in the sense that they make the same truth tables. In other words, the statements $P \Rightarrow Q$, (2.2) and (2.3) in classical logic are equivalent. This is not true in case of fuzzy logic, when we can interpret the fuzzy if-then rules by transformation NOT, AND, OR to fuzzy complement, fuzzy union (t-conorm), fuzzy intersection (t-norm), respectively.

There is a variety of fuzzy unions, intersections and complements, and different interpretations of fuzzy if-then rules are possible. For example in fuzzy logic expressions:

$$N\big(\mu_A(x)\big) \star_S \mu_B(y),\tag{2.4}$$

and

$$\big(\mu_A(x) \star_T \mu_B(y)\big) \star_S N\big(\mu_B(y)\big),\tag{2.5}$$

are generally not equivalent; $\star_T$, $\star_S$ are t-norm T and t-conorm S.

The above expression describes a relation between variables X and Y. A fuzzy if-then rule may be defined as a binary relation R of product space $X \times Y$:

$$A \Rightarrow B = R.\tag{2.6}$$

This relation is called the fuzzy implication. An axiomatic approach to fuzzy implications is presented in the next section. This is a logical interpretation of if-then rules. The second interpretation of if-then rules is a conjunction interpretation. In this case an if-then rule is defined by the relation:

$$A \Rightarrow B = R = A \star_T B.\tag{2.7}$$

The minimum (Mamdani) and product (Larsen) t-norms T are commonly used.

An investigation of inference processes when premises and/or conclusions in if-then rules are fuzzy is still a subject of many papers (see Fodor 1991; Fodor and Roubens 1994; Kerre 1992; Maeda 1996; Yager 1996; Dubois and Prade 1996). In such processes, a sound and proper choice of logical operators plays an essential role. The theoretical (mathematical) and the practical (computational) behavior of logical operators in inference processes has to be known before such a choice is made. Both types of the above mentioned knowledge related to well-known families of triangular norms and implications can also be found in literature (Weber 1983; Fodor and Roubens 1994).

Some selected logical operators and fuzzy implications were also investigated with respect to their behavior in the inference processes. On one hand the fuzzy if-then rules have a conjunction interpretation and on the other hand the interpretation in terms of classical logical implication. The inference algorithms based on conjunctive implication interpretation of if-then rules were simpler and faster with relation to algorithms used for the logical interpretation of such rules. Additionally, the application of conjunctive implication interpretation of if-then rules leads to intuitively better inference results. In the chapter we present an inference with specific defuzzification that leads to simpler, faster and intuitively acceptable results.

2.2
An approach to axiomatic definition of fuzzy implication

We recall an axiomatic approach (formulated by Fodor cf. Fodor 1991, 1995, 1996; Fodor and Roubens 1994) to the definition of fuzzy implication, which considers an implication to be a connective and seems to possess its most general and characteristic properties.

A fuzzy implication is a function I: $[0,1]^2 \rightarrow [0,1]$ satisfying the following conditions:

I1. if $x \leq z$ then $I(x, y) \geq I(z, y)$, for all $x, y, z \in [0, 1]$,

I2. if $y \leq z$ then $I(x, y) \leq I(x, z)$, for all $x, y, z \in [0, 1]$,

I3. $I(0, y) = 1$, for all $y \in [0, 1]$,   (falsity implies anything),

I4. $I(x, 1) = 1$, for all $x \in [0, 1]$,   (anything implies tautology),

I5. $I(1, 0) = 0$,   (booleanity).

Assuming that N: $[0, 1] \rightarrow [0, 1]$ is a strictly decreasing continuous function (a strong negation, $N(0) = 1$, $N(1) = 0$, $N(N(x)) = x$, for all $x \in [0, 1]$), the N- reciprocal of $I(x, y)$ defined by

$$I_N(x, y) = I(N(y), N(x)), \quad x, y \in [0, 1] \tag{2.8}$$

is also considered to be a fuzzy implication.

Now let us recall further properties, in terms of function $I(x, y)$, which could also be important in some applications:

I6. $I(1, x) = x$, for all $x \in [0, 1]$,   (tautology cannot justify anything),

I7. $I(x, I(y, z)) = I(y, I(x, z))$, for all $x, y, z \in [0,1]$,   (exchange principle),

I8. $x \leq y$ if and only if $I(x, y) = 1$ for all $x, y \in [0, 1]$, (implication defines ordering),

I9. $N(x) = I(x, 0)$, for all $x \in [0,1]$ is a strong negation,

I10. $I(x, y) \geq y$, for all $x, y \in [0, 1]$,

I11. $I(x, x) = 1$, for all $x \in [0, 1]$,   (identity principle),

I12. $I(x, y) = I(N(y), N(x))$ with a strong negation $N(x)$ for all $x, y \in [0, 1]$,

I13. $I(x, y)$ is a continuous function.

The two most important families of such implications are related either to the formalism of Boolean logic or to the residuation concept from intuitionistic logic. For the concepts mentioned above, a suitable definition is introduced below (see Mizumoto and Zimmermann 1982, Fodor 1995): an S-implication associated with a t-conorm S and a strong negation $N(x)$ is defined by

$$I_{S,N}(x, y) = S(N(x), y), \quad x, y \in [0, 1].$$

(2.9)

An R-implication associated with a t-norm T is defined by

$$I_T(x, y) = \sup_z \{z \mid T(x, z) \leq y\}, \quad x, y \in [0, 1].$$

(2.10)

The last expression can be justified by the following classical set-theoretic identities (Fodor and Roubens 1994):

$$\bar{A} \cup B = \overline{(A \setminus B)} = \bigcup \{Z \mid A \cap Z \subseteq B\}.$$

(2.11)

where \ denotes a set-difference operator.

We can see that both $I_{S,N}$ and I_T satisfy conditions I1-I5 for any t-norm T, t-conorm S and strong negation $N(x)$, thus they are fuzzy implications.

For the sake of completeness we mention a third type of implications used in quantum logic and called QL-implication

$$I_{T,S,N}(x, y) = S(N(x), T(x, y)), \quad x, y \in [0, 1].$$

(2.12)

Generally, $I_{T,S,N}$ violates property I1. However, requirements under which I1 is satisfied by a QL-implication can be found in Fodor (1991).

Considering a connection between implications and negation we notice that $I(\cdot, 0)$ is non-increasing and continuous. However, it is neither strictly decreasing nor continuous in general. Continuity of the implication is sufficient but not necessary to obtain strong negation via residuation. As an example, a particular t-norm (called nilpotent minimum) and t-conorm (called nilpotent maximum) are considered in Fodor (1991, 1995) and recalled below:

$$x \wedge_0 y = \min_0(x, y) = \begin{cases} 0, & \text{if } (x + y) \leq 1, \\ \min(x, y), & \text{if } (x + y) > 1. \end{cases}$$

(2.13)

and

$$x \vee_1 y = \max_1(x, y) = \begin{cases} 1, & \text{if } (x + y) \geq 1, \\ \max(x, y), & \text{if } (x + y) < 1. \end{cases}$$

(2.14)

Then the residuated implication is of the form:

$$I_{\min_0}(x, y) = I_{Fo}(x, y) = \begin{cases} 1, & \text{if } x \le y, \\ \max(1 - x, y), & \text{if } x > y. \end{cases} \tag{2.15}$$

Although I_{Fo} is not continuous, $I_{Fo}(x, 0) = 1 - x$, $x \in [0, 1]$, is the standard strong negation. Fuzzy implication (2.15) has been introduced by Fodor (1991) and will be also taken into account in further considerations.

Since t-norms (e.g. M-, Π-, W-, Z-norms), t-conorms (e.g. M'-, Π'-, W'-, Z'-conorms) and strong negation (e.g. $N(x) = 1 - x$) are well established models for AND, OR, NOT respectively, fuzzy implications should be regarded as closely related to those models. The most important fuzzy implications representing the classes of fuzzy implications discussed above are juxtaposed in Table 2.2.

We may also classify and order fuzzy implications using an integrated index obtained from the location of fuzzy implications versus fuzzy operations within the interval $[0,1]$.

Let $I_1, I_2: [0,1] \times [0,1] \to [0,1]$ be measurable functions treated as two-argument operations in $[0,1]$. The distance between the operations I_1 and I_2 with respect to the values of their arguments is calculated as follows:

$$d(I_1, I_2) = \int_0^1 \int_0^1 | I_1(x, y) - I_2(x, y) | \, dx \, dy, \tag{2.16}$$

where $d(\bullet, \bullet)$ is a pseudometric distance here.

For constant operations, i.e. for $I_1(x, y) = 0$, $I_2(x, y) = 1$, for all $x, y \in [0,1]$ we get $d(I_1, I_2) = 1$. Because constant operations differ from drastic operations only by boundary conditions we also obtain the distance for drastic operations as follows: $d(Z, Z') = 1$, where Z and Z' are drastic product and drastic sum, respectively.

As an example, let us locate two products (algebraic product $x \bullet y = xy$ and bold product $x \odot y = 0 \vee (x + y - 1)$) within the $[0,1]$ interval according to the pseudometric distance. For the algebraic product the calculated distance is $d(\sqcap, \bullet) = 1/4$ and for bounded product we get $d(\sqcap, \odot) = 1/6$. By analogy, we get locations for the probabilistic sum $x + y = x + y - xy$ and bounded sum $x \oplus y = 1 \wedge (x + y)$ which are symmetric to the corresponding products with respect to ½ in the $[0,1]$ interval. These and some additional known results are illustrated in Fig 1.16.

We can also classify and order other families of operations which can be obtained using algebraic product and bounded product (e.g. Yager operations, Schweizer and Sklar operations, Frank operations, Hamacher operations and others).

Regarding a fuzzy implication as a two argument function we can also find its location within the interval $[0,1]$ using the above mentioned pseudometric distance in the same way as for fuzzy operations.

Table 2.2.   Selected fuzzy implications.

Implication Name	Implication Form	Implication Type	Properties
Łukasiewicz	$\min(1 - x + y, 1)$	S with $S = W'$ R with $T = W$ QL with $S = W'$, $T = \min$	1-13
Fodor	$\begin{cases} 1, & \text{if } x \le y, \\ \max(1 - x, y), & \text{if } x > y. \end{cases}$	R with $T = \min_0$ S with $S = \max_1$ QL with $T = \min$, $S = \max_1$	1-12
Reichenbach	$1 - x + x y$	S with $S = \Pi'$	1-7, 9, 10, 12, 13
Kleene-Dienes	$\max(1 - x, y)$	S with $S = \max$ QL with $S=W'$, $T=W$	1-7, 9, 10, 12, 13
Zadeh	$\max\{1 - x, \min(x, y)\}$	QL with $S = \max$, $T = \min$	2, 3, 5, 6, 9, 13
Goguen	$\min(y / x, 1)$	R with $T = \Pi$	1-8, 10, 11
Gödel	$\begin{cases} 1, & \text{if } x \le y, \\ y, & \text{if } x > y. \end{cases}$	R with $T = \min$	1-8, 10, 11
Rescher	$\begin{cases} 1, & \text{if } x \le y, \\ 0, & \text{if } x > y. \end{cases}$	----------------	1-5, 8, 11, 12

In Fig. 2.9. we illustrate the computed distance $d(\sqcap, I)$ for the above considered fuzzy implications. Such determined distance may be also regarded as the volume under implication functions which are shown in Figs. 2.1 - 2.8, respectively. The full collection of results of pseudometric distance between fuzzy implications are presented in Table 2.3. However, the above mentioned distance is integrated index characterizing a fuzzy implication, and also deliver indirect information for the selection of other operations.

2.3
Compositional rule of inference

The compositional rule of inference is a generalization of a procedure well-known from mathematics. Suppose that we have a curve $y = g(x)$ from $x \in X$ to $y \in Y$ describing relation between X and Y. If we are given $x = x'$, then from function g we

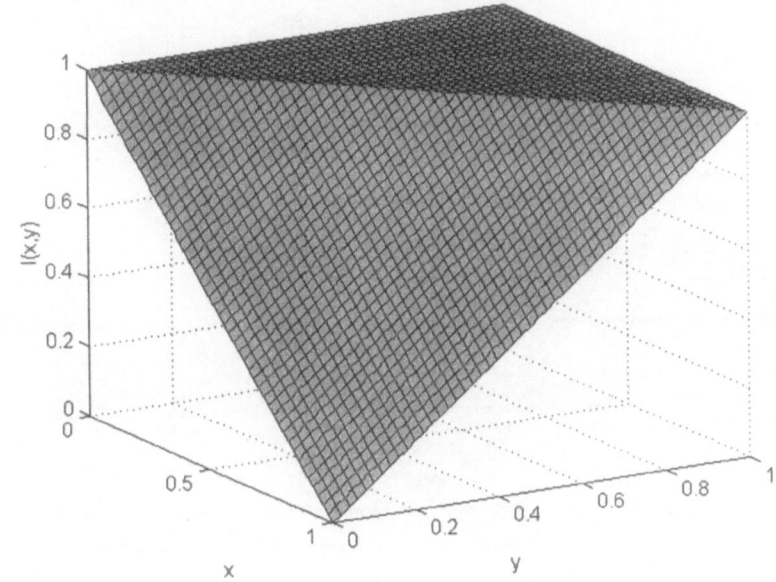

Fig. 2.1. Graphical illustration of Łukasiewicz fuzzy implication.

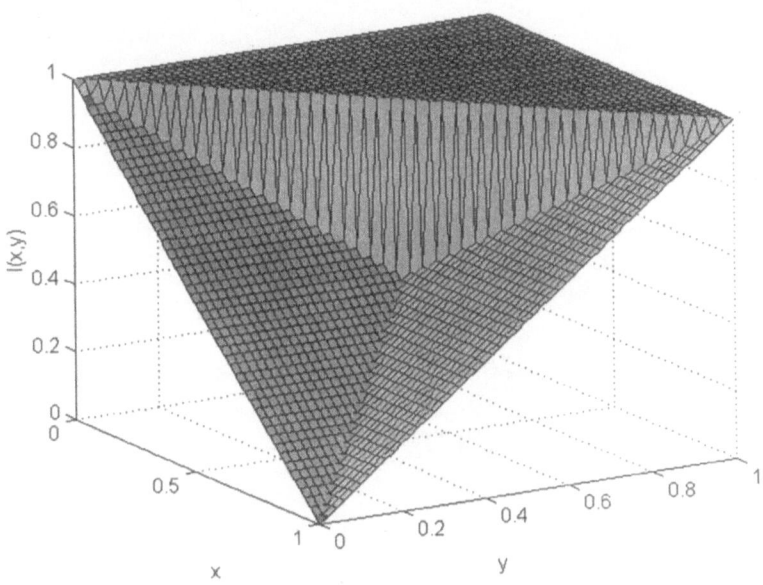

Fig. 2.2. Graphical illustration of Fodor fuzzy implication.

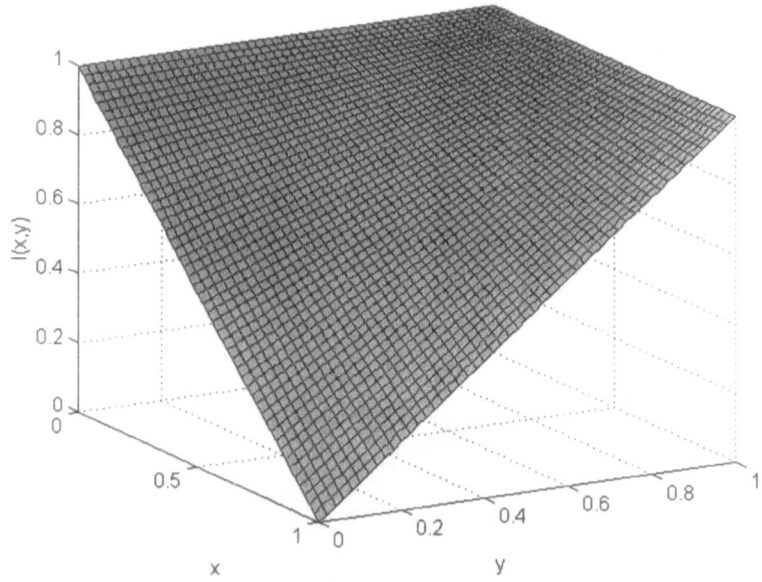

Fig. 2.3. Graphical illustration of Reichenbach fuzzy implication.

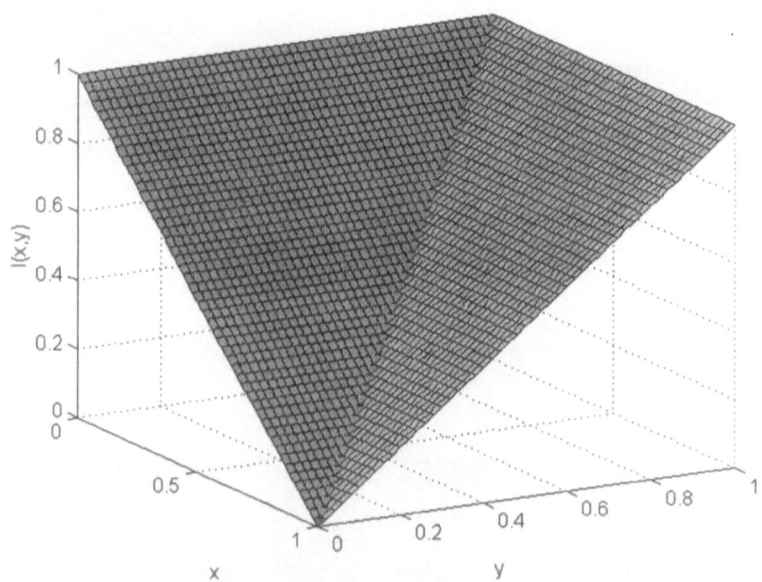

Fig. 2.4. Graphical illustration of Kleene-Dienes fuzzy implication.

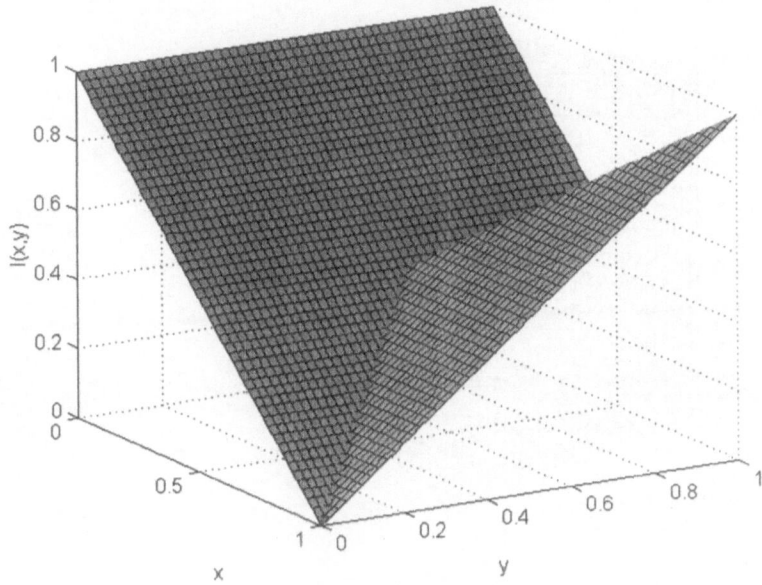

Fig. 2.5. Graphical illustration of Zadeh fuzzy implication.

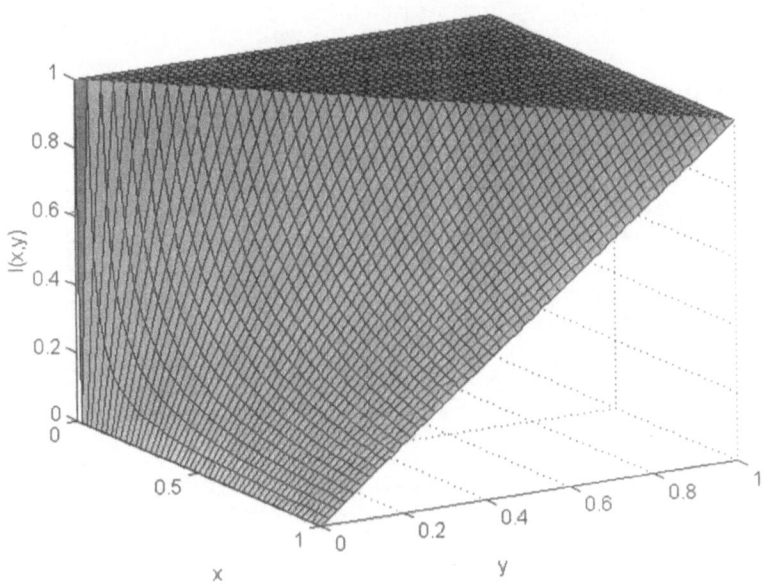

Fig. 2.6. Graphical illustration of Goguen fuzzy implication.

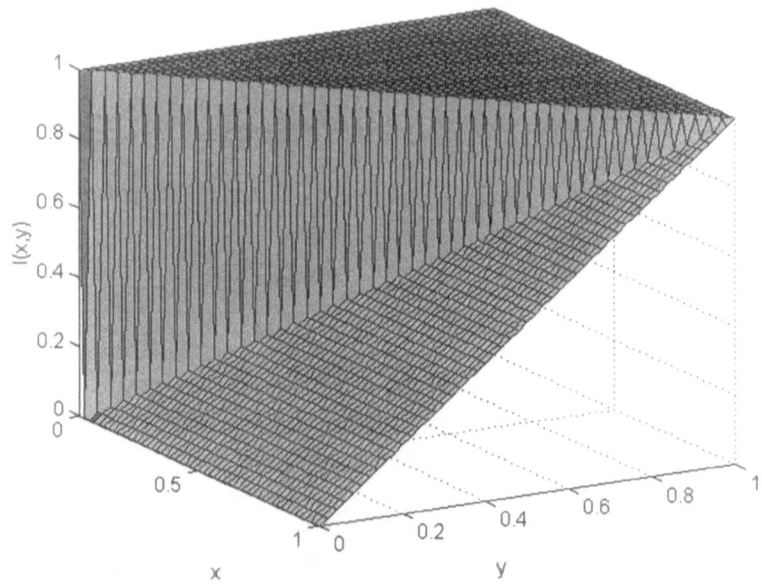

Fig. 2.7. Graphical illustration of Gödel fuzzy implication.

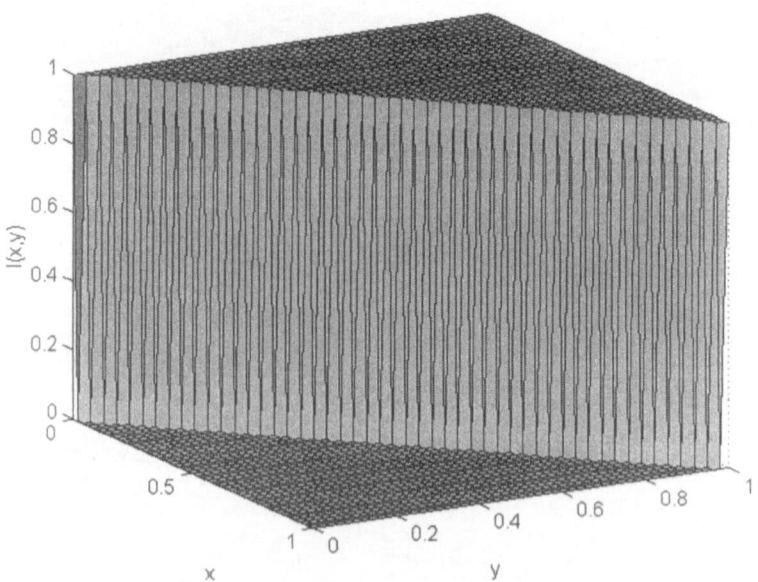

Fig. 2.8. Graphical illustration of Rescher fuzzy implication.

infer that $y' = g(x')$.

The extension of the above mentioned procedure from point in X to fuzzy set A is presented in Section 1.9.

Table 2.3. Pseudometric distance between fuzzy implications.

$d(I_1, I_2)$	Łukasiewicz	Fodor	Reichenbach	Kleene-Dienes	Zadeh	Goguen	Gödel	Rescher
Łukasiewicz	0	1/12	1/12	1/6	5/24	1/12	1/6	1/3
Fodor		0	1/12	1/12	1/8	1/12	1/12	1/4
Reichenbach			0	1/12	1/8	11/96	1/6	1/3
Kleene-Dienes				0	1/24	1/6	1/6	1/3
Zadeh					0	5/24	5/24	3/8
Goguen						0	1/12	1/4
Gödel							0	1/6
Rescher								0

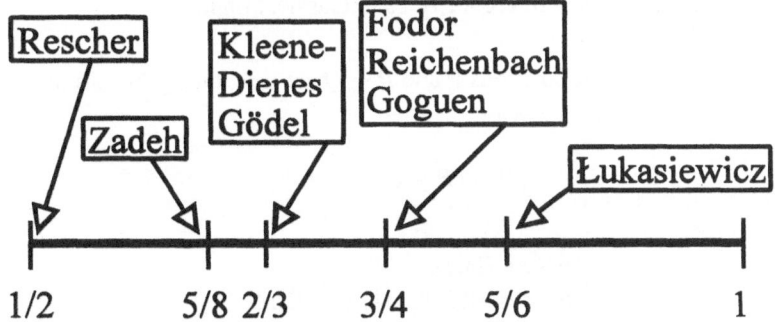

Fig. 2.9. Pseudometric distance from drastic product to fuzzy implications.

The above-mentioned cases are examples of the use of the compositional rule of inference. In this general case we have fuzzy set $A'(x)$ on X, fuzzy relation $R(x, y)$ on $X \times Y$, and we want to compute fuzzy set $B'(y)$ on Y. To find this fuzzy set we construct a cylindrical extension $Ce(A')$ (see Section 1.8) of fuzzy set A':

$$\mu_{Ce(A')}(x, y) = \mu_{A'}(x).$$ (2.17)

In this way we have a two-dimensional fuzzy set defined on $X \times Y$, and we make intersection $Ce(A')$ and relation $R(x, y)$ using t-norm T:

$$\mu_{Ce(A') \cap R}(x, y) = T(\mu_{A'}(x), \mu_R(x, y)) = \mu_{A'}(x) \star_T \mu_R(x, y).$$ (2.18)

Then, if we project this intersection on the Y axis (see Section 1.8), we obtain the resulting fuzzy set $B'(y)$:

$$\mu_{B'}(y) = \sup_{x \in X} [\mu_{A'}(x) \star_T \mu_R(x, y)].$$ (2.19)

The above formula is called the compositional rule of inference or sup-star composition introduced by Zadeh (1973). If we see a composition of fuzzy relations (1.56) or (1.57), then fuzzy set B' can be expressed as composition of A' (a unary fuzzy relation) and R (binary fuzzy relation):

$$B' = A' \circ R,$$ (2.20)

where $\circ$ is the composition operator.

2.4
Fuzzy reasoning

The most commonly used inference rules in classical logic are:

1. Modus Ponens: if propositions P and $P \rightarrow Q$ are true, then propositions Q is also true. Symbolically, we can write:

$$(P \wedge (P \rightarrow Q)) \rightarrow Q,$$ (2.21)

or

Premise I (fact):	P
Premise II (rule):	**IF P THEN Q**
Conclusion:	Q

(2.22)

2. Modus Tollens: if propositions not(P) ($\neg P$) and $P \rightarrow Q$ are true, then proposition not(Q) ($\neg Q$) is also true:

$$(\neg P \wedge (P \rightarrow Q)) \rightarrow \neg Q,$$ (2.23)

or

Premise I (fact): $\neg P$
Premise II (rule):   **IF P THEN Q**   (2.24)
Conclusion: $\neg Q$

3. Hypothetical Syllogism: if propositions $P \rightarrow Q$ and $Q \rightarrow S$ are true, then $P \rightarrow S$ is also true:

$$((P \rightarrow Q) \wedge (Q \rightarrow S)) \rightarrow (P \rightarrow S),$$ (2.25)

or

Premise I: **IF P THEN Q**
Premise II: **IF Q THEN S**   (2.26)
Conclusion: **IF P THEN S**

For example in classical logic if we have propositions "tomato is red" and "IF Tomato is red THEN tomato is ripe", then we conclude proposition "tomato is ripe". In case of fuzzy logic (and real human reasoning) we may have imprecise proposition "tomato is very red". Using intuition we conclude that "tomato is very ripe".

Symbolically, we can write:

Premise I (fact): P'
Premise II (rule):   **IF P THEN Q**   (2.27)
Conclusion: Q'

where propositions P and P', Q and Q' are similar (closer).

This type of inference procedure is called generalized modus ponens. The detailed formulas for computing proposition Q' are obtained using the compositional rule of inference. From the previous section we know that the if-then rule can be interpreted as a fuzzy relation, and propositions as fuzzy sets (unary fuzzy relation). Then we obtain basic methods of inference in fuzzy logic:

1. Generalized Modus Ponens. Let fuzzy set A' (which represents the premise P') be defined on X, fuzzy relation R (which represents IF P THEN Q) on $X \times Y$, and conclusion fuzzy set B' (which represents the conclusion Q') is inferred as:

$$\mu_{B'}(y) = \sup_{x \in X} [\mu_{A'}(x) \star_T \mu_R(x, y)],$$ (2.28)

or, equivalently

$$B' = A' \circ R = A' \circ (A \rightarrow B).$$ (2.29)

2. Generalized Modus Tollens, can be written symbolically:

Premise *I* (fact): Q'
Premise *II* (rule):   **IF** *P* **THEN** *Q*   (2.30)
Conclusion: P'

Let fuzzy set B' be defined on Y (which represents the premise Q'), fuzzy relation R on $X \times Y$ (which represents the premise IF P THEN Q), and fuzzy set A' be defined on X (which represents the conclusion) is inferred as:

$$\mu_{A'}(x) = \sup_{y \in Y} [\mu_R(x, y) \star_T \mu_{B'}(y)],$$ (2.31)

or, equivalently

$$A' = R \circ B' = (A \rightarrow B) \circ B'.$$ (2.32)

3. Generalized Hypothetical Syllogism, which can be written symbolically:

Premise *I*:   **IF** *P* **THEN** *Q*
Premise *II*:   **IF** Q' **THEN** *S*   (2.33)
Conclusion: **IF** *P* **THEN** S'

Let fuzzy relations R_1 on $X \times Y$ (which represents premise IF P THEN Q), R_2 on $Y \times Z$ (which represents premise IF Q' THEN S), and R_3 on $X \times Z$ (which represents conclusion IF P THEN S') be inferred as:

$$\mu_{R_3}(x, z) = \sup_{y \in Y} [\mu_{R_1}(x, y) \star_T \mu_{R_2}(y, z)],$$ (2.34)

or, equivalently

$$R_3 = R_1 \circ R_2.$$ (2.35)

2.5
Canonical fuzzy if-then rule

The main component of each fuzzy system is the rule base. This rule base constitutes a convenient form for expressing pieces of knowledge while a set of it-then rules forms a fuzzy rule base. Let us consider fuzzy rule base R, which consists of a set of I fuzzy if-then rules $R^{(i)}$ ($i = 1, 2, ..., I$):

$$R^{(i)}: \textbf{IF } X_1 \text{ is } A_1^{(i)} \textbf{ and } X_2 \text{ is } A_2^{(i)} \textbf{ and } ... \textbf{ and } X_N \text{ is } A_N^{(i)}$$
$$\textbf{THEN } Y_1 \text{ is } B_1^{(i)}, \ Y_2 \text{ is } B_2^{(i)}, ..., Y_P \text{ is } B_P^{(i)},$$ (2.36)

or, in compact form:

$$R = \left\{R^{(i)}\right\}_{i=1}^{I} = \left\{ \mathbf{IF} \;\; \underset{n=1}{\overset{N}{\mathbf{and}}} \; X_n \text{ is } A_n^{(i)} \;\; \mathbf{THEN} \; \left\{Y_p \text{ is } B_p^{(i)}\right\}_{p=1}^{P} \right\}_{i=1}^{I}, \qquad (2.37)$$

where $X_1, X_2, ..., X_N$ are input linguistic variables, $Y_1, Y_2, ..., Y_P$ are output linguistic variables, $A_1^{(i)}, A_2^{(i)}, ..., A_N^{(i)}, B_1^{(i)}, B_2^{(i)}, ..., B_P^{(i)}$ are linguistic values (terms) defined by fuzzy sets on $X_1, X_2, ..., X_N, Y_1, Y_2, ..., Y_P$, respectively.

The formula (2.37) describes fuzzy if-then rules from the multi-input-multi-output (MIMO) fuzzy system. Such a system can always be decomposed into a collection of P multi-input-single-output (MISO) systems described by the rule base:

$$R_p = \left\{ \mathbf{IF} \;\; \underset{n=1}{\overset{N}{\mathbf{and}}} \; X_n \text{ is } A_n^{(i)} \;\; \mathbf{THEN} \; Y_p \text{ is } B_p^{(i)} \right\}_{i=1}^{I}, \qquad (2.38)$$

and

$$R = \left\{R_p\right\}_{p=1}^{P}. \qquad (2.39)$$

In future considerations we describe only one system and index p is omitted. Finally, we obtain the fuzzy rule base:

$$R = \left\{R^{(i)}\right\}_{i=1}^{I} = \left\{ \mathit{IF} \;\; \underset{n=1}{\overset{N}{\mathit{and}}} \; X_n \text{ is } A_n^{(i)} \;\; \mathit{THEN} \; Y \text{ is } B^{(i)} \right\}_{i=1}^{I}. \qquad (2.40)$$

Rule $R^{(i)}$ in form (2.40) is called a canonical fuzzy if-then rule. These rules include many other types of fuzzy rules:

1. "Rules with or":

$$\mathbf{IF} \;\; \underset{n=1}{\overset{N'}{\mathbf{and}}} \; X_n \text{ is } A_n^{(i)} \;\; \mathbf{or} \;\; \underset{n=N'+1}{\overset{N}{\mathbf{and}}} \; X_n \text{ is } A_n^{(i)} \;\; \mathbf{THEN} \; Y \text{ is } B^{(i)}, \qquad (2.41)$$

where $N' < N$. This rule can be decomposed to canonical form:

$$\mathbf{IF} \;\; \underset{n=1}{\overset{N'}{\mathbf{and}}} \; X_n \text{ is } A_n^{(i)} \;\; \mathbf{THEN} \; Y \text{ is } B^{(i)},$$

$$\mathbf{IF} \;\; \underset{n=N'+1}{\overset{N}{\mathbf{and}}} \; X_n \text{ is } A_n^{(i)} \;\; \mathbf{THEN} \; Y \text{ is } B^{(i)}. \qquad (2.42)$$

2. "Partial rule":

$$\text{IF } \mathbf{and}_{n=1}^{N'} X_n \text{ is } A_n^{(i)} \text{ THEN } Y \text{ is } B^{(i)}, \tag{2.43}$$

where $N' < N$. The above rule is equivalent to rule in canonical form:

$$\text{IF } \mathbf{and}_{n=1}^{N'} X_n \text{ is } A_n^{(i)} \text{ and } \mathbf{and}_{n=N'+1}^{N} X_n \text{ is } \tilde{I}_n \text{ THEN } Y \text{ is } B^{(i)}, \tag{2.44}$$

where $\tilde{I}_\xi$ is a fuzzy set on X_ξ defined as $\mu_I(x_\xi) = 1$ for all $x_\xi \in X_\xi$.

The collection of fuzzy if-then rules in a rule base must be complete and consistent. The completeness means that at any inputs $X_1, X_2, ..., X_N$ there is at least one rule that is active (the membership functions in a premise part of an if-then rule are non-zero for that input). The rule base is consistent if there are no rules with the same premise parts but different consequences.

The canonical fuzzy if-then rule in linguistic form (2.40) can be represented by $(N+1)$-nary fuzzy relation:

$$R^{(i)} = A_1^{(i)} \times A_2^{(i)} \times ... \times A_N^{(i)} \rightarrow B^{(i)}, \tag{2.45}$$

or in terms of membership functions:

$$\mu_{R^{(i)}}(x_1, x_2, ..., x_N, y) = \mu_{A_1^{(i)} \times A_2^{(i)} \times ... \times A_N^{(i)}}(x_1, x_2, ..., x_N) \rightarrow \mu_{B^{(i)}}(y) \tag{2.46}$$

defined on $X_1 \times X_2 \times ... \times X_N \times Y$.

If we use pseudo-vector notation, then:

$$\underline{A}^{(i)} = A_1^{(i)} \times A_2^{(i)} \times ... \times A_N^{(i)} \tag{2.47}$$

is a fuzzy relation in $\underline{X} = X_1 \times X_2 \times ... \times X_N$. Equations (2.45) and (2.46) can be written in the form:

$$R^{(i)}: \underline{A}^{(i)} \rightarrow B^{(i)}, \tag{2.48}$$

and

$$\mu_{R^{(i)}}(\underline{x}, y) = \mu_{\underline{A}^{(i)}}(\underline{x}) \rightarrow \mu_{B^{(i)}}(y), \tag{2.49}$$

defined on $\underline{X} \times Y$, where $\underline{x} = [x_1, x_2, ..., x_N]^T$.

The AND operator in the premise of an if-then rule is represented by t-norm T, thus we obtain:

$$\mu_{A_1^{(i)} \times A_2^{(i)} \times ... \times A_N^{(i)}}(x_1, x_2, ..., x_N) = \mu_{\underline{A}^{(i)}}(\underline{x}) =$$
$$\mu_{A_1^{(i)}}(x_1) \star_T \mu_{A_2^{(i)}}(x_2) \star_T ... \star_T \mu_{A_N^{(i)}}(x_N), \tag{2.50}$$

where $A_1^{(i)}, A_2^{(i)}, ..., A_N^{(i)}$ are fuzzy sets which represent linguistic terms in the premise of i-th if-then rule, $B^{(i)}$ is a fuzzy set representing linguistic terms in consequence of that rule.

Additionally, if we use a logical interpretation of the if-then rule, then:

$$\mu_{R^{(i)}}(\underline{x}, y) = \mu_{R^{(i)}}(x_1, x_2, ..., x_N, y) = I(\mu_{\underline{A}^{(i)}}(\underline{x}), \mu_{B^{(i)}}(y)) =$$
$$I(\mu_{A_1^{(i)}}(x_1) \star_T \mu_{A_2^{(i)}}(x_2) \star_T ... \star_T \mu_{A_N^{(i)}}(x_N), \mu_{B^{(i)}}(y)), \qquad (2.51)$$

where $I(\bullet, \bullet)$ is a fuzzy implication.

If we use conjunction interpretation of if-then rules represented by t-norm marked $T1$ then we get:

$$\mu_{R^{(i)}}(\underline{x}, y) = \mu_{R^{(i)}}(x_1, x_2, ..., x_N, y) = \mu_{\underline{A}^{(i)}}(\underline{x}) \star_{T1} \mu_{B^{(i)}}(y)) =$$
$$\mu_{A_1^{(i)}}(x_1) \star_T \mu_{A_2^{(i)}}(x_2) \star_T ... \star_T \mu_{A_N^{(i)}}(x_N) \star_{T1} \mu_{B^{(i)}}(y). \qquad (2.52)$$

The generalized modus ponens inference method in case we use the canonical fuzzy if-then rule takes the form:

$$B^{(i)'} = \underline{A}' \circ R^{(i)} = \underline{A}' \circ (\underline{A}^{(i)} \rightarrow B^{(i)}), \qquad (2.53)$$

where $\underline{A}' = A_1' \times A_2' \times ... \times A_N'$ is a premise defined on $\underline{X}$, and $R^{(i)}$ is a fuzzy relation representing the i-th if-then rule. The membership function of fuzzy set $B^{(i)'}$ defined on Y is computed from sup-t-norm $T2$ composition:

$$\mu_{B^{(i)'}}(y) = \sup_{\underline{x} \in \underline{X}} \left[\mu_{A'}(\underline{x}) \star_{T2} \mu_{R^{(i)}}(\underline{x}, y) \right] =$$
$$\sup_{\underline{x} \in \underline{X}} \left[\mu_{A_1'}(x_1) \star_T \mu_{A_2'}(x_2) \star_T ... \star_T \mu_{A_N'}(x_N) \star_{T2} \mu_{R^{(i)}}(x_1, x_2, ... x_N, y) \right]. \qquad (2.54)$$

2.6
Aggregation operation

We consider I fuzzy relations $R^{(1)}, R^{(2)}, ..., R^{(I)}$ and aggregation operation $\oplus: [0, 1]^I \rightarrow [0, 1]$ which produce single fuzzy relation R:

$$R = \bigoplus_{i=1}^{I} R^{(i)} = \oplus(R^{(1)}, R^{(2)}, ..., R^{(I)}). \qquad (2.55)$$

We are using an operation which is continuous, i.e. react infinitesimally to a infinitesimal change of arguments. The aggregation operation will also be neutral, i.e. $\oplus$ is independent of any permutation of arguments. Finally, $\oplus$ presents a non-negative response to any increase of the arguments.

There are two contradicting arguments about what a collection of fuzzy relation (if-then rules) may be aggregated. The first argument treats the relations as a representation of independent conditional statements. In this case reasonable operation for an aggregation is a union (t-conorm). This method is called Mamdani combination. The second argument treats relations as coupled conditional statements. In this case the intersection (t-norm) is a reasonable operation for the aggregation of relations. This method is called Gödel combination.

From Chapter 1 we know that the min and max operations divide fuzzy connectives into products, sums and averages. The averages are found between products and sums in accordance with Fig. 1.16. As a result, taking into account both contradict arguments with different weights we can use averaging as an aggregation operation. Most often we use arithmetic, harmonic and geometric mean or generally the root-power mean with α parameter:

$$\boxplus_{(\alpha)}(x_1, x_2, ..., x_I) = \boxplus_{(\alpha)} \underset{i=1}{\overset{I}{}} x_i = \left(\frac{1}{I} \sum_{i=1}^{I} x_i^{\alpha} \right)^{\frac{1}{\alpha}} \qquad (2.56)$$

for $-\infty < \alpha < +\infty$.

This operation includes:

- for $\alpha \to -\infty$, the conjunctive mean:

$$\boxplus_{(-\infty)}(x_1, x_2, ..., x_I) = \min_{i=1}^{I} x_i, \qquad (2.57)$$

- for $\alpha = -1$, the harmonic mean:

$$\boxplus_{(-1)}(x_1, x_2, ..., x_I) = \left(\frac{1}{I} \sum_{i=1}^{I} \frac{1}{x_i} \right)^{-1}, \qquad (2.58)$$

- for $\alpha = 0$, the geometric mean:

$$\boxplus_{(0)}(x_1, x_2, ..., x_I) = \left(\prod_{i=1}^{I} x_i \right)^{\frac{1}{I}}, \qquad (2.59)$$

- for $\alpha = 1$, the arithmetic mean:

$$\boxplus_{(1)}(x_1, x_2, ..., x_I) = \frac{1}{I} \sum_{i=1}^{I} x_i, \qquad (2.60)$$

- for $\alpha = 2$, quadratic mean:

$$\boxplus_{(2)}(x_1, x_2, ..., x_I) = \sqrt{\frac{1}{I} \sum_{i=1}^{I} x_i^2}, \qquad (2.61)$$

• for $\alpha \to +\infty$, the disjunctive mean:

$$\uplus_{(+\infty)}(x_1, x_2, ..., x_I) = \max_{i=1}^{I} x_i. \tag{2.62}$$

2.7
Approximate reasoning using a fuzzy rule base

Approximate reasoning is usually executed in a fuzzy inference system which performs a mapping from an input fuzzy set $\underline{A}'$ in $\underline{X}$ to a fuzzy set B' in Y via a fuzzy rule base. Two methods of approximate reasoning are mostly used: composition based inference (first aggregate then inference - FATI) and individual-rule based inference (first inference then aggregate - FITA).

In a composition based inference, a finite number of rules $i = 1,..., I$ is aggregated via union, intersection or average operations, i.e.

$$R = \bigoplus_{i=1}^{I} R^{(i)}, \tag{2.63}$$

where $\oplus$ denotes the symbol of aggregation operation using t-norm $T3$ or t-conorm S or averages $\uplus_{(\alpha)}$ for the aggregation of respective membership functions:

$$R(\underline{x}, y) = R^{(1)}(\underline{x}, y) \left\|\begin{matrix} \bigstar_{T3} \\ \bigstar_S \\ \uplus_{(\alpha)} \end{matrix}\right\| R^{(2)}(\underline{x}, y) \left\|\begin{matrix} \bigstar_{T3} \\ \bigstar_S \\ \uplus_{(\alpha)} \end{matrix}\right\| ... \left\|\begin{matrix} \bigstar_{T3} \\ \bigstar_S \\ \uplus_{(\alpha)} \end{matrix}\right\| R^{(I)}(\underline{x}, y), \tag{2.64}$$

where $\| : \|$ symbol denotes alternatives in aggregation operation.

Taking into account an arbitrary input fuzzy set $\underline{A}'$ in $\underline{X}$ and using the generalized modus ponens we obtain the output of fuzzy inference (FATI):

$$B'_{FATI} = \underline{A}' \circ \left[\bigoplus_{i=1}^{I} R^{(i)} \right] = \underline{A}' \circ \left[\bigoplus_{i=1}^{I} \left(\underline{A}^{(i)} \to B^{(i)} \right) \right], \tag{2.65}$$

or in terms of membership functions:

$$\mu_{B'_{FATI}}(y) = \sup_{x \in X} [\mu_{A'}(x) \star_{T2} \mu_R(x, y)] =$$

$$= \sup_{x \in X} [\mu_{A'}(x) \star_{T2} \left\| \begin{array}{c} \overset{I}{\underset{i=1}{\star}}_{T3} \\ \overset{I}{\underset{i=1}{\star}}_S \\ \overset{I}{\underset{i=1}{\uplus}}_{(\alpha)} \end{array} \right\| \mu_{R^{(i)}}(x, y)] = \sup_{x \in X} [\mu_{A'}(x) \star_{T2} \overset{I}{\underset{i=1}{\bigoplus}} \mu_{R^{(i)}}(x, y)], \qquad (2.66)$$

where $\star_{T3}$, $\star_{T2}$ denote t-norms ($T3$, $T2$) for aggregation operation and composition, respectively. The $\star_S$, $\uplus_{(\alpha)}$ denote s-norm S and averaging operation for aggregation.

In individual - rule based inference (FITA) each rule in the fuzzy rule base determines an output fuzzy set and after that an aggregation via intersection, union or average operation is performed. So the output fuzzy set is expressed by means of the formulas:

$$B'_{FITA} = \overset{I}{\underset{i=1}{\bigoplus}} \left[A' \circ R^{(i)} \right] = \overset{I}{\underset{i=1}{\bigoplus}} \left[A' \circ (A^{(i)} \rightarrow B^{(i)}) \right], \qquad (2.67)$$

or:

$$\mu_{B'_{FATI}}(y) = \overset{I}{\underset{i=1}{\bigoplus}} \sup_{x \in X} \left[\mu_{A'}(x) \star_{T2} \mu_{R^{(i)}}(x, y) \right]. \qquad (2.68)$$

It can be proved that B'_{FITA} is more specified than B'_{FATI}, i.e.

$$B'_{FATI} \subseteq B'_{FITA}, \quad \text{or} \quad \underset{y \in Y}{\forall} \mu_{B'_{FATI}}(y) \leq \mu_{B'_{FATI}}(y). \qquad (2.69)$$

It means that the consequent B'_{FATI} is equal to or contained in the intersection of fuzzy inference results - B'_{FITA}. For simplicity of calculation the consequent B'_{FATI} is replaced by B'_{FITA}, under the assumption that the differences are not big.

2.8
Approximate reasoning with singletons

If the input fuzzy sets $A'_1, A'_2, \ldots, A'_N$ or A' are singletons in points $x_{10}, x_{20}, \ldots, x_{N0}$ or x_0 then the consequence B'_{FATI} is equal to:

$$\mu_{B'_{FATI}}(y) = [1 \star_{T2} \mu_R(\underline{x}_0, y)] \bigvee \sup_{\substack{\underline{x} \in \underline{X} \\ \underline{x} \neq \underline{x}_0}} [0 \star_{T2} \mu_R(\underline{x}, y)] =$$

$$= \mu_R(\underline{x}_0, y) = \bigoplus_{i=1}^{I} \mu_{R^{(i)}}(\underline{x}_0, y), \tag{2.70}$$

and in case of FITA inference:

$$\mu_{B'_{FITA}}(y) = \bigoplus_{i=1}^{I} \left\{ [1 \star_{T2} \mu_{R^{(i)}}(\underline{x}_0, y)] \bigvee \sup_{\substack{\underline{x} \in \underline{X} \\ \underline{x} \neq \underline{x}_0}} [0 \star_{T2} \mu_{R^{(i)}}(\underline{x}, y)] \right\} =$$

$$= \bigoplus_{i=1}^{I} \mu_{R^{(i)}}(\underline{x}_0, y) = \mu_R(\underline{x}_0, y). \tag{2.71}$$

From equations (2.70) and (2.71) we see that for singletons FATI and FITA inference results are the same. Finally, if we use interpretations of fuzzy relation representing if-then rules discussed in previous sections, then we get:

$$\mu_{B'}(y) = \bigoplus_{i=1}^{I} \left\{ \mu_{A^{(i)}}(\underline{x}_0) \star_{T1} \mu_{B^{(i)}}(y) \right\}, \tag{2.72}$$

for conjunction interpretation, and:

$$\mu_{B'}(y) = \bigoplus_{i=1}^{I} I(\mu_{A^{(i)}}(\underline{x}_0), \mu_{B^{(i)}}(y)), \tag{2.73}$$

for logical interpretation of if-then rules.

2.9
Fuzzifiers and defuzzifiers

The fuzzifiers are defined as a mapping from real-valued point $\underline{x}_0 \in \underline{X} \subset R^N$ to a fuzzy set $\underline{A}'$ defined on $\underline{X}$. The most frequently used fuzzifiers are:

1. Singleton fuzzifiers, maps point $\underline{x}_0 \in \underline{X}$ into a fuzzy singleton $\underline{A}'$ defined on $\underline{X}$, which have a membership function equal to 1 for $\underline{x} = \underline{x}_0$, and 0 for any other point:

$$\mu_{A'}(\underline{x}) = \begin{cases} 1, & \underline{x} = \underline{x}_0, \\ 0, & \underline{x} \neq \underline{x}_0. \end{cases} \tag{2.74}$$

2. Triangular fuzzifier, maps point $\underline{x}_0 \in \underline{X}$ into a fuzzy set $\underline{A}'$, which have the triangular membership function:

$$\mu_{\underline{A}'}(\underline{x}) = \bigstar_T \max_{n=1}^{N} \left[\min\left(\frac{x_n - a_n}{x_{n0} - a_n}, \frac{b_n - x_n}{b_n - x_{n0}} \right), 0 \right], \tag{2.75}$$

where $\bigstar_T$ is t-norm T representing AND operator, a_n, b_n are parameters.

3. Gaussian fuzzifiers, maps point $\underline{x}_0 \in \underline{X}$ into a fuzzy set $\underline{A}'$, which have the Gaussian membership function:

$$\mu_{\underline{A}'}(\underline{x}) = \bigstar_T^{N} \left[e^{-\frac{1}{2}\left(\frac{x_n - x_{n0}}{\sigma_n} \right)^2} \right], \tag{2.76}$$

where σ_n is a parameter. If we use algebraic product as t-norm T then we get:

$$\mu_{\underline{A}'}(\underline{x}) = e^{-\frac{1}{2} \sum_{n=1}^{N} \left(\frac{x_n - x_{n0}}{\sigma_n} \right)^2}. \tag{2.77}$$

We see that the above fuzzifiers satisfy $\mu_{\underline{A}'}(\underline{x}_0) = 1$.

Fuzzy systems generate inference results based on fuzzy if-then rules. These results are mainly fuzzy sets. In many applications crisp results are required instead of fuzzy ones. The transformation of fuzzy results into crisp results is performed by a defuzzification method generally expressed as:

$$\delta: \mathscr{F}(Y) \rightarrow Y, \tag{2.78}$$

or, using membership functions:

$$\delta_{mf}: \left\{ \mu_{B'}(y) \mid B' \in \mathscr{F}(Y), y \in Y \right\} \rightarrow Y, \tag{2.79}$$

where symbols δ, δ_{mf} stand for defuzzification mapping.

That defuzzification is defined as a mapping from fuzzy set B' which is the output of the fuzzy inference to crisp point $y^* \in Y$. This also implies that a defuzzification method should be chosen. Although many various defuzzification methods (defuzzifiers) may be proposed, we will recall the most important ones from the class of standard defuzzifiers (SD).

1. The center of gravity (COG) defuzzifier specifies the y^* as the center of the area covered by the membership function of B', i.e.

$$y^* = \frac{\int\limits_Y y\,\mu_{B'}(y)\,dy}{\int\limits_Y \mu_{B'}(y)\,dy}.$$ (2.80)

2. Sometimes it is necessary to eliminate the $y \in Y$, whose membership values in B' are too small or equal in all Y (indeterminant part of membership function). In this case we use the indexed center of gravity (ICOG) defuzzifier which results in:

$$y^* = \frac{\int\limits_{Y_\alpha} y\,\mu_{B'}(y)\,dy}{\int\limits_{Y_\alpha} \mu_{B'}(y)\,dy}.$$ (2.81)

where α is constant and Y_α is defined as:

$$Y_\alpha = \left\{ y \in Y \mid \mu_{B'}(y) \geq \alpha \right\}.$$ (2.82)

The value $\alpha \in [0,1]$ describes the indeterminancy that accompanies the corresponding part of information. To eliminate the indeterminant part under membership function where $B'(y) > \alpha$, the informative part or operative part of the membership function where $B'(y) > 0$, has to be parallely shifted downward by the value of α according to the formula:

$$\mu_{B \cdot}(y) = \begin{cases} \mu_{B'}(y) - \alpha, & \text{if } \mu_{B'}(y) > \alpha, \\ 0, & \text{if } \mu_{B'}(y) \leq \alpha. \end{cases}$$ (2.83)

In such a case we may build a modified indexed center of gravity defuzzifier denoted by $MICOG_\alpha$ which may be expressed in the form:

$$y^* = \frac{\int\limits_{Y_\alpha} y\,\mu_{B \cdot}(y)\,dy}{\int\limits_{Y_\alpha} \mu_{B \cdot}(y)\,dy} = \frac{\int\limits_{Y_\alpha} y\left(\mu_{B'}(y) - \alpha\right)dy}{\int\limits_{Y_\alpha} \left(\mu_{B'}(y) - \alpha\right)dy}.$$ (2.84)

The last modification can also be obtained considering ordinal COG defuzzifier on bounded difference, i.e.

$$y^* = COG\left[\max(0, \mu_{B'}(y) - \alpha)\right].$$ (2.85)

Other modifications are obtained when two cutting levels α_L (left-sided) and β_R (right-sided), $(\alpha_L > \beta_R)$ for $B'(y)$, appear. Denoting the cutting points for constant levels with $B'(y)$, by y_α and y_β respectively, we get:

$$y^* = \text{COG}\left[\mu_{B'}(y) - \beta_R \, \mathbb{I}(y - y_\beta) - \alpha_L \, \mathbb{I}(y_\alpha - y)\right] \qquad (2.86)$$

denoted shortly $\text{MICOG}_{\alpha\beta}$, and

$$y^* = \text{COG}\left[\mu_{B'}(y) - \beta_R \, \mathbb{I}(y - y_\alpha) - \alpha_L \, \mathbb{I}(y_\alpha - y)\right] \qquad (2.87)$$

denoted $\text{MICOG}_{\alpha\alpha}$, where $\mathbb{I}(\cdot)$ denotes the Heaviside unit step pseudo-function. The interpretation of the above introduced defuzzifiers is obvious.

3. If $y^{(i)}$ is denoted as the center of the i-th output fuzzy set and τ_i as its height, the center average defuzzifier (CAD) or height method (HM) determines y^* as

$$y^* = \frac{\sum\limits_{i=1}^{I} \tau_i \, y^{(i)}}{\sum\limits_{i=1}^{I} \tau_i}. \qquad (2.88)$$

As an example, let us consider the i-th output fuzzy set as a trapezoid (Fig. 2.10). Its center of gravity $y^{(i)}$ may be computed by means of the formula:

$$y^{(i)} = \text{COG}[\mu_{B^{(i)}{'}}(y)] = \frac{a_m(m_1 - a_m/3) - m_1^2 + m_2^2 + b_m(m_2 + b_m/3)}{a_m + 2(m_2 - m_1) + b_m}. \qquad (2.89)$$

4. The maximum defuzzifier (MD) chooses the y^* as the point in Y at which $B'(y)$ achieves its maximum value, i.e. defining the set of all points in Y at which $B'(y)$ achieves its maximum value

$$Y(B') = \left\{y \in Y \,\middle|\, \mu_{B'}(y) = \sup_{y \in Y} \mu_{B'}(y)\right\}. \qquad (2.90)$$

The maximum defuzzifier determines y^* as an arbitrary element in $Y(B')$.

The mean of maximum (MOM) defuzzifier is defined as

$$y^* = \frac{\int\limits_{Y(B')} y \, dy}{\int\limits_{Y(B')} dy}, \qquad (2.91)$$

where the integral denotes the conventional integration for the continuous part of $Y(B')$ (or summation for the discrete part of $Y(B')$). The modifications applied to defuzzifier 2, can also be applied to defuzzifiers 3 and 4 denoted shortly as MISD_α, $\text{MISD}_{\alpha\alpha}$, $\text{MISD}_{\alpha\beta}$.

2.10
Equivalence of approximate reasoning results using different interpretations of if-then rules

In many applications crisp results are required instead of fuzzy results. An output fuzzy set $B'(y)$ obtained from inference system based on fuzzy implication interpretation of if-then rules is different from the resulting fuzzy set obtained from the inference system based on the conjunctive interpretation of fuzzy if-then rules. Hence, a question arises whether it is possible to get the same or approximately the same crisp results from inference system when defuzzification is applied. The answer is positive under the respective circumstances. The point of departure of our considerations is the equality expressed in the form:

$$
\delta_{mf_L}\left\{\sup_{x\in X}\left[\mu_{A'}(x)\star_{T2}\bigoplus_{i=1}^{I} I\big(\mu_{A^{(i)}}(x),\mu_{B^{(i)}}(y)\big)\right]\right\} =
$$
$$
= \delta_{mf_R}\left\{\sup_{x\in X}\left[\mu_{A'}(x)\star_{T2}\bigoplus_{i=1}^{I}\big(\mu_{A^{(i)}}(x)\star_{T1}\mu_{B^{(i)}}(y)\big)\right]\right\}. \tag{2.92}
$$

The left-side part of that equality represents the defuzzified output of fuzzy implication based inference system whereas the right-side part represents an inference system based on Mamdani's composition (conjunctive interpretation of if-then rules).

The problem is to find such fuzzy implications (for the left-side part of the last equality), conjunctive operators (in the right-side of this equality), aggregation operations and defuzzification methods for both sides of the last equality in order to get the same crisp results. Generally, solving such a problem causes difficulties. One of the most important reasons is the different nature of fuzzy implication and conjunction (cf. different truth tables in classical logic). However, in special cases, under some assumptions, a pragmatic solution exists. To show such a solution let us assume for simplicity that the input fuzzy sets A' are singletons in x_0 (in this particular case FATI is equivalent to FITA). The last equality can be rewritten in the simplified form:

$$
\delta_{mf_L}\left\{\bigoplus_{i=1}^{I} I(\mu_{A^{(i)}}(x_0),\mu_{B^{(i)}}(y))\right\} =
$$
$$
= \delta_{mf_R}\left\{\bigoplus_{i=1}^{I}\big(\mu_{A^{(i)}}(x_0)\star_{T1}\mu_{B^{(i)}}(y)\big)\right\}. \tag{2.93}
$$

Because of the differences in aggregation operations, we accept the same for both sides of the equality aggregation operation i.e. normalized arithmetic sum. Additionally, we assume different defuzzification methods for both sides of the last equality, e.g. $MISD_\alpha$ (modified indexed standard defuzzifier) for the left-side and SD (standard defuzzifier) for the right-side. For our purposes we will use as the left-side defuzzification method, the method presented in the previous section named $MICOG_\alpha$. For some fuzzy implications (e.g. Kleene-Dienes, Łukasiewicz, Reichenbach, Zadeh and Fodor) we have:

$$\alpha = \frac{1}{I} \sum_{i=1}^{I} \alpha_i = \frac{1}{I} \sum_{i=1}^{I} \left(1 - \mu_{A'}(\underline{x}_0)\right) = \frac{1}{I} \sum_{i=1}^{I} \left(1 - \tau_i\right), \tag{2.94}$$

where τ_i stands for firing degree of the i-th rule.

However, for other fuzzy implications (e.g. Gödel, Rescher and Goguen) α equals zero.

As the right side defuzzification method the well known COG method can be used. Taking into account the above mentioned assumptions and simplifications the last equality may be written as

$$MICOG_\alpha \left(\frac{1}{I} \sum_{i=1}^{I} I(\mu_{A^{(i)}}(\underline{x}_0), \mu_{B^{(i)}}(y)) \right) =$$
$$= COG \left(\frac{1}{I} \sum_{i=1}^{I} (\mu_{A^{(i)}}(\underline{x}_0) \star_{TI} \mu_{B^{(i)}}(y)) \right). \tag{2.95}$$

It should be pointed out here that the modification in $MICOG_\alpha$ is responsible for the elimination of the indeterminant part of output membership function $B'(y)$ (if such a part exists).

The specific equivalence of inference results mentioned above can be seen straight on, if we take e.g. Reichenbach fuzzy implication on the assumption that α is computed by means of formula (2.94), as aggregation operation, a normalized arithmetic sum is applied and the defuzzification method $MICOG_\alpha$ is represented by formula (2.84) or (2.85). On the right side of formula (2.95) algebraic product operation is taken in order to get Larsen's inference system with normalized arithmetic sum as aggregation operation and COG as defuzzification method. The above mentioned equivalence can also be described by the identity:

$$MICOG_\alpha \left(\frac{1}{I} \sum_{i=1}^{I} (1 - \mu_{A^{(i)}}(\underline{x}_0) + \mu_{A^{(i)}}(\underline{x}_0) \mu_{B^{(i)}}(y)) \right)_{\text{Reichenbach}} =$$
$$= COG \left(\frac{1}{I} \sum_{i=1}^{I} (\mu_{A^{(i)}}(\underline{x}_0) \mu_{B^{(i)}}(y)) \right)_{\text{Larsen}} \tag{2.96}$$

A similar equivalence can be shown in the case of Łukasiewicz fuzzy implication and Mamdani's minimum.

Considering the Łukasiewicz fuzzy implication and assuming that α is also computed using formula (2.94), aggregation operation and $MICOG_\alpha$ are the same as in the previous case and on the right side of formula (2.95), $\star_{TI}$ represents minimum, we get a well-known Mamdani's inference system with a normalized arithmetic sum as an aggregation operation and COG as a defuzzification method. This equivalence can be described as follows:

$$
MICOG_\alpha \left(\frac{1}{I} \sum_{i=1}^{I} \min(1, \ 1 - \mu_{A^{(i)}}(\underline{x}_0) + \mu_{B^{(i)}}(y)) \right)_{\text{Łukasiewicz}} =
$$
$$
= COG \left(\frac{1}{I} \sum_{i=1}^{I} \min(\mu_{A^{(i)}}(\underline{x}_0), \ \mu_{B^{(i)}}(y)) \right)_{\text{Mamdani}}
$$

(2.97)

The equivalence formulated in such a way may be also shown using the generalized bounded difference (cf. Yager 1996). In order to illustrate the considerations presented above some numerical examples will be discussed below.

2.11
Numerical results

A fuzzy knowledge base presented in Fig. 2.11 is taken as a basis of numerical calculation carried out here. Such a knowledge base consisting of 9 fuzzy if-then rules may have practical meaning in many fields, e.g. fuzzy control, fuzzy modeling, decision support systems and others. Each rule consists of two premises (e.g. error and change of error) in the antecedent part of the rule and one conclusion (e.g. control) in the consequent part. The fuzzy sets representing possible values of the respective linguistic variables are also shown in Fig. 2.11. Using such a knowledge base we can geometrically illustrate the above discussed equivalence. For all numerical examples the "AND" connective is considered to be an algebraic product.

Considering Reichenbach implication with the normalized arithmetic sum as the aggregation operation and defuzzifier of $MICOG_\alpha$ type (αs are computed from formula (2.94)), the equivalence of inference results with those obtained on the basis of Larsen's product is illustrated in Fig. 2.12. Taking into account the Łukasiewicz fuzzy implication with the same aggregation operation and defuzzifier of $MICOG_\alpha$ type for the same αs as in the previous case, the equivalence of inference results with inference results obtained on the basis of Mamdani's minimum is shown in Fig. 2.13.

If we use the defuzzifier $MIHM_\alpha$ instead of $MICOG_\alpha$ in the last case, we get the same results as we got for Reichenbach implication. It means that the reduced (clipped) conclusion fuzzy sets are transformed into scaled conclusion fuzzy sets. Let us notice that the reduced fuzzy sets obtained using Łukasiewicz fuzzy implication include the scaled fuzzy sets.

In Fig. 2.14. the inference results obtained on the basis of Kleene-Dienes fuzzy implication are shown. However, the equivalence between the inference results obtained on the basis of this fuzzy implication and inference results obtained using a conjunction is not found, but applying the defuzzifier $MIHM_\alpha$ instead of $MICOG_\alpha$ we get the same results as for Reichenbach fuzzy implication (cf. Fig. 2.12). Because of the inclusion of Kleene-Dienes conclusion fuzzy sets in Reichenbach conclusion fuzzy sets the Kleene-Dienes conclusion fuzzy sets have to be respectively rescaled in order to get the last ones.

An analogous situation occurs if Fodor fuzzy implication is considered (cf. Fig. 2.15). The equivalence between the inference results obtained on the basis of this implication and results obtained by means of a conjunction is also not found. However, using $MIHM_\alpha$ defuzzifier instead of $MICOG_\alpha$ we get the same results as for Reichenbach fuzzy implication. Additionally, it should be also pointed out that conclusion fuzzy sets obtained on the basis of Fodor fuzzy implication are not included in conclusion fuzzy sets obtained on the basis of Reichenbach fuzzy implication.

The rule base depicted in Fig. 2.11 was tested by means of a complete set of singletons for the reason of fuzzy modeling of the function:

$$z = f(x, y) = -\frac{x + y}{2}. \tag{2.98}$$

Eight fuzzy implications (Reichenbach, Łukasiewicz, Kleene-Dienes, Fodor, Gödel, Standard Sequence, Goguen and Zadeh) were applied in inference system with the normalized arithmetic sum as an aggregation operation and defuzzifier of $MICOG_\alpha$ type, where α is computed from (2.94) as well. For the above mentioned fuzzy implications the resulting surfaces are presented in Figs. 2.16 - 2.23. These surfaces correspond to the surfaces obtained from the conjunctive based inference system. The indexes (λ_{MSE}, λ_{MAX}) characterizing the quality of inference system may be defined as follows:

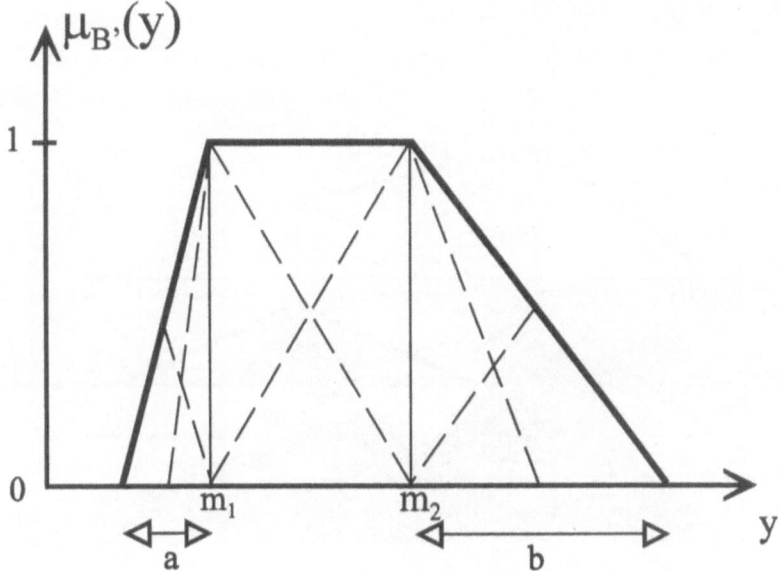

Fig. 2.10. An example of a trapezoidal membership function.

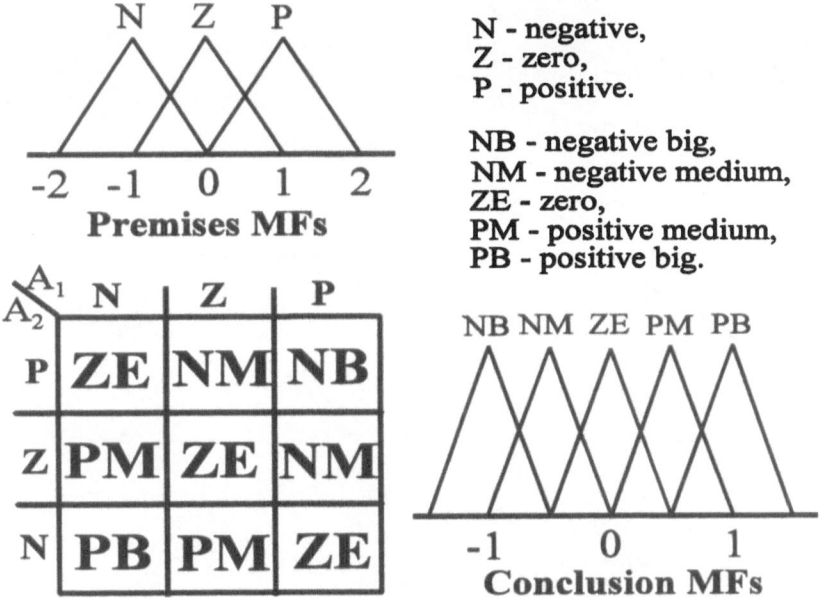

N - negative,
Z - zero,
P - positive.

NB - negative big,
NM - negative medium,
ZE - zero,
PM - positive medium,
PB - positive big.

Fig. 2.11. Knowledge base and related membership functions.

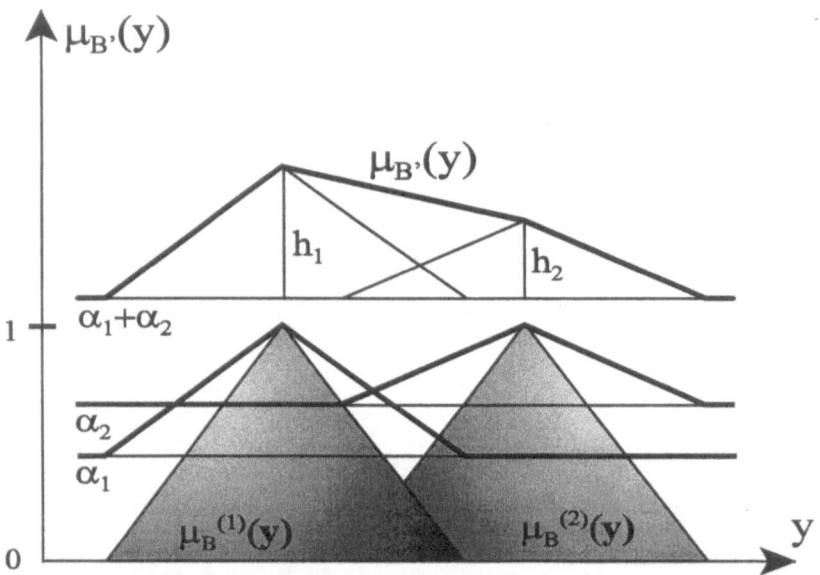

Fig. 2.12. An illustration of the inference results using Reichenbach fuzzy implication and Larsen product.

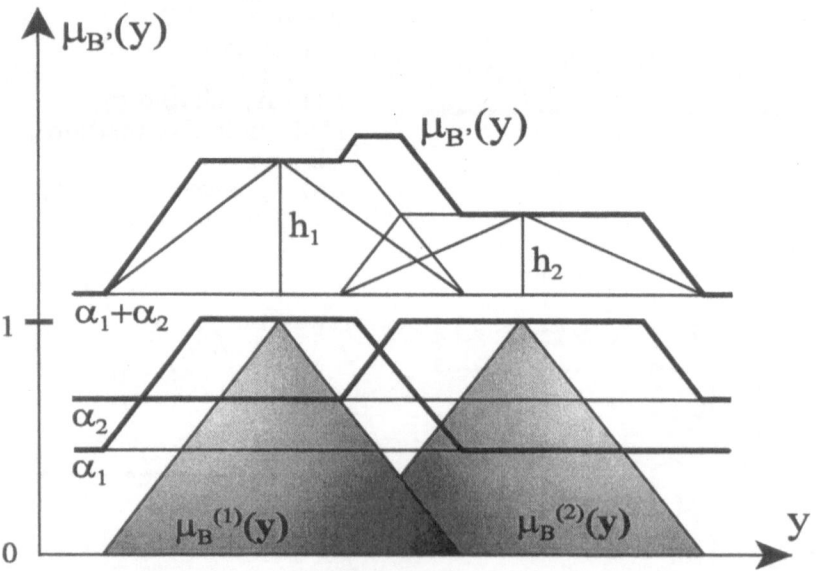

Fig. 2.13. An illustration of the inference results using Łukasiewicz fuzzy implication and Mamdani's minimum.

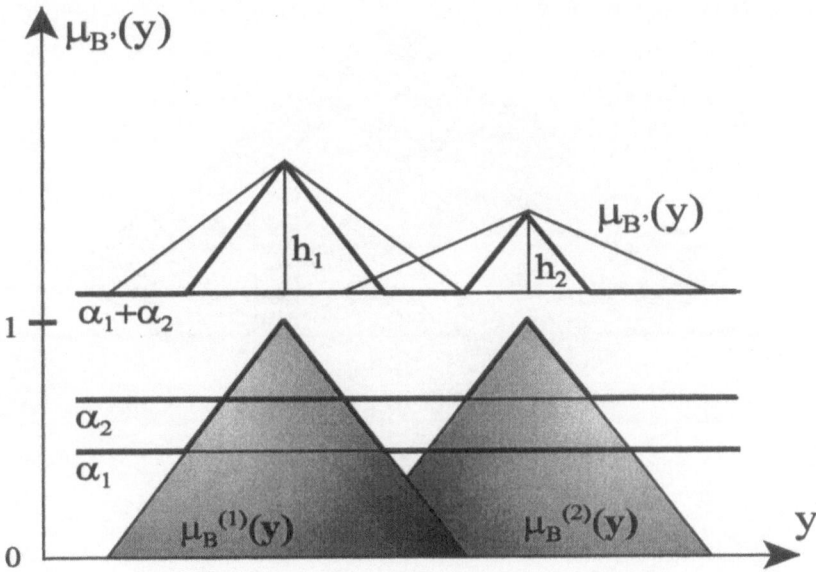

Fig. 2.14. An illustration of the inference results using Kleene-Dienes fuzzy implication and Reichenbach fuzzy implication.

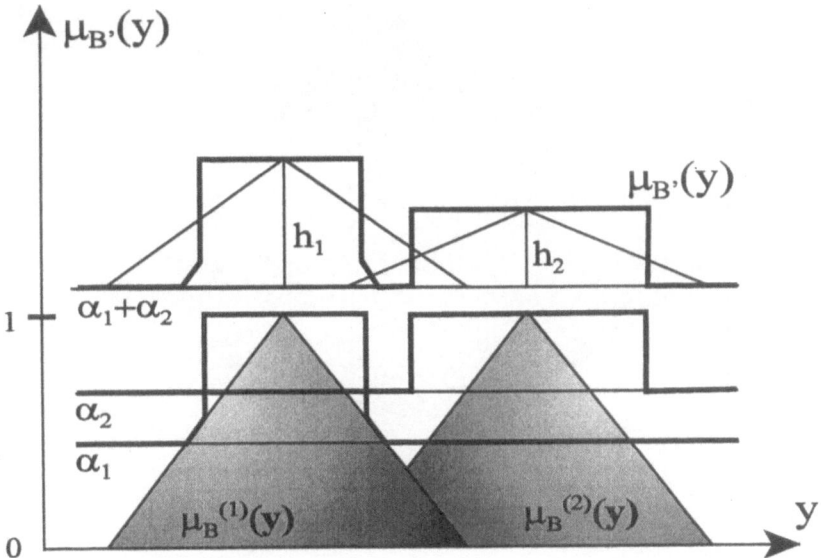

Fig. 2.15. An illustration of the inference results using Fodor fuzzy implication and Reichenbach fuzzy implication.

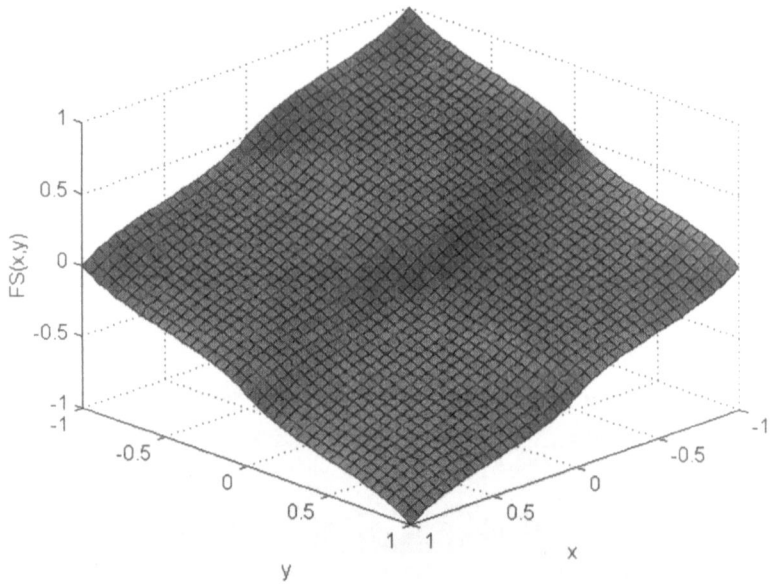

Fig. 2.16. The output surface for Łukasiewicz fuzzy implication.

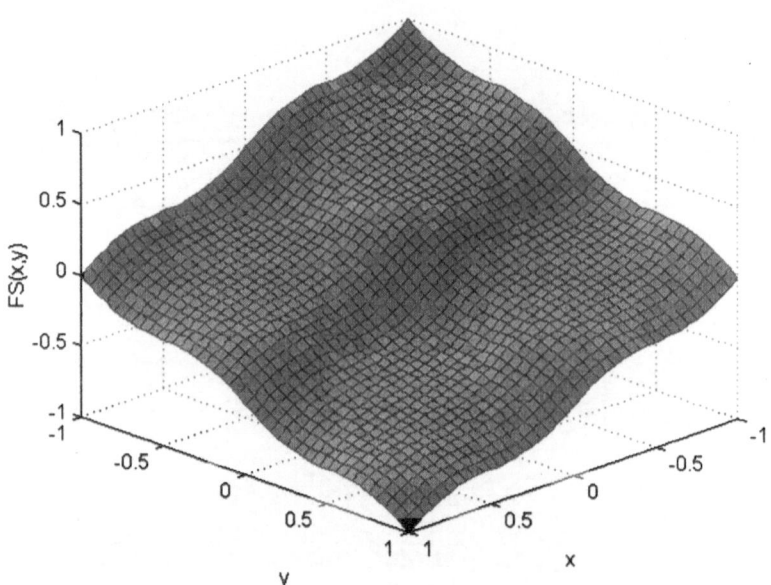

Fig. 2.17. The output surface for Fodor fuzzy implication.

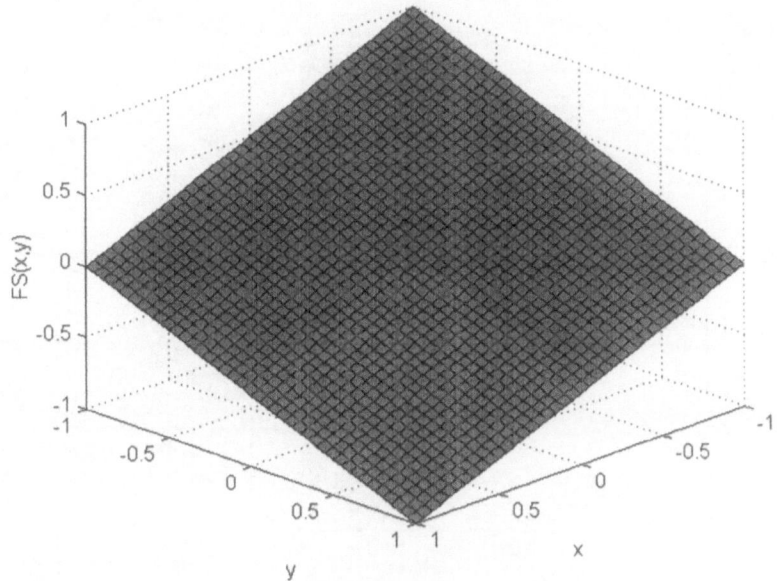

Fig. 2.18. The output surface for Reichenbach fuzzy implication.

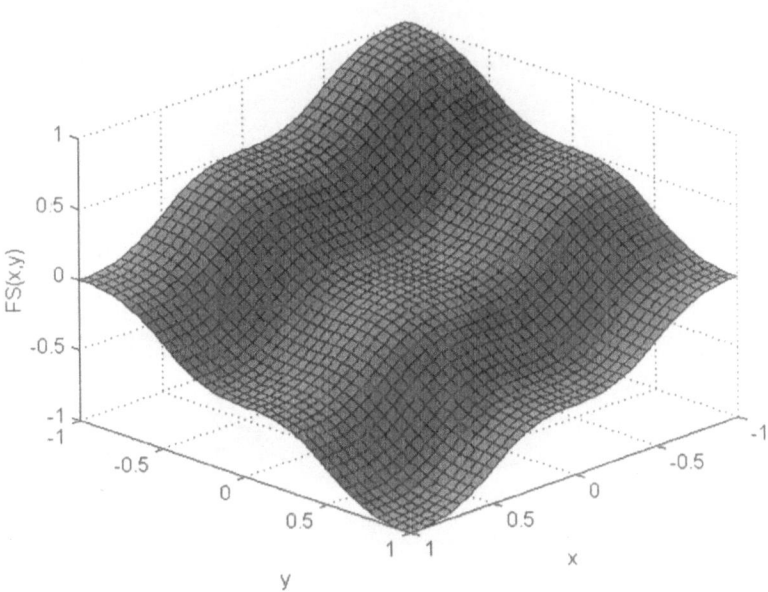

Fig. 2.19. The output surface for Kleene-Dienes fuzzy implication.

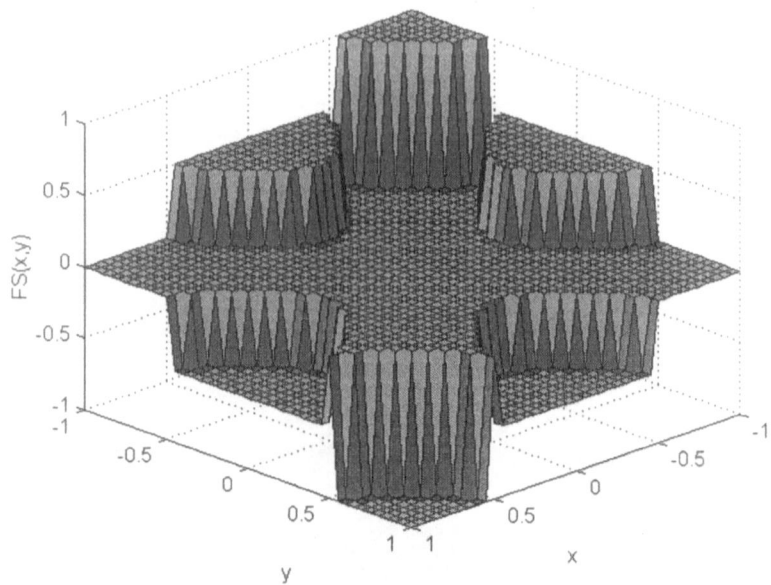

Fig. 2.20. The output surface for Zadeh fuzzy implication.

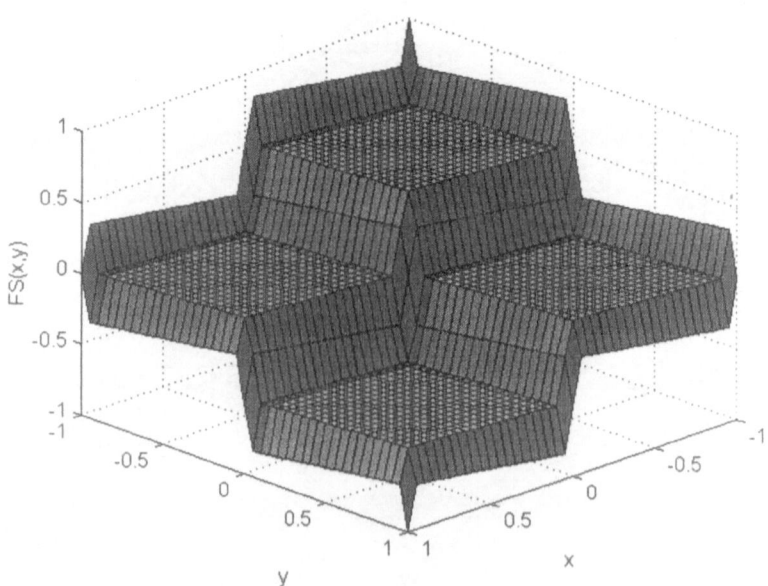

Fig. 2.21. The output surface for Goguen fuzzy implication.

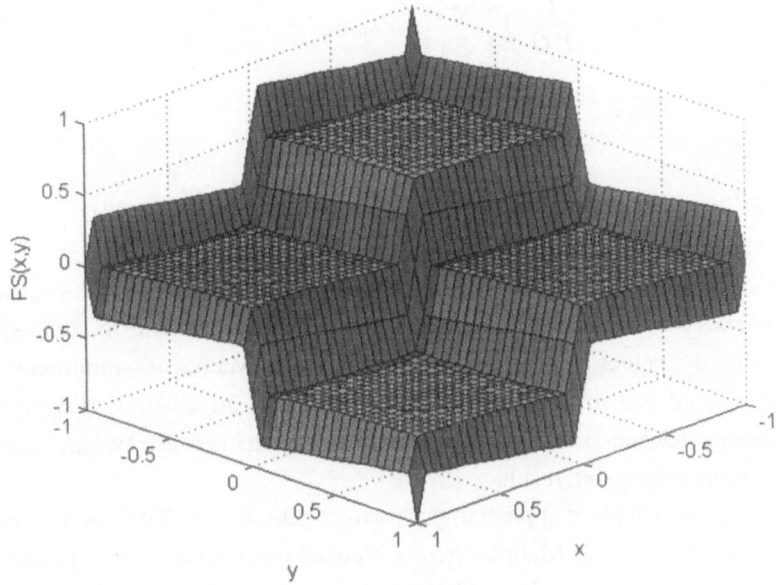

Fig. 2.22. The output surface for Gödel fuzzy implication.

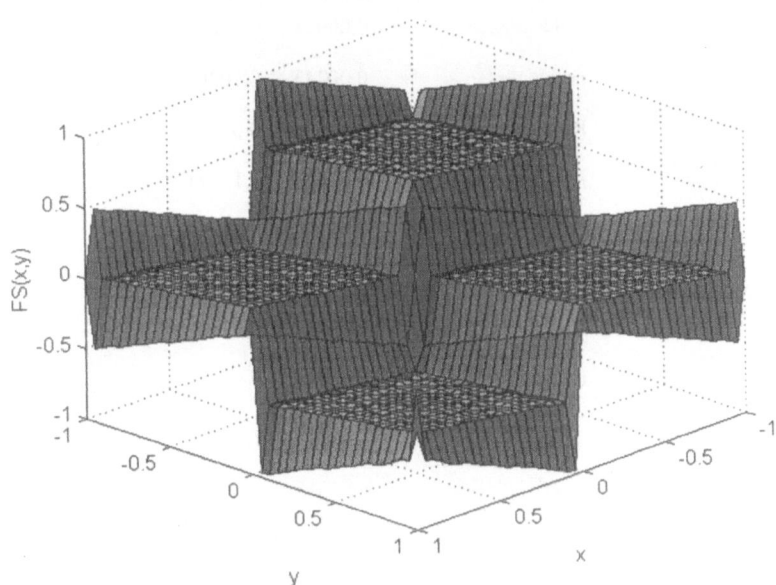

Fig. 2.23. The output surface for Rescher fuzzy implication.

$$\lambda_{MSE} = \frac{1}{PQ} \sum_{p=1}^{P} \sum_{q=1}^{Q} \left[FS(x_p, y_q) + \frac{x_p + y_q}{2} \right]^2,$$

$$\lambda_{MAX} = \max_{\substack{1 \le p \le P \\ 1 \le q \le Q}} \left| FS(x_p, y_q) + \frac{x_p + y_q}{2} \right|,$$

(2.99)

where $FS(x_p, y_q)$ denotes fuzzy system which modeled function (2.98); $x_p = -1 + 2p/P$, $y_q = -1 + 2q/Q$; $P = Q = 100$.

The values of the above mentioned indexes are gathered in Table 2.4. As expected, both indexes for Reichenbach implication are equal to zero and for Łukasiewicz implication the values of indexes are the same as for Mamdani's minimum. It can also be noticed that in this example only four fuzzy implications (Reichenbach, Łukasiewicz, Kleene-Dienes and Fodor) applied in the inference system mentioned above deliver reasonable results.

The programming tool applied to these investigations was FDSS Fuzzy-Flou and Fuzzy Logic toolbox for Matlab systems. Special procedures (m-files) concerning fuzzy implications and modified COG methods were added to the last mentioned toolbox.

Table 2.4. Values of quality indexes.

Implication name	λ_{MSE}	λ_{MAX}
Łukasiewicz	0.00051	0.04612
Fodor	0.00243	0.10364
Reichenbach	0.0	0.0
Kleene-Dienes	0.00555	0.15031
Zadeh	0.06952	0.75000
Goguen	0.04662	0.51597
Gödel	0.05185	0.52537
Rescher	0.06941	0.99979

2.12
Summary

In this chapter we have presented the following:

- interpretations of classical and fuzzy conditional statements,
- different (logical and conjunction) interpretations of if-then rules,
- axiomatic definition of fuzzy implications and its properties,
- the idea of compositional rule of inference,
- basic classical rule of inference as: Modus Ponens, Modus Tollens and Hypotetical Syllogism,
- basic fuzzy rule of inference as: Generalized Modus Ponens, Generalized Modus Tollens and Generalized Hypotetical Syllogism,
- canonical form of fuzzy if-then rules and properties of a set of rules (database),
- aggregation operations for fuzzy relations; Mamdani and Gödel combinations using generalized mean to aggregation,
- two methods of approximate reasoning: composition based inference (first aggregate then inference - FATI) and individual-rule based inference (first inference then aggregate - FITA),
- approximate reasoning with singletons,
- basic fuzzifiers including singleton, triangular and Gaussian fuzzifiers,
- basic defuzzification methods including: center of gravity (COG), indexed center of gravity (ICOG), height method (HM), maximum defuzzification (MD),
- modified version of defuzzification which eliminates a non-informative part of membership function named a modified indexed center of gravity (MICOG) method,
- an equivalence of approximate reasoning results using logical and conjunctive interpretations of if-then rules,
- numerical investigations of approximate reasoning methods using different fuzzy implications,

The most important result of this chapter is showing a specific type of equivalence of inference results using fuzzy implication interpretation and the respective conjunctive interpretation of the if-then rules. Such an equivalence is important regarding the inference algorithm development. The inference algorithm based on conjunctive operators (minimum, product) usually seem to be simpler, faster and more exact than the algorithms of fuzzy implications based inference systems. However, the interpretation of the fuzzy if-then rules based on fuzzy implications is sounder from the logical point of view.

Bibliographical notes

The Zadeh (1973) paper was an outstanding milestone for approximate reasoning. This paper introduced the generalization of classical logic principles to fuzzy logic. A mathematical analysis of the fuzzy inference process were also presented by: Bouchon-Meunier (1991), Demirli and Türksen (1994), Emami et al. (1998), Fodor and Keresztfalvi (1996), Klement and Navara (1999), Kóczy and Hirota (1993), Kundu and Chen (1998), Maeda and Nobusada (1997), Mouzouris and Mendel (1997), Türksen (1988), Türksen (1989), Yager and Larsen (1991).

Fuzzy relational equations are in Drewniak (1989), Drewniak (1995), Pedrycz (1984), Pedrycz (1993). For an exposition of aggregation operations the reader may consult Fodor and Roubens (1994), Marichal and Mathonet (1999), Yager (1996).

There is an extensive literature on the fuzzy implications. Our exposition is based on: Fodor (1991), Fodor (1993), Fodor (1993a), Fodor (1995), Fodor (1996), Fodor and Roubens (1994), Dubois and Prade (1991), Dubois and Prade (1996), Türksen et al. (1998), Whalen and Schott (1992), Czogała and Łęski (1999).

3 Artificial neural networks

3.1
Introduction

Artificial neural networks are systems whose structure is inspired by the action of the nervous system and the human brain. A neuron is the basic unit of a biological neural network. This neuron is shown in Fig. 3.1.a. The neuron consists of inputs called dendrites and output (to other neurons) called axon. The transmission of a signal from an axon to dendrites of other neurons goes through synaptic contacts. The signals transmitted from the synapse to dendrites are modified according to the synaptic strength of connection (synaptic weight). This biological motivation leads McCulloch and Pitts (1943) to publishing the model of a neuron as a binary thresholding device shown in Fig. 3.1.b. and described by:

$$y = f\left(\sum_{i=1}^{N'} w_i\, u_i - \theta \right),$$ (3.1)

where f is the activation function, w_is are the synaptic weights and θ is the threshold parameter. Originally, McCulloch and Pitts used the Heaviside pseudo-function. In this case the neuron is fired (activated) when the weighted sum of input is greater than parameter θ.

Real neurons are more complicated than those shown by McCulloch and Pitts, and can perform a more general non-linear function of their inputs. Usually, we use the following activation functions: threshold function

$$f(x) = I(x) = \begin{cases} 1, & x \geq 0, \\ 0, & x < 0, \end{cases}$$ (3.2)

or, sigmoid function (s-sharped)

$$f(x) = \frac{1}{1 + e^{-ax}},$$ (3.3)

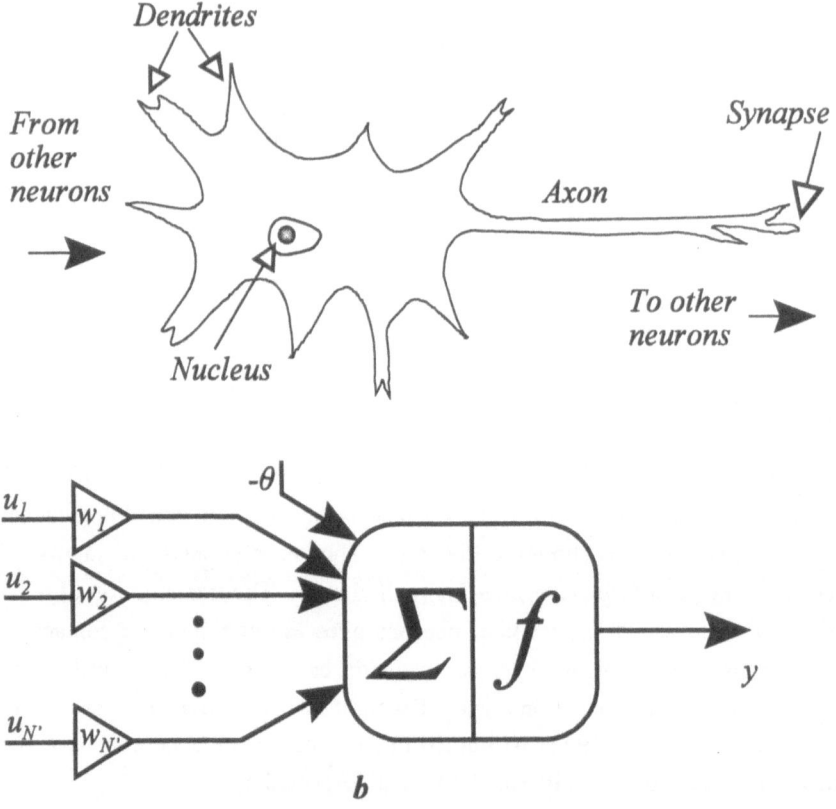

Fig. 3.1. Biological (**a**) and artificial (**b**) neurons.

or

$$f(x) = \frac{1 - e^{-ax}}{1 + e^{-ax}} \qquad (3.4)$$

for $a > 0$. When we use (3.2) the neuron is called perceptron.

Artificial neural networks are architectures composed of the series, parallel and feedback interconnections of artificial neurons. These networks may be quite different from biological ones. It is difficult to give a clear definition of an artificial neural network, due to a variety of their structures. However, the following three major advantages distinguish them from other systems:

- adaptivity: it can learn from the new data, i.e. can adjust local processing parameters and global configurations of processors to accommodate changes in inputs,

- parallelism: as opposed to performing a program of sequential instructions (von Neumann computers), neural networks explore instructions simultaneously using massively parallel nets of many interconnected neurons,
- fault tolerance: resistance to noisy, missing and confusing data.

The artificial neural networks can be classified as:

- feedforward networks, where neurons are organized in layers,
- recurrent networks, where the outputs of some neurons are feedback to input of other neurons,
- self-organizing networks, where neurons are organized on "maps" transformed by input data,
- associative memory networks, where a recurrent neural network is used to memorize information in the steady-state of the network.

Artificial neural networks can only imitate a small portion of the behaviors of biological networks. The most powerful computer used to implement artificial neural networks is far less effective than the brain of a primitive human being. However, these networks can be useful to solve some problems, such as system identification, pattern recognition and prediction.

3.2
Artificial neural networks topologies

3.2.1
Feedforward multilayer networks

This type of artificial neural network has neurons which have one-way connections to other neurons. Neurons are organized in a sequence of layers. The layers are labeled as: input, hidden and output. A network with one hidden layer with N' neurons, input layer with P neurons and output layer with K neurons is shown in Fig. 3.2. Neurons on the same layer do not link with each other. Neurons in input layer only distribute the input signals u_i. The neurons whose outputs are set to one (bias neurons) have connection weights equal to $-\theta_i$ (associated with i-th neuron). If we denote the weight on link from i-th neuron to j-th neuron (in next layer) as w_{ij},

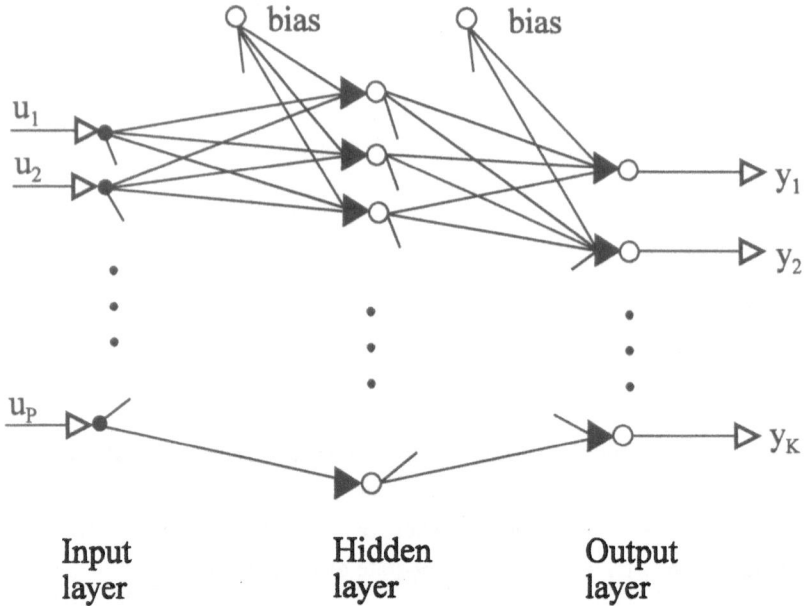

Fig. 3.2. An example of a feedforward multilayer network.

then using neuron model from (3.1) the network represents the function:

$$y_k = f_k\left(\sum_{j=1}^{N'} w_{jk} f_j\left(\sum_{i=1}^{P} w_{ij} u_i - \theta_j \right) - \theta_k \right), \quad 1 \le k \le K, \qquad (3.5)$$

where θ_k are threshold parameters (biases), f_k are activation functions.

If we introduce notation $w_{0j} = -\theta_j$, $u_0 = 1$ and additionally assume that $j \to k$ denotes indexes of neurons j connected to k-th neuron then (3.5) takes the form:

$$y_k = f_k\left(\sum_{j \to k} w_{jk} f_j\left(\sum_{i \to j} w_{ij} u_i \right) \right), \quad 1 \le k \le K. \qquad (3.6)$$

If we denote any continuous function $g: R^P \to R$ on compact set $\underline{K} \subset R^P$, and f is a sigmoid function, then for any $\varepsilon > 0$ there exists a positive integer N' (a number of neurons in hidden layer) and a neural network described by (3.6) with one hidden layer and no activation function at the output layer denoted as $ANN(\underline{u})$ such that:

$$\underset{\underline{u} \in \underline{K}}{\forall} \ | g(\underline{u}) - ANN(\underline{u}) | < \varepsilon. \qquad (3.7)$$

In other words, any continuous function can be uniformly approximated on compact set by a feedforward multilayer neural network with a single hidden layer. The proof of above proposition is given in Kalouptsidis (1997).

3.2.2
Radial basis function networks

A radial basis function network (RBFN) is a feedforward network with a single hidden layer. Such a network with a single output is presented in Fig.3.3. The hidden layer consist of neurons described by function:

$$z_j = R\left(\underline{u} - \underline{m}_j,\ \underline{s}_j\right), \tag{3.8}$$

where $\underline{m}_j$, $\underline{s}_j$ denote vectors of parameters of j-th neuron, R is function $R: R^P \rightarrow R$, with the maximal value for $\underline{u} = \underline{m}_j$ and decreasing as the absolute value of its argument grows. Finally, the input-output function represented by the network is:

$$y = \sum_{j=1}^{Q} a_j\ R\left(\underline{u} - \underline{m}_j,\ \underline{s}_j\right), \tag{3.9}$$

where a_j are parameters (weights) of output neuron.

The common choices for R are a Gaussian function:

$$R(\underline{x},\ \underline{s}) = e^{-\frac{1}{2}\underline{x}^T \underline{s}^{-1} \underline{x}}, \tag{3.10}$$

or a logistic function:

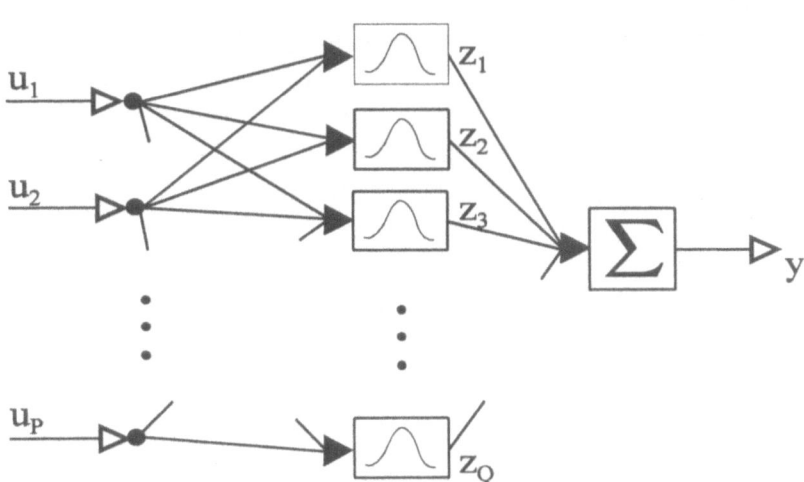

Fig. 3.3. An example of radial basis function network.

$$R(\underline{x}, \underline{s}) = \frac{2}{1 + e^{\underline{x}^T \underline{s}^{-1} \underline{x}}},$$

(3.11)

where $\underline{s}$ is a positive definite matrix of parameters. Functions R are radially symmetric and this clarifies the name radial basis network. Like a multilayer neural network, radial networks are also universal approximators (see Kalouptsidis 1997).

3.2.3
Recurrent networks

Recurrent neural networks are systems of neurons where outputs of some neurons are feedback to input of some other neurons. An example of that network is shown in Fig. 3.4. This network consists of $K+P+Q$ inputs, Q hidden and K output neurons. Symbol z^{-1} denotes one-step time delay. This network is called a real time recurrent network (RTRN). Signals in input layer can be written as P external signals $u_1, u_2,...u_P$, Q delayed signals from hidden neurons $x_1, x_2,...x_Q$ and K delayed signals from output layer $y_1, y_2,...y_K$.

The input-output function realized by the network from Fig. 3.4. can be written as:

$$y_i(n) = \sum_{j \to i} w_{ji}^{(1)} u_j(n) + \sum_{j \to i} w_{ji}^{(2)} x_j(n-1) + \sum_{j \to i} w_{ji}^{(3)} y_j(n-1),$$

(3.12)

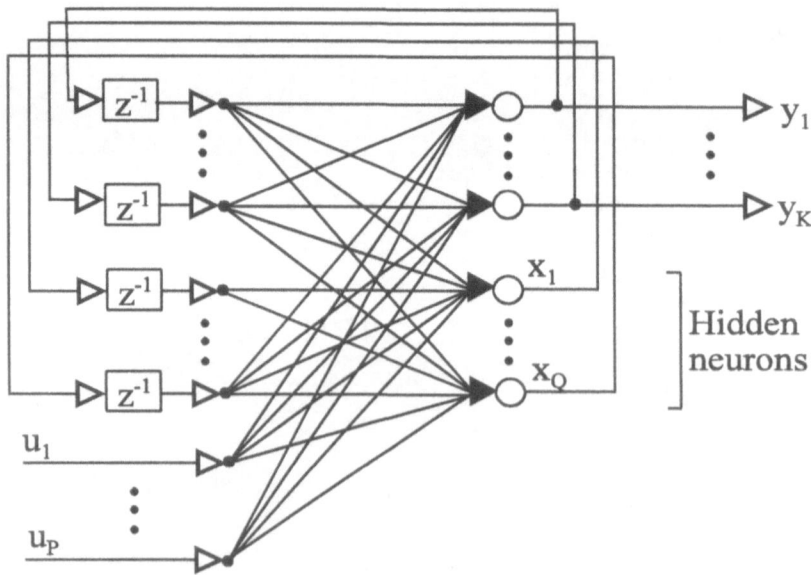

Fig. 3.4. An example of recurrent network.

where $w_{ij}^{(1)}$, $w_{ij}^{(2)}$, $w_{ij}^{(3)}$ are neurons weights from input, delayed hidden and delayed output signals, respectively. The use of $j \rightarrow i$ symbol implies that not all connections of neurons exist. The same effect is obtained by setting some weights to zero. All signals are determined in discrete time n = 0, 1, 2, ... Eq. (3.12) describes a dynamical system whose outputs can be determined if we know initial conditions and input signals. If we construct a network without input signals ($P = 0$) and without a hidden layer ($Q = 0$) we get the so-called Hopfield network. In this case external signals are put in as initial conditions. The output signals are obtained after a number of iterations. This network has a finite number of steady-state output vectors and can be viewed as an associative memory system.

3.3
Learning in artificial neural networks

Human beings can learn tasks such as for example letter recognition, car driving and searching faults in electronic circuits. Something changes (is modified) in our neural network during experience (training). This is a change of connection strength (including adding and removing connections or/and neurons) between neurons.

Like in biological neural networks artificial networks also have learning features. Learning is the process by which the neural networks adapt themselves to producing desired behaviors. There are different methods of learning in artificial neural networks. The most popular methods are:

- a supervised learning process requiring a teacher or supervisor who inform what is a target response of the network. During learning input signals are presented to the network, which results in output response. Error signal is defined as a difference between this response and target response. Network's synaptic weights are modified in such a way that error signal is minimized,
- unsupervised learning does not require a teacher. In this case we do not know the target response of the network. The input signals (patterns) are grouped into similar classes. During the learning process new input patterns presented to the network are included in existing classes or a new class is created,
- reinforced learning is a type of supervised learning, where teachers do not grade the alignment between actual and target outputs of the network. Teachers indicate the effect on network's output as "good" or "bad". Network's synaptic weights are corrected if the teachers indicate "bad" network response,
- competitive learning is the next type of supervised learning, where output neurons

compete with each other. When input patterns are presented to the network the output neurons produce responses. The winning neuron is the neuron that produces the smallest error signal. This is often called specialization process, where each output is taught to respond to other type of input patterns.

Historically, first method of network learning was written by Hebb (1949). In his approach the synaptic weights between neurons should be increased if they are fired together. He also suggested that corrections of weights are proportional to the product of the neurons output signals:

$$w_{jk} \leftarrow w_{jk} + \eta \, y_j \, y_k, \qquad (3.13)$$

where η is learning rate, $\leftarrow$ denotes updating symbol.

This is known as the Hebbian learning rule.

Another learning rule was developed by Rosenblatt (1958), Widrow and Hoff (1960). Let us write equation (3.1) in vector form assuming that $f(x) = x$:

$$y = \underline{w}^T \underline{u}, \qquad (3.14)$$

where $\underline{w}$, $\underline{u}$ are vectors of weights and input signals, respectively, and superscript T denotes vector transposition. If we denote target value on output of that linear neuron as t, then Widrow-Hoff (or delta) learning rule is:

$$\underline{w} \leftarrow \underline{w} - \eta\left(\underline{w}^T \underline{u} - t\right), \qquad (3.15)$$

where η is learning rate (a small positive value).

In the case of Rosenblatt perceptron the output signal from the neuron is a sign of linear combination from (3.14). The sign indicates the class of patterns to which the input pattern belongs. The perceptron learning rule has the form (see Ripley 1996):

$$\underline{w} \leftarrow \underline{w} + \eta \, \varphi \, \underline{u} \, I(-\varphi \, \underline{w}^T \underline{u}), \qquad (3.16)$$

where I is Heaviside pseudo-function, φ is parameter 1 or -1 for input pattern from class one or two, respectively.

These simple learning rules were an inspiration for Rumelhart and McClelland (1986) when they proposed the back-propagation learning rule.

3.4
Back-propagation learning rule

The idea of back-propagation first occurred in control theory (Bryson and Ho 1969).

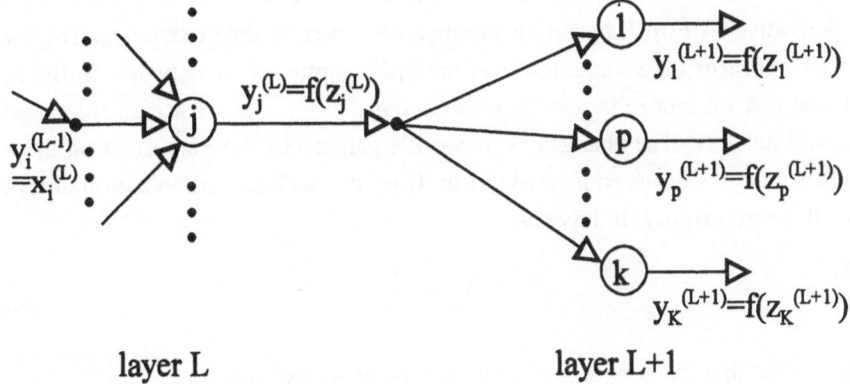

layer L   **layer L+1**

Fig. 3.5. Fragment of a neural network.

These ideas were used by Rumelhart et al. (1986a), Rumelhart and McClelland (1986) in the learning process of artificial neural networks. Back-propagation is a supervised method of learning, and let us suppose that we have N examples of input data denoted $\underline{x}(n)$; $n=1, 2, ..., N$ and the same number of target responses of neural network given by supervisor (a teacher): $\underline{t}(n)$; $n = 1, 2, ..., N$. These data create the so-called training set (set of ordered pairs):

$$\left\{ \left(\underline{x}(n), \underline{t}(n) \right) \right\}_{n=1}^{N}. \tag{3.17}$$

If we denote an input-output relation in a trained neural network as a parameterized function $\underline{y} = g(\underline{x}, \underline{\theta})$, where $\underline{y}$ is network output vector, then $\underline{\theta}$ denotes the vector of parameters in a network (i.e., weights of connections, parameter of radial functions) to optimize. By minimization the total error on training set:

$$E(\underline{\theta}) = \frac{1}{2} \sum_{i=1}^{N} \left\| \underline{t}(i) - g\left(\underline{x}(i), \underline{\theta} \right) \right\|^2, \tag{3.18}$$

where $\|\bullet\|$ denotes the norm of vector, we chose parameter vector $\underline{\theta}$. Scalar index (least-square criterion) $E(\underline{\theta})$ is generally a non-linear function of parameter vector $\underline{\theta}$.

So, we can use to minimize $E(\underline{\theta})$ any algorithm from unconstrained non-linear optimization. Rumelhart and colleagues used the steepest descent method to minimize (3.18), with the updating rule:

$$\underline{\theta} \leftarrow \underline{\theta} - \eta \, \frac{\partial E(\underline{\theta})}{\partial \underline{\theta}}. \tag{3.19}$$

Note that $g(\underline{x}, \underline{\theta})$ must be differentiable if $E(\underline{\theta})$ should be differentiable. This implies that activation function in neuron model must be differentiable, and (3.3),

(3.4) functions are commonly used. Criterion (3.18) is a sum over all training data, so derivatives $\partial E(\theta) \,/\, \partial\theta$ can be summed also over all data examples. The same remark concerns the summation over multiple outputs of the network. In the next calculations we ignore index i in training data. In Fig. 3.5 we see an fragment of a neural network. The changes of network's parameters have an effect on the j-th neuron and all neurons connected to j-th. If we denote linear combination of inputs for j-th neuron from L-th layer as:

$$z_j^{(L)} = \sum_{p \sim j} w_{pj}\, x_p^{(L)},$$
(3.20)

then for the derivative with respect to parameter w_{ij} we have:

$$\frac{\partial E}{\partial w_{ij}} = \frac{\partial E}{\partial y_j^{(L)}} \frac{\partial y_j^{(L)}}{\partial w_{ij}} = \frac{\partial E}{\partial y_j^{(L)}} \frac{\partial f(z_j^{(L)})}{\partial z_j^{(L)}} \frac{\partial z_j^{(L)}}{\partial w_{ij}},$$
(3.21)

where $y_j^{(L)} = f(z_j^{(L)})$, f is neuron activation function. Denoting:

$$\delta_j^{(L)} = \frac{\partial E}{\partial y_j^{(L)}} \frac{\partial f(z_j^{(L)})}{\partial z_j^{(L)}}$$
(3.22)

we have:

$$\frac{\partial E}{\partial w_{ij}} = \delta_j^{(L)} \frac{\partial z_j^{(L)}}{\partial w_{ij}} = \delta_j^{(L)}\, y_j^{(L-1)}.$$
(3.23)

However, in the next layer $(L+1)$ there are some neurons connected with j-th neuron.

If we denote neurons connected with output of j-th neuron as $k \sim j$, then criterion (3.18) can be expressed as function ξ of neuron outputs from layer $L+1$ which are connected with j-th neuron from layer L:

$$E = \xi(\, y_k^{(L+1)} \mid k \sim j) = \xi(\, f(z_k^{(L+1)}) \mid k \sim j).$$
(3.24)

But $z_k^{(L+1)}$ depends on $y_j^{(L)}$, hence:

$$E = \xi\!\left(f(w_{jk} y_j^{(L)} + c) \mid k \sim j \right),$$
(3.25)

where c represents the rest of inputs independent from $y_j^{(L)}$. Using the ordered derivative (Werbos 1974) we obtain:

$$\frac{\partial E}{\partial y_j^{(L)}} = \frac{\partial \xi(f(w_{jk} y_j^{(L)} + c) \mid k \leftarrow j)}{\partial y_j^{(L)}} =$$

$$= \sum_{k \leftarrow j} \frac{\partial \xi(y_k^{(L+1)} \mid k \leftarrow j)}{\partial y_k^{(L+1)}} \frac{\partial f(z_k^{(L+1)})}{\partial z_k^{(L+1)}} \frac{\partial z_k^{(L+1)}}{\partial y_j^{(L)}}. \tag{3.26}$$

Hence, using (3.20) and (3.26):

$$\frac{\partial E}{\partial y_j^{(L)}} = \sum_{k \leftarrow j} \frac{\partial E}{\partial y_k^{(L+1)}} \frac{\partial f(z_k^{(L+1)})}{\partial z_k^{(L+1)}} w_{jk}, \tag{3.27}$$

And finally using (3.22) we have:

$$\delta_j^{(L)} = \frac{\partial f(z_j^{(L)})}{\partial z_j^{(L)}} \sum_{k \leftarrow j} w_{jk} \delta_k^{(L+1)}. \tag{3.28}$$

From this equation we see that $\delta_j^{(L)}$ from layer L can be expressed by δs from the next layer $(L+1)$. Hence, partial derivatives of criterion E with respect to parameters can be calculated from output to input of the network. So, outputs of the network are calculated by forward pass, and derivatives by backward pass.

There are two basic types of learning using back-propagation:

- batch (off-line) learning method, where parameter w_{ij} is updated by Δw_{ij} after presentation all patterns (signals) from training set into neural network:

$$\Delta w_{ij} = -\eta \frac{\partial E}{\partial w_{ij}} = -\eta \sum_{i=1}^{N} \frac{\partial E_i}{\partial w_{ij}}, \tag{3.29}$$

where (see (3.18)):

$$E_i = \frac{1}{2} \| t(i) - f(x(i), \theta) \|^2; \tag{3.30}$$

each presentation all data from training set to network is called epoch,
- on-line learning method, where parameter w_{ij} is updated after each pattern (signal) from the training set is presented into network. This method is described by equation (3.19) with E replaced by E_i. This method can converge faster than off-line version.

3.5

Modifications of the classic back-propagation method

In original Rumelhart and McClelland's (1986) work in contrast to (3.29) the idea of "momentum" was proposed. This method of network learning can be written as:

$$\left(\Delta w_{ij}\right)_{new} = \alpha \eta \left(\Delta w_{ij}\right)_{old} - \eta \left(1 - \alpha\right) \frac{\partial E}{\partial w_{ij}}, \tag{3.31}$$

where parameter $\alpha \in (0,1)$. This method can be seen as low-pass filtering of the corrections term Δw_{ij}. There are several problems connected with back-propagation algorithms, such as: parameter initialization, stopping rule, the choice of learning rate. Calculations are usually initialized from a random set of weights. As a stopping rule, the examination of total error on the test set or execution of pre-specified number of iterations are executed. Another problem is the selection of the learning rate η. If we use a large value of η then local minimum of criterion E can be obtain in a few steps, but if small η is used, this minimum is archived with great precision. But application of a fixed learning rate causes that the algorithm gets stuck in a local minimum. Generally in (3.19) the learning rate can change with iteration index:

$$\underline{\theta}^{(k+1)} = \underline{\theta}^{(k)} - \eta^{(k)} \left. \frac{\partial E(\underline{\theta})}{\partial \underline{\theta}} \right|_{\underline{\theta} = \underline{\theta}^{(k)}}, \tag{3.32}$$

where $\eta^{(k)}$ is the learning rate in k-th iteration step. There are many methods of selection of $\eta^{(k)}$ values. Some of them use results from stochastic approximation theory: $\eta^{(k)} \sim k^{-\zeta}$, $0 < \zeta < 1$. The above series of $\eta^{(k)}$ satisfies stochastic approximation criteria: $\Sigma_k \eta^{(k)} = \infty$, $\Sigma_k (\eta^{(k)})^2 < \infty$.

Another group of methods uses the learning rate minimizing criterion E in the direction of gradient $\partial E / \partial w_{ij}$. These methods are presented in Section 3.6.

Other methods use heuristically obtained learning rules. A classical example is Quickprop by Fahlman (1989). In this case the modification of weights can be written as:

$$\left(\Delta w_{ij}\right)_{new} = \alpha_{ij} \left(\Delta w_{ij}\right)_{old} - \eta \left[\frac{\partial E}{\partial w_{ij}} + \gamma w_{ij} \right], \tag{3.33}$$

where γ is weight decay parameter (typically 10^{-4}). Learning rate η takes pre-specified value (typically 0.55) in the following situations: algorithm start, $(\Delta w_{ij})_{old} = 0$,

$$\left(\frac{\partial E}{\partial w_{ij}} + \gamma w_{ij} \right) \left(\Delta w_{ij}\right)_{old} > 0, \tag{3.34}$$

and, otherwise, zero value. The "momentum" coefficients α_{ij} are calculated individually for each learned parameter. If:

$$g = \frac{\partial E}{\partial w_{ij}} + \gamma w_{ij}; \quad \alpha' = \frac{g}{(g)_{old} - g}, \tag{3.35}$$

then

$$\alpha_{ij} = \begin{cases} \alpha_{max}, & \alpha' > \alpha_{max} \text{ or } g(\Delta w_{ij})_{old} \; \alpha' < 0, \\ \alpha', & \text{otherwise.} \end{cases} \tag{3.36}$$

Typical value for $\alpha_{max} = 1.75$. The above algorithm speeds up convergence and decreases probability of stick in local minimum.

A very simple operation speeding up convergence is proposed by Amari (1967). If in two successive steps Δw has an angle in parameter space less than $90°$ than η is increased. In other cases the learning rate is decreases.

Another very useful technique is proposed by Jang (1993a):

- if in pre-specified number of successive steps criterion E decreases then increase normalized parameter updating,
- if in other pre-specified number of successive steps criterion E increases and decreases commutatively then normalized parameter updating decreases.

Normalized updating takes the following form:

$$\Delta w_{ij} = -\frac{\upsilon}{\sqrt{\sum_{(ij)} \left(\frac{\partial E}{\partial w_{ij}}\right)^2}} \frac{\partial E}{\partial w_{ij}}, \tag{3.37}$$

where υ is the step size, and the sum takes over all optimized parameters. In this case updating is done along the steepest descent by Euclidean distance υ.

Another modification is weight decay proposed by Hinton (1986). The method tries to reduce weights in each step. This prevents saturation of neurons output. The original criterion (3.18) is replaced by E':

$$E' = E + \varsigma \sum_i \sum_j w_{ij}^2, \tag{3.38}$$

where ς is a parameter. If we use the steepest descent method for the modified criterion (3.38) then parameter updating takes the form:

$$w_{ij} \leftarrow w_{ij} - \eta \frac{\partial E}{\partial w_{ij}} - 2\varsigma \eta w_{ij}. \qquad (3.39)$$

In several cases network output is a linear combination of some optimized parameters. When additionally, we use least-square criterion (3.18) then this parameters optimization is a linear least-square problem. These methods are briefly discussed in Section 3.7.

3.6
Optimization methods in neural networks learning

In this section we review fundamental methods of minimizing criterion function $E(\underline{\theta})$ which has a nonlinear form with respect to parameter vector $\underline{\theta}=[\theta_1, \theta_2,..., \theta_q]^T$. These methods are iterative. Generally, minimization algorithm is of the form:

$1°$ choose initial point $\underline{\theta}^{(0)}$,

$2°$ determine search direction $\underline{d}^{(k)}$ in $\underline{\theta}^{(k)}$ point (for k-th iteration step),

$3°$ minimize criterion $E(\underline{\theta})$ along $\underline{d}^{(k)}$ direction (line minimization):

$$\min_{\eta > 0} E(\underline{\theta}^{(k)} + \eta \underline{d}^{(k)}) \to \eta^{(k)}, \qquad (3.40)$$

$4°$ update parameter vector:

$$\underline{\theta}^{(k+1)} = \underline{\theta}^{(k)} + \eta^{(k)} \underline{d}^{(k)}, \qquad (3.41)$$

$5°$ goto $2°$ unless the convergence conditions are met.

Minimization procedure is stopped when one of following condition is satisfied:

- criterion function E is small,
- gradient vector is small,
- a pre-specified number of iterations is attained.

Let us suppose that criterion $E(\underline{\theta})$ is a differentiable function with respect to $\underline{\theta}$:

$$\nabla E(\underline{\theta}) = \left[\frac{\partial E(\underline{\theta})}{\partial \theta_1} \quad \frac{\partial E(\underline{\theta})}{\partial \theta_2} \quad \cdots \quad \frac{\partial E(\underline{\theta})}{\partial \theta_q}\right]^T. \qquad (3.42)$$

A first-order Taylor expansion of $E(\underline{\theta})$ about point $\underline{\theta}^{(k)}$ gives:

$$E(\underline{\theta}^{(k)} + \eta \underline{d}^{(k)}) = E(\underline{\theta}^{(k)}) + \eta \left[\nabla E(\underline{\theta}^{(k)})\right]^T \underline{d}^{(k)}. \qquad (3.43)$$

If we want to have $E(\underline{\theta}^{(k)}+\eta\, \underline{d}^{(k)}) < E(\underline{\theta}^{(k)})$ then second term in (3.43) must be negative. Usually we choose:

$$\underline{d}^{(k)} = -\nabla E(\underline{\theta}^{(k)}). \tag{3.44}$$

This method of choosing direction is known as the steepest descent. The Taylor expansion (3.43) gives no idea how to select learning rate η. Several methods are presented in the previous section, and another one is to perform line minimization (3.40). These so-called gradient methods are frequently used due their simplicity, but slow convergence is their main disadvantage. If criterion $E(\underline{\theta})$ is twice differentiable and has Hessian matrix $H(\underline{\theta})$:

$$H(\underline{\theta}) = \begin{bmatrix} \dfrac{\partial^2 E}{\partial\theta_1\,\partial\theta_1} & \cdots & \dfrac{\partial^2 E}{\partial\theta_q\,\partial\theta_1} \\ \cdot & \cdots & \cdot \\ \dfrac{\partial^2 E}{\partial\theta_1\,\partial\theta_q} & \cdots & \dfrac{\partial^2 E}{\partial\theta_q\,\partial\theta_q} \end{bmatrix}, \tag{3.45}$$

then second-order Taylor expansion is given by:

$$E(\underline{\theta}^{(k)} + \underline{d}^{(k)}) = E(\underline{\theta}^{(k)}) + \left[\nabla E(\underline{\theta}^{(k)})\right]^T \underline{d}^{(k)} + \frac{1}{2}\, \underline{d}^{(k)\,T} H(\underline{\theta}^{(k)})\, \underline{d}^{(k)}. \tag{3.46}$$

The necessary condition for minimum (3.46) is $\partial E(\underline{\theta}^{(k)}+\underline{d}^{(k)}) / \partial\underline{\theta}^{(k)} = \underline{0}$, that leads to:

$$\nabla E(\underline{\theta}^{(k)}) + H(\underline{\theta}^{(k)})\, \underline{d}^{(k)} = \underline{0}, \tag{3.47}$$

so, finally we get:

$$\underline{d}^{(k)} = -\left[H(\underline{\theta}^{(k)})\right]^{-1} \nabla E(\underline{\theta}^{(k)}). \tag{3.48}$$

This direction is the so-called Newton's direction. If criterion $E(\underline{\theta})$ is a quadratic function then the minimum is given in a single step. However, in practice this quadratic approximation is not adequate and we do not have Hessian matrix. Then we use modifications of Newton's method, called quasi-Newton (or variable metric) ones. Hessian can be interpreted as a gradient between gradients determined in successive points $\underline{\theta}^{(k)}$. If matrix M denotes approximation of inverse Hessian matrix then:

$$\underline{\theta}^{(k+1)} - \underline{\theta}^{(k)} = M^{(k+1)}\left(\nabla E(\underline{\theta}^{(k+1)}) - \nabla E(\underline{\theta}^{(k)})\right). \tag{3.49}$$

Let us additionally denote: $\underline{s}^{(k)} = \underline{\theta}^{(k)} - \underline{\theta}^{(k-1)}$, $\underline{r}^{(k)} = \nabla E(\underline{\theta}^{(k)}) - \nabla E(\underline{\theta}^{(k-1)})$. Quasi-Newton method uses (3.49) to built up approximation M of H^{-1}. There are many ways of using this information. The most effective is the Broyden-Fletcher-Goldfarb-Shanno (BFGS) method, where:

$$M^{(k)} = M^{(k-1)} + \left[1 + \frac{\underline{r}^{(k)T} M^{(k-1)} \underline{r}^{(k)}}{\underline{s}^{(k)T} \underline{r}^{(k)}}\right] \frac{\underline{s}^{(k)} \underline{s}^{(k)T}}{\underline{s}^{(k)T} \underline{r}^{(k)}} - \frac{\underline{s}^{(k)} \underline{r}^{(k)T} M^{(k-1)} + M^{(k-1)} \underline{r}^{(k)} \underline{s}^{(k)T}}{\underline{s}^{(k)T} \underline{r}^{(k)}}, \quad (3.50)$$

or, for Davidon-Fletcher-Powell (DFP) method we have:

$$M^{(k)} = M^{(k-1)} + \frac{\underline{s}^{(k)} \underline{s}^{(k)T}}{\underline{s}^{(k)T} \underline{r}^{(k)}} - \frac{M^{(k-1)} \underline{r}^{(k)} \underline{r}^{(k)T} M^{(k-1)}}{\underline{r}^{(k)} M^{(k-1)} \underline{r}^{(k)}}. \quad (3.51)$$

When initial $M^{(0)}$ is chosen as identity matrix I, and we use line minimization in each step then approximated Hessian is positive definite. The tests show that the BFGS method is more tolerant to inaccuracy of line minimization. BFGS is probably the best method of non-linear optimization, but this method is rarely used in neural network learning due to its memory and computation burdens.

When the Hessian matrix is inconvenient to compute, an approximation is determined (called a pseudo-Hessian). A reasonable approximation of the Hessian can be computed using for example a gradient with a low burden of additional computations. If we use direction selection from (3.40), the Hessian must be positive definite, so that its inverse is computable. To make a pseudo-Hessian positive definite, it is altered by adding a positive definite matrix (usually identity matrix). So, in place of the Hessian in (3.48) we put $H + \lambda^{(k)} I$, where $\lambda^{(k)}$ is a nonnegative parameter for k-th step. This method is known as the Levenberg-Marquardt algorithm. If $\lambda \to 0$ the method is the Newton's method, if $\lambda \to \infty$ is the steepest descent method. There is a variety of methods of selecting λ parameter. For example in k-th iteration $\lambda^{(k)}$ can be determined as:

$$\lambda^{(k)} = \lambda^{(k-1)} \left/ \left(1 - \frac{\| \nabla E(\underline{\theta}^{(k-1)}) \|^2}{\| \nabla E(\underline{\theta}^{(k)}) - \nabla E(\underline{\theta}^{(k-1)}) \|^2} \right) \right., \quad (3.52)$$

and $\lambda^{(0)}$ is larger than the magnitude of the most negative eigenvalue of the approximated Hessian. Generally λ decreases if the distance of $\underline{\theta}$ from the local minimum decreases.

A very useful method of solving a large non-linear optimization problem is conjugate gradient method. This method has the power of second-order method without calculating the Hessian matrix. In this method consecutive search directions $\underline{d}^{(k)}$ are mutually conjugated with respect to matrix H, i.e.

$$\underset{i \neq j}{\forall} \quad \underline{d}^{(i)T} H \underline{d}^{(j)} = 0. \quad (3.53)$$

It can be shown (see Gill et al. 1981) that:

$$\underline{d}^{(k)} = -\nabla E(\underline{\theta}^{(k)}) + \sum_{j=0}^{k-1} \alpha_{kj} \underline{d}^{(j)}, \tag{3.54}$$

where αs are coefficients. If we use conditions (3.53) then we have:

$$\underline{d}^{(k)} = -\nabla E(\underline{\theta}^{(k)}) + \beta^{(k-1)} \underline{d}^{(k-1)}. \tag{3.55}$$

A new direction of search depends on only actual gradient and previous direction. There are several methods determining βs, i.e.
Polak-Ribiere method:

$$\beta^{(k-1)} = \frac{\nabla E(\underline{\theta}^{(k)})^T \left(\nabla E(\underline{\theta}^{(k)}) - \nabla E(\underline{\theta}^{(k-1)}) \right)}{\nabla E(\underline{\theta}^{(k-1)})^T \nabla E(\underline{\theta}^{(k-1)})}, \tag{3.56}$$

the Fletcher-Reeves method:

$$\beta^{(k-1)} = \frac{\nabla E(\underline{\theta}^{(k)})^T \nabla E(\underline{\theta}^{(k)})}{\nabla E(\underline{\theta}^{(k-1)})^T \nabla E(\underline{\theta}^{(k-1)})}, \tag{3.57}$$

and Beale-Sovenson method:

$$\beta^{(k-1)} = \frac{\nabla E(\underline{\theta}^{(k)})^T \left(\nabla E(\underline{\theta}^{(k)}) - \nabla E(\underline{\theta}^{(k-1)}) \right)}{\underline{d}^{(k-1)T} \left(\nabla E(\underline{\theta}^{(k)}) - \nabla E(\underline{\theta}^{(k-1)}) \right)}. \tag{3.58}$$

The above methods determine only direction and usually step size is calculated with line minimization. The conjugate gradient method assumes that calculation of directions is re-started ($\beta=0$) for every q iteration (q is the number of optimized parameters). This is relevant only for large q.

In the above described minimization algorithms the most effective way to determine the learning rate is line minimization. Line minimization is a one-dimensional search along previously determined direction $\underline{d}^{(k)}$ (in k-th iteration):

$$\min_{\eta>0} E(\underline{\theta}^{(k)} + \eta \, \underline{d}^{(k)}) = \min_{\eta>0} \rho(\eta) \to \eta^*. \tag{3.59}$$

Three problems are merged with this minimization: initial bracketing, line search method and stopping criteria. Initial bracketing is determination the interval in which minimum η (η^*) must be. Line search is the process of determining η^* that minimizes one-argument function $\rho(\eta)$. Generally, this method can be divided into: sectioning, Newton's method and polynomial interpolation. Sectioning method includes well-known bisection, Fibonacci and golden section search. Newton's method can be written as:

$$\eta \rightarrow \eta - \frac{\rho'(\eta)}{\rho''(\eta)}, \tag{3.60}$$

where ρ', ρ'' are first and second derivatives, respectively. Polynomial interpolation method is based on $\rho(\eta)$ curve fitting. For example second-order polynomial is given by: $\tilde{\rho}(\eta) = a_2 \eta^2 + a_1 \eta + a_0$, where a_0, a_1, a_2 are parameters determined from conditions: $\rho_1 = \tilde{\rho}(\eta_1)$, $\rho_2 = \tilde{\rho}(\eta_2)$, $\rho_3 = \tilde{\rho}(\eta_3)$. By solving $\partial \tilde{\rho}(\eta) / \partial \eta = 0$, we obtain:

$$\eta = -\frac{a_1}{2a_2} = \eta_2 - \frac{1}{2} \frac{(\eta_2 - \eta_1)^2 (\rho_2 - \rho_3) - (\eta_2 - \eta_3)^2 (\rho_2 - \rho_1)}{(\eta_2 - \eta_1)(\rho_2 - \rho_3) - (\eta_2 - \eta_3)(\rho_2 - \rho_1)}. \tag{3.61}$$

Line minimization is stopped when some criteria are met. Usually these criteria take the form:

$$\begin{aligned} (\rho(\eta) - \rho(0)) &\geq \zeta_1 \, \eta \, \nabla E(\underline{\theta}^{(k)}) \, \underline{d}^{(k)}, \\ \nabla E(\underline{\theta}^{(k)} + \eta \underline{d}^{(k)}) \, \underline{d}^{(k+1)} &\geq \zeta_2 \, \nabla E(\underline{\theta}^{(k)}) \, \underline{d}^{(k)}, \end{aligned} \tag{3.62}$$

where ζ_1, ζ_2 are parameters from $(0, 1)$ interval.

3.7
Networks with output linearly depending on parameters

In some cases artificial neural network output is a linear combination of some optimized parameters. Let us denote the input-output relation in a neural network as $\underline{y} = g(\underline{x}, \underline{\theta}_L, \underline{\theta})$, where $\underline{\theta}_L$, $\underline{\theta}$ are vectors of unknown parameters for which output $\underline{y}$ depends linearly and non-linearly, respectively. Let dimension of $\underline{\theta}_L$ be p. If we assume that estimation of $\underline{\theta}$ is known, then we can write a simpler form $\underline{y} = g(\underline{x}, \underline{\theta}_L) = \underline{a}(\underline{x})^T \underline{\theta}_L$, where $\underline{a}(\underline{x})$ is a vector depending on input vector $\underline{x}$. If the training set is given by (3.17) (but with scalar target output) then we have a set of N linear equations:

$$\begin{cases} t(1) = \underline{a}(\underline{x}(1))^T \underline{\theta}_L = a_1(\underline{x}(1)) \, \theta_{L1} + \ldots + a_p(\underline{x}(1)) \, \theta_{Lp}, \\ \vdots \\ t(N) = \underline{a}(\underline{x}(N))^T \underline{\theta}_L = a_1(\underline{x}(N)) \, \theta_{L1} + \ldots + a_p(\underline{x}(N)) \, \theta_{Lp}. \end{cases} \tag{3.63}$$

Using a matrix notation we have:

$$T = A \underline{\theta}_L, \tag{3.64}$$

where $T = [t(1), t(2), \ldots, t(N)]^T$ is output vector, $\underline{\theta}_L = [\theta_{L1}, \theta_{L2}, \ldots, \theta_{Lp}]^T$ is vector of unknown parameters, and A is $N{\times}p$-dimensional matrix in a form:

$$A = \begin{bmatrix} a_1(\underline{x}(1)) & a_2(\underline{x}(1)) & \ldots & a_p(\underline{x}(1)) \\ \vdots & & & \vdots \\ a_1(\underline{x}(N)) & a_2(\underline{x}(N)) & \ldots & a_p(\underline{x}(N)) \end{bmatrix}. \tag{3.65}$$

If A is a square ($p = N$) and nonsingular matrix (i.e., determinant not equal to zero) then we have the solution: $\underline{\theta}_L = A^{-1}T$. In practical cases we have $N > p$, and

$$T = A\,\underline{\theta}_L + \underline{e}, \tag{3.66}$$

where $\underline{e}$ is an N-dimensional error vector which represents measurement or model (3.64) errors. We define a weighted least-square criterion:

$$\min_{\underline{\theta}_L} \underline{e}^T Q \underline{e} = \min_{\underline{\theta}_L} \left[T - A\,\underline{\theta}_L \right]^T Q \left[T - A\,\underline{\theta}_L \right], \tag{3.67}$$

where Q is diagonal matrix with weights, i.e. $Q = \text{diag}[q_1, q_2, ..., q_N]$. The q_i is a large value when noise (or other errors) in i-th training data is low. In other words these weights are large when we associate great certainty to data. The minimization of this criterion is made by its differentiating with respect to unknown parameter vector $\underline{\theta}_L$ and equaling the result to zero, i.e.

$$-2A^T Q \left[T - A\,\underline{\theta}_L \right] = 0. \tag{3.68}$$

Solving this equation for $\underline{\theta}_L$ yields the weighted least-square estimator:

$$\hat{\underline{\theta}}_L = (A^T Q A)^{-1} A^T Q T. \tag{3.69}$$

Because usually we do not have information about noise level (or certainty) we use $Q = \mathbb{I}$. In this case we get the well-known least-square estimator:

$$\underline{\theta}_L = (A^T A)^{-1} A^T T = A^{\#} T, \tag{3.70}$$

where $A^{\#}$ denotes the so-called pseudo-inverse matrix, which also exist when $(A^T A)$ is singular (for details see Fukunaga 1990).

In general, when an artificial neural network has K outputs then:

$$\underline{T} = A\,\underline{\Theta}_L + E, \tag{3.71}$$

where $T = [\underline{t}(1), \underline{t}(2), ..., \underline{t}(N)]^T$ is $N \times K$ target output matrix,

$$\underline{\Theta}_L = \begin{bmatrix} \theta_{L11} & \ldots & \theta_{L1K} \\ \vdots & & \vdots \\ \theta_{Lp1} & \ldots & \theta_{LpK} \end{bmatrix} \tag{3.72}$$

is $p{\times}K$ matrix of unknown parameters. All previously obtained results can be generalized to multi-output case. In this case (3.70) takes the form:

$$\underline{\Theta}_L = A^{\#} \underline{T}. \tag{3.73}$$

Using (3.70) is not useful for a large training data set (a large N) because we must store all data and computation involves matrices of high dimension. An alternative is a recursive form (3.70) which use only the last data and previous estimate. Let us rewrite (3.70) using a block matrix form:

$$\hat{\underline{\theta}}_L^{(k+1)} = \left(\begin{bmatrix} A^{(k)} \\ \underline{a}(\underline{x}(k+1))^T \end{bmatrix} \begin{bmatrix} A^{(k)} \\ \underline{a}(\underline{x}(k+1))^T \end{bmatrix}^T \right)^{-1} \begin{bmatrix} A^{(k)} \\ \underline{a}(\underline{x}(k+1))^T \end{bmatrix}^T \begin{bmatrix} T^{(k)} \\ (t(k+1))^T \end{bmatrix}, \tag{3.74}$$

where superscript (k) denotes that matrix A and T are constructed using data from the training set with indexes from 1 to k. After some matrix manipulations, especially using block matrix inversion lemma, the estimator can be expressed in the form:

$$\hat{\underline{\theta}}_L^{(k+1)} = \hat{\underline{\theta}}_L^{(k)} + K^{(k+1)} \left[t(k+1) - \underline{a}(\underline{x}(k+1))^T \hat{\underline{\theta}}_L^{(k)} \right], \tag{3.75}$$

where $K^{(k+1)}$ is called gain matrix:

$$K^{(k+1)} = P^{(k)} \underline{a}(\underline{x}(k+1))^T \left(\underline{a}(\underline{x}(k+1))^T P^{(k)} \underline{a}(\underline{x}(k+1)) + \mathbb{I} \right)^{-1}, \tag{3.76}$$

where:

$$P^{(k)} = \left(A^{(k)T} A^{(k)} \right)^{-1}. \tag{3.77}$$

This matrix can be also computed recursively:

$$P^{(k+1)} = P^{(k)} \left(\mathbb{I} - K^{(k+1)} \underline{a}(\underline{x}(k+1)) P^{(k)} \right). \tag{3.78}$$

Equations (3.75), (3.76) and (3.78) are usually in the form of two recursive equations (see i.e., Larminat and Thomas 1977), and forms recursive least-square estimator. To start computations of this algorithm we need $P^{(0)}$ and $\hat{\underline{\theta}}_L^{(0)}$. In practice we set $\hat{\underline{\theta}}_L^{(0)} = \underline{0}$ and $P^{(0)} = \alpha \, \mathbb{I}$, where α is a large positive value, and $\mathbb{I}$ is an identity matrix. Another method starts from $(k+1)$-th iteration using exact solution for first k training data by means of (3.70).

Generally, we can use estimation theory to obtain $\hat{\underline{\theta}}_L$ parameters. There are two approaches to this estimate:

- general or Bayesian, assuming that $\underline{\theta}_L$ is a random vector. In this case minimized criterion is expressed in probabilistic terms:

$$\min E\left[L(\underline{\theta}_L - \hat{\underline{\theta}}_L) \right], \tag{3.79}$$

where $\underline{\theta}_L$ is true value of parameter vector, E is expectation operator, L is a loss function, usually $L(\underline{x}) = \underline{x}^T Q \underline{x}$, Q is a positive semidefinite matrix. Minimization of criterion (3.79) leads to unbiased estimator:

$$E[\hat{\underline{\theta}}_L] = \underline{\theta}_L, \tag{3.80}$$

and minimal variance estimator, which for any other estimate $\underline{\theta}^*$:

$$\operatorname{tr} \Sigma_{\hat{\underline{\theta}}_L} \le \operatorname{tr} \Sigma_{\underline{\theta}_L^*}, \tag{3.81}$$

where for some vector $\underline{\alpha}$

$$\Sigma_{\underline{\alpha}} = E\left[(\underline{\theta}_L - \underline{\alpha})(\underline{\theta}_L - \underline{\alpha})^T \right] \tag{3.82}$$

is covariance matrix, tr is trace of matrix (sum of diagonal elements). Orthogonality principle is very useful to solve problems in this theory. Estimation $\hat{\underline{\theta}}_L$ is optimal when estimation error $\hat{\underline{\theta}}_L - \underline{\theta}_L$ is uncorrelated to output data (measurements):

$$E[(\hat{\underline{\theta}}_L - \underline{\theta}_L) T^T] = 0. \tag{3.83}$$

In other words, we do not inference anything about estimation error from data, and it's not possible to correct estimate.

- classical or Fisherian, assuming that $\underline{\theta}_L$ is deterministic, unknown parameter vector. A likelihood function ℓ plays here a fundamental role:

$$\ell(\underline{\theta}_L, \underline{T}) = f_{\underline{T}}(\underline{T}, \underline{\theta}_L), \tag{3.84}$$

where $f_{\underline{T}}$ is probabilistic density function of random variable $\underline{T}$ with $\underline{\theta}_L$ as parameter. Maximum likelihood estimate is achieved for $\hat{\underline{\theta}}_L$ which maximizes ℓ function and which can be obtained as a solution of equation:

$$\frac{\partial \ell(\underline{\theta}_L, \underline{T})}{\partial \underline{\theta}_L} = 0. \tag{3.85}$$

Maximum likelihood estimators are consistent, i.e.

$$\underset{\varepsilon > 0}{\forall} \ \lim_{N \to \infty} P\left[\left| \hat{\underline{\theta}}_L - \underline{\theta}_L \right| \ge \varepsilon \right] = 0, \tag{3.86}$$

where P denotes probability. An unbiased estimate is efficient when the variance of estimate error equals to its minimum possible value. This value is called Cramer-Rao lower bound.

If we assume in (3.66) that error vector $\underline{e}$ has Gaussian distribution with statistical characteristic: $E(\underline{e}) = \underline{0}$, $E(\underline{e}\,\underline{e}^T) = \Sigma_{\underline{e}}$ and unknown parameter $\underline{\theta}_L$ are deterministic (or random with infinity elements on diagonal covariance matrix), then using general or classical estimation theory we get the estimate:

$$\hat{\underline{\theta}}_L = \left(A^T \Sigma_{\underline{e}}^{-1} A\right)^{-1} A^T \Sigma_{\underline{e}}^{-1} T, \tag{3.87}$$

and covariance matrix of estimation error:

$$\Sigma_{\hat{\underline{\theta}}_L} = \left(A^T \Sigma_{\underline{e}}^{-1} A\right)^{-1}. \tag{3.88}$$

This estimator called the Markov one, is unbiased with minimal variance. When distribution of $\underline{e}$ is non-Gaussian then estimator (3.88) is the best in the class of linear estimators with minimal error variance.

In the most general case unknown parameter vector $\underline{\theta}_L$ is a time varying sequence, and the problem is to estimate this parameter from the sequence of training data. Let us assume the following model:

$$\begin{cases} \underline{\theta}_L^{(k+1)} = F^{(k)} \underline{\theta}_L^{(k)} + \underline{v}^{(k)}, \\ t(k) = \underline{a}(\underline{x}(k))^T \underline{\theta}_L^{(k)} + \underline{e}^{(k)}, \end{cases} \tag{3.89}$$

where $F^{(k)}$ is $p \times p$ matrix, $\underline{v}^{(k)}$, $\underline{e}^{(k)}$ are random vectors with zero mean and following covariance matrix:

$$\underset{k,l}{\forall} \ E\left\{ \begin{bmatrix} \underline{v}^{(k)} \\ \underline{e}^{(k)} \end{bmatrix} \begin{bmatrix} \underline{v}^{(k)} \\ \underline{e}^{(k)} \end{bmatrix}^T \right\} = \begin{bmatrix} Q^{(k)} & \underline{0} \\ \underline{0} & R^{(k)} \end{bmatrix} \delta_{k,l}, \tag{3.90}$$

where $\delta_{k,l}$ denotes Kronecker symbol. Equations (3.89) are initialized at the random vector $\underline{\theta}_L^{(0)}$ with mean $E[\underline{\theta}_L^{(0)}] = \bar{\underline{\theta}}_L^{(0)}$ and covariance matrix $P^{(0)}$. This initial state is uncorrelated with $\underline{v}$ and $\underline{e}$:

$$\underset{k}{\forall} \ E\left\{ \begin{bmatrix} \underline{v}^{(k)} \\ \underline{e}^{(k)} \end{bmatrix} \underline{\theta}_L^{(0)T} \right\} = \underline{0}. \tag{3.91}$$

The problem is how to create the estimator minimizing criterion (3.79) using output sequence $t(k)$. The best estimator from class of linear estimators with minimal variance is given by:

$$\hat{\underline{\theta}}_L^{(k+1)} = \hat{\underline{\theta}}_L^{(k)} + K^{(k+1)}\left[t(k+1) - \underline{a}(\underline{x}(k+1))^T F^{(k)} \hat{\underline{\theta}}_L^{(k)}\right], \tag{3.92}$$

where $K^{(k+1)}$ is a gain matrix with the form:

$$K^{(k+1)} = \left(F^{(k)} P^{(k)} F^{(k)T} + Q^{(k)}\right) \underline{a}(\underline{x}(k+1)) \times$$
$$\times \left[\underline{a}(\underline{x}(k+1))^T\left(F^{(k)} P^{(k)} F^{(k)T} + Q^{(k)}\right) \underline{a}(\underline{x}(k+1)) + R^{(k+1)}\right]^{-1}, \tag{3.93}$$

where $\times$ denotes algebraic multiplication in this case, $P^{(k)}$ is covariance matrix of estimation error, defined as:

$$P^{(k)} = E\left\{(\underline{\theta}_L - \hat{\underline{\theta}}_L^{(k)})(\underline{\theta}_L - \hat{\underline{\theta}}_L^{(k)})^T\right\}, \tag{3.94}$$

which can be computed recursively:

$$P^{(k+1)} = \left(\mathbb{I} - K^{(k+1)} \underline{a}(\underline{x}(k+1))^T\right)\left(F^{(k)} P^{(k)} F^{(k)T} + Q^{(k)}\right). \tag{3.95}$$

If first output value is $t(1)$ then we start recursions from $\bar{\underline{\theta}}_L^{(0)}$ and $P^{(0)}$. Equations (3.92), (3.93) and (3.95) are called the Kalman filter. Estimator (3.92) is optimal in the sense of criterion (3.79) when initial state, $\underline{v}$ and $\underline{e}$ vectors are Gaussian. When $F^{(k)} = \mathbb{I}$ and $\underline{v} = \underline{0}$, we get a recursive least-square weighted estimator. Moreover, if error $\underline{e}$ is uncorrelated ($R^{(k)} = \mathbb{I}$) then we get recursive least-square method (compare with (3.75)). It can be proved that (3.92) minimizes criterion:

$$J_{k+1} = \frac{1}{2}\left(\hat{\underline{\theta}}_L^{(0)} - \underline{\theta}_L^{(0)}\right)^T \left(P^{(0)}\right)^{-1}\left(\hat{\underline{\theta}}_L^{(0)} - \underline{\theta}_L^{(0)}\right) +$$
$$\frac{1}{2}\sum_{i=1}^{k+1} \underline{v}^{(i)T}\left(Q^{(i)}\right)^{-1} \underline{v}^{(i)} + \tag{3.96}$$
$$\frac{1}{2}\sum_{i=1}^{k+1}\left(t(i) - \underline{a}(\underline{x}(i))^T \hat{\underline{\theta}}_L^{(i)}\right)^T\left(R^{(i)}\right)^{-1}\left(t(i) - \underline{a}(\underline{x}(i))^T \hat{\underline{\theta}}_L^{(i)}\right),$$

with constraints (3.89).

3.8
Global optimization methods

Optimization methods presented in Section 3.6 are based on gradient-direction search on parameter space $\underline{\theta}$ minimizing criterion $E(\underline{\theta})$. However, in case of multimodal $E(\underline{\theta})$ the local minimas are usually obtained. In artificial neural networks the criterion function (3.18) is typically multimodal. Global optimization methods lead to a global minimum (or maximum) of criterion function. For this feature we pay the price of a higher computational burden. This methods are sometimes called a derivative free optimization methods, because it does not need functional derivative of $E(\underline{\theta})$. The simplest method for this class is random search. This method finds the minimum of criterion function sequentially, investigating in random fashion the parameter space $\underline{\theta}$ using the following algorithm:

    1°   select random initial point $\underline{\theta}$,
    2°   select random modification vector $\Delta\underline{\theta}$,
    3°   if $E(\underline{\theta} + \Delta\underline{\theta}) < E(\underline{\theta})$ then $\underline{\theta} \leftarrow \underline{\theta} + \Delta\underline{\theta}$,
    4°   if stopping criteria are not met goto 2°.

Frequently used stopping criteria are: pre-specified number of iterations or criterion function is small. Modification vector $\Delta\underline{\theta}$ is chosen:

- randomly, where vector elements are independent uniformly distributed random variables,
- by the best trial, where we get m trials in random directions with constant length. We choose direction where criterion function is the smallest,
- by statistically determined (estimated) gradient, where we get m trials in random direction $\underline{d}(i)$ with constant length δ. We determine direction of search as:

$$\underline{d} = \frac{\nabla \hat{E}(\underline{\theta})}{\| \nabla \hat{E}(\underline{\theta}) \|}, \tag{3.97}$$

where gradient is estimated by the formula:

$$\nabla \hat{E}(\underline{\theta}) = \frac{1}{\delta} \sum_{i=1}^{m} \left[E(\underline{\theta} + \delta \underline{d}(i)) - E(\underline{\theta}) \right] \underline{d}(i). \tag{3.98}$$

There are many modifications of the above presented basic method. For example a method with memory, where after successful direction selection we search this direction further along.

Another global optimization method is simulated annealing presented by Metropolis et al. (1953), and Kirkpatrick et al. (1983). This method is derived from statistical physics, and its principles are analogous to behavior of materials whose temperature is cooled at some rate. If cooling is slow then material goes to low energetic state. If cooling is rapid material goes to amorphic structure with increased energy. Our minimized criterion $E(\underline{\theta})$ is analogous to the energetic state of material. In simulated annealing, when material is cooled, the global energy is decreased, but it is possible to increase this energy temporarily, leaving local minimum. Simulated annealing optimization algorithm can be described as:

1°   select starting point $\underline{\theta}$, and starting temperature T,

2°   select $\underline{\Delta\theta}$ with probability distribution given by the so-called generation function $g(\underline{\Delta\theta}, T)$, and compute: $\Delta E = E(\underline{\theta} + \underline{\Delta\theta}) - E(\underline{\theta})$,

3°   assign $\underline{\theta} \leftarrow \underline{\theta} + \underline{\Delta\theta}$ with probability given by the so-called acceptance function $a(\Delta E, T)$,

4°   if pre-set number of iterations in temperature T is archived then decrease temperature: $T \leftarrow \lambda T$, where $\lambda \in [0, 1]$. This operation is called annealing schedule,

5°   if stopping criteria are not met goto 2°.

In typical simulated annealing (called Boltzmann machine) the generation function has Gaussian distribution:

$$g(\underline{\Delta\theta}, T) = (2\pi)^{-\frac{p}{2}} T^{-\frac{1}{2}} \exp\left\{ -\frac{1}{2} \frac{\|\Delta\theta\|^2}{T} \right\}, \qquad (3.99)$$

and acceptance function is given by:

$$a(\Delta E, T) = \frac{1}{1 + \exp(\beta \Delta E / T)}, \qquad (3.100)$$

where p is dimension of $\underline{\theta}$ and β is constant.

It can be proved that this algorithm finds global minimum when $\lambda_k = \ln(k) / \ln(k+1)$, where k is iteration index. There are some variants of the above mentioned algorithm, for example the so-called Cauchy machine or fast simulated annealing described by Szu and Hartley (1987), where generation function is:

$$g(\underline{\Delta\theta}, T) = \frac{T}{\left(\|\Delta\theta\|^2 + T^2 \right)^{(p+1)/2}}. \qquad (3.101)$$

In many practical applications simulated annealing is not realistic, because to find global minimum we must set very slow rate at which the temperature is lowered. In the same way as thermodynamics principles can be obtained from statistical mechanics, the deterministic annealing is obtained from simulated annealing. Deterministic annealing tries to connect the best feature from simulated annealing and deterministic optimization method. Deterministic annealing replaces stochastic movement on parameter space by using expectation. In other words, criterion function $E(\underline{\theta})$ is optimized by deterministic fashion at each successively decreased temperature level. The principle of deterministic annealing was given by Rose

(1991), and applied to clustering, vector quantization, classification, piecewise regression and mixture of experts. Some principles of deterministic annealing will be described in Section 6.4 in application to neuro-fuzzy system training.

At the end of this section let us recall other important method of global optimization, i.e. genetic algorithm. The genetic algorithm was introduced by Holland (1975). This algorithm is based on principles of natural selection, evolution and genetics to imitate behavior of biological systems. Genetic algorithms operate on population, which is transformed (evolves) to obtain members with higher fitness values. The members of population are called chromosomes. Using previous notations, $\underline{\theta}_i$ is i-th chromosome, and population is a set of N chromosomes $\Theta = \{\underline{\theta}_1, \underline{\theta}_2,..., \underline{\theta}_N\}$. Each chromosome is characterized by fitness value $F(\underline{\theta}_i)$. Genetic algorithms find a chromosome that maximizes F. Typically, following transformation criterion $E(\underline{\theta})$ from (3.18) to fitness is used:

$$F(\underline{\theta}) = \begin{cases} C_{max} - E(\underline{\theta}), & E(\underline{\theta}) < C_{max}, \\ 0, & \text{otherwise}. \end{cases} \tag{3.102}$$

The C_{max} is chosen as maximum value of E in previously generated population. Genetic algorithms can be described as:

1°   randomly generate an initial N chromosome population Θ,

2°   compute the fitness of each chromosome $\underline{\theta}_i$ in the current population,

3°   create new chromosomes Θ_{new} by mating current ones,

4°   delete some chromosomes from current population to make place for the new ones,

5°   insert new chromosomes to current population,

6°   if stopping criteria are not met goto 2° else return the best chromosome as result $\underline{\theta}$.

One of the main features of genetic algorithms is that it uses an encoding scheme. This is a method of transformation point in parameter space to bit-string format. The chromosomes are usually expressed as string of variables, called genes. The variable is mostly represented by binary forms, but real numbers or other forms can be used. Generation of new chromosomes consists of the selection of parents and application of genetic operations. The probability of selecting chromosomes as parents is usually proportional to their fitness value (Darwinian model). Genetic operations include crossover and mutation. Crossover is an operation that combines subpart of two parents chromosomes and procreates offspring which contains some parts of genetic material from both parents. This operation is applied with probability called

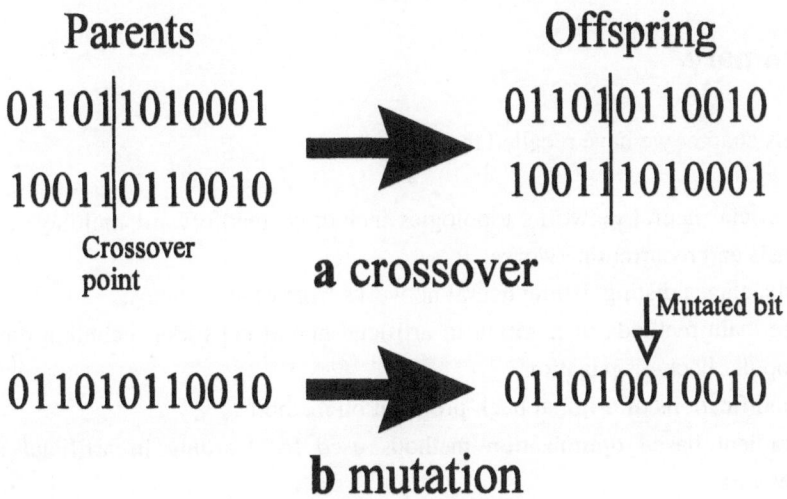

Parents   Offspring

01101|1010001   01101|0110010

10011|0110010   10011|1010001

Crossover point

a crossover

|Mutated bit

011010110010   ➤   011010010010

b mutation

Fig. 3.6. Examples of the genetic operations: crossover (**a**), mutation (**b**).

crossover rate. Commonly, the offspring is created by randomly selecting a crossover point and exchanging the portion of parents chromosomes. An example of crossover operation is shown in Fig. 3.4a. We note that sometimes m-point crossover operation is used. Mutation is an operation that introduces spontaneous variations into the chromosomes. In practice, we use flip bits (0 is replaced by 1, and 1 is replaced by 0) with some very small probability. Example of this operation is presented in Fig. 3.4b. After the generation of offspring many strategies can be proposed for the replacement of current population. For example, in generational-replacement the entire population is replaced by generated offspring, in steady-state reproduction only a few chromosomes are replaced by new ones. Generational-replacement technique is frequently associated with elitist strategy, where a few of the best (having highest fitness) chromosomes are copied into the next population. The genetic algorithm is very useful to imprecise localization of global extremum, and then we may use derivative based optimization method to "fine tune" the optimal solution in parameter space.

3.9
Summary

In this chapter we have recalled the following:

- artificial neural networks topologies including: feedforward multilayer, radial basis and recurrent networks,
- advantages distinguishing neural networks from other systems,
- the main methods of learning in artificial neural networks including the most popular back-propagation,
- modifications of original back-propagation method,
- gradient based optimization methods used for learning in artificial neural networks,
- optimization of the parameters which linearly depend on the network's output,
- global (derivative-free) optimization methods including: random search, simulated annealing and genetic algorithms.

Bibliographical notes

Artificial neural networks and radial basis functions are discussed in Haykin (1999), Hertz et al. (1991), Kartalopoulos (1996), Khanna (1990) and Maren et al. (1990). Tutorial overview is presented in Lippmann (1986).

Artificial neural network application to pattern recognition and bioinformatics are demonstrated in Ripley (1996), Baldi and Brunak (1998) and Pao (1989). Connections of neural networks theory with fuzzy logic and wavelets are presented in Takagi and Hayashi (1991), Zhang and Benveniste (1992), Zhang (1998), Buckley et al. (1993), Keller and Takagi (1992).

For mathematical foundations of universal approximation theory see Rudin (1976).

For further reading about optimization theory the reader is refereed to Gill et al. (1981) and Scales (1985). The exposition on estimation theory is based on Deutsch (1965), Larminat and Thomas (1977), Elbert (1984).

System identification is treated in Söderström and Stoica (1994) and Eykhoff (1974). Kalman filtering is studied in Anderson and Moore (1979) and Meditch (1969).

Sources for deterministic annealing are Rose (1991), Rose (1993) and Rose (1998). See also Hofmann and Buhmann (1997). Genetic algorithms are considered in Holland (1975) and Goldberg (1989).

4 Unsupervised learning
Clustering methods

4.1
Introduction

In the learning method described in the previous chapter we assume that we have target (desired) output of network for inputs from training data set. In contrast to that, in this chapter we use data set without the desired output of network. Such an approach to network learning without a teacher or supervisor is called an unsupervised method. The effect of that learning are features, regularities and structure of data extraction, and sometimes it is called a method that search for structures of data. For example in biology and medicine, where sets of physical and biochemical measurements define species and diseases, respectively, unsupervised methods are very useful. In this book unsupervised methods will be used to search fuzzy if-then rules. Grouping found by unsupervised methods is frequently referred to as clusters. The cluster is a natural and homogeneous subset of data. The data in each cluster are as similar as possible to each other, and as different (dissimilar) as possible from other cluster's data.

4.2
Self-organizing feature map

The self-organizing map is an algorithm developed by Kohonen (1982). This algorithm map a set of input data (patterns) onto output vectors. In that way the output signals of the network reflect some feature of input data. The basis of learning in this method is the competition between output neurons. Basic self-organizing network consists of two layers: input and output. The output layer is organized in a regular grid in one or two dimensions. Each output neuron is connected to each input neuron. We denote connection strength between i-th input and j-th output as w_{ij}.

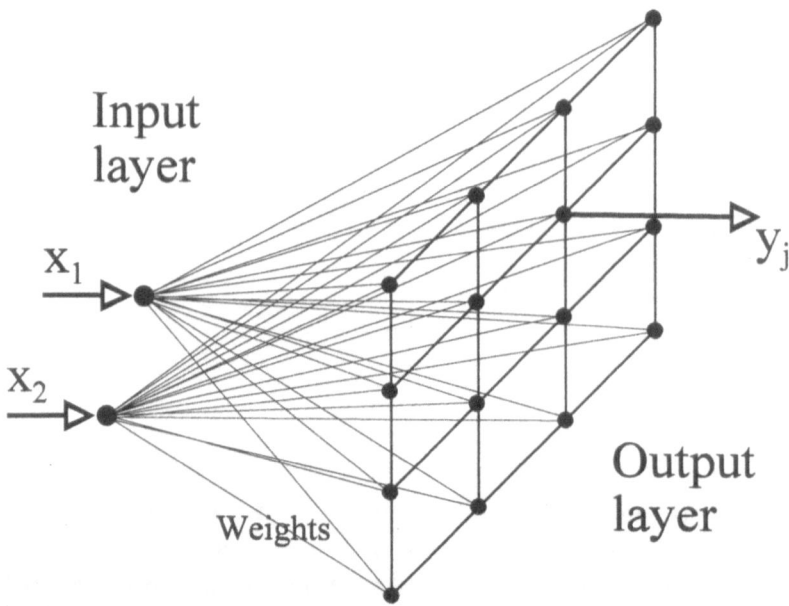

Fig. 4.1. Connection scheme in 2 inputs and 16 outputs Kohonen network.

An example of Kohonen network with two input and 16 output neurons is shown in Fig. 5.1. The output of j-th neuron is given by:

$$y_j = \underline{w}_j^T \underline{x} = [w_{j1}, w_{j2}, \ldots w_{jp}] [x_1, x_2, \ldots x_p]^T, \qquad (4.1)$$

where p is a number of input neurons. The y_j is the so-called activation of j-th output neuron. For further processing a neuron with the highest activation (called winner) is selected. If we assume that the weight vector is normalized, then the winner neuron has minimal dissimilarity to $\underline{x}$ in the sense of Euclidean distance:

$$d_2^2(\underline{x}, \underline{w}_j) = \| \underline{x} - \underline{w}_j \| = \underline{x}^T \underline{x} - 2\underline{w}_j^T \underline{x} + \underline{w}_j^T \underline{w}_j, \qquad (4.2)$$

because the first element is independent from index j, and the last one is equal to one.

Thus the result depends only on $\underline{w}_j^T \underline{x}$. Distance (4.2) is a specific case of general the Minikovsky distance:

$$d_b(\underline{x}, \underline{w}_j) = \left(\sum_{i=1}^{p} \left(x_i - w_{ij} \right)^b \right)^{\frac{1}{b}}, \qquad (4.3)$$

where parameter $b \geq 1$. For $b = 1$ we obtain the Manhattan distance, for $b = 2$ Euclidian distance, and finally for $b \to \infty$ the Chebyshev distance.

The learning of the Kohonen self-organizing network can be described in following steps:

1° randomly initialize weights $\underline{w}_j^{(0)}$, $1 \leq j \leq c$, where c is the number of neurons in output layer,

2° for current input vector (pattern) select the winning neuron (with index h) as the one with smallest dissimilarity measure (largest similarity):

$$d_b(\underline{x}, \underline{w}_h^{(k)}) = \min_{1 \leq i \leq c} d_b(\underline{x}, \underline{w}_i^{(k)}).$$ (4.4)

The superscript (k) denotes iteration index.

3° update winning neuron and neighboring neurons according to the formula:

$$\underline{w}_j^{(k+1)} = \underline{w}_j^{(k)} + \eta_i^{(k)} N^{(k)}(i, h)\,(\underline{x} - \underline{w}_i),$$ (4.5)

where $N^{(k)}(i, h)$ is neighborhood function, $\eta_i^{(k)}$ is learning rate for i-th neuron.

4° if all input vectors are presented to network goto 2°,

5° if stopping criteria are not met then modify neighborhood function, learning rate and goto 2°.

One of the following formulas is commonly used as a neighborhood function:

- rectangular neighborhood, where:

$$N^{(k)}(i, h) = \begin{cases} 1, & \text{for } d_b(i,h) \leq \lambda^{(k)}, \\ 0, & \text{otherwise,} \end{cases}$$ (4.6)

where $\lambda^{(k)}$ determines the size of winner neuron neighborhood and generally is decreased with iteration index k,

- Gaussian neighborhood, where :

$$N^{(k)}(i, h) = \exp\left\{ -\frac{1}{2} \frac{d_b^2(i, h)}{(\lambda^{(k)})^2} \right\}.$$ (4.7)

This is the so-called winner-takes-most type of neighborhood.

- winner-takes-all type of neighborhood, where:

$$N^{(k)}(i, h) = \delta_{i,h},$$ (4.8)

δ is the Kronecker delta.

- stochastic relaxation type of neighborhood, where:

$$N^{(k)}(i, h) = \begin{cases} 1, & \text{for } G^{(k)}(i) > G, \\ 0, & \text{otherwise,} \end{cases}$$ (4.9)

G is a random number from [0, 1] interval, and $G^{(k)}(i)$ is Gibbs probability distribution given by:

$$G^{(k)}(i) = \frac{\exp\left\{-\dfrac{d_2^2(\underline{x}, \underline{w}_i)}{T^{(k)}}\right\}}{\displaystyle\sum_{j=1}^{c} \exp\left\{-\dfrac{d_2^2(\underline{x}, \underline{w}_j)}{T^{(k)}}\right\}},\qquad(4.10)$$

where $T^{(k)}$ is pseudo-temperature parameter.

- soft competition scheme type of neighborhood, where:

$$N^{(k)}(i, h) = G^{(k)}(i).\qquad(4.11)$$

For each neuron the learning rate depends on previous values of neighborhood functions:

$$\eta_i^{(k)} = 1 \left/ \left(1 + \sum_{j=1}^{k-1} N^{(j)}(i, h)\right)\right.,\qquad(4.12)$$

This algorithm gives a chance for neurons with low activity.

- neural-gas type of neighborhood, where output neurons are sorted by activation value:

$$\mathop{\forall}_{1 \le i < c} \quad d_b(\underline{x}, \underline{w}_{s(i)}^{(k)}) \le d_b(\underline{x}, \underline{w}_{s(i+1)}^{(k)}),\qquad(4.13)$$

where $s(i)$ is a sort function. Finally, neighborhood function has the form:

$$N^{(k)}(i, h) = e^{-\frac{s(i)}{\lambda^{(k)}}}.\qquad(4.14)$$

$\lambda^{(k)}$ is a parameter which decreases with iteration index k as:

$$\lambda^{(k)} = \lambda_{max}\left(\frac{\lambda_{min}}{\lambda_{max}}\right)^{\frac{k}{k_{max}}},\qquad(4.15)$$

where k_{max} is target number of iterations, λ_{min}, λ_{max} are minimal and maximal values of λ parameter, respectively.

Generally, the learning rate $\eta_i^{(k)}$ is a decreasing function of iteration index k:

$$\begin{cases} \eta_i^{(k)} = \eta_i^{(0)} e^{-\alpha k}, & \alpha > 0, \\ \eta_i^{(k)} = \eta_i^{(0)} k^{-\alpha}, & \alpha \le 1, \\ \eta_i^{(k)} = \eta_i^{(0)} (1 - \alpha k), & 0 < \alpha < 1/k_{max}, \\ \eta_i^{(k)} = \eta_i^{(0)} (\eta_{min}/\eta_i^{(0)})^{k/k_{max}}. \end{cases} \tag{4.16}$$

The η_{min} denotes minimal value of learning rate. Sometimes the so-called conscience mechanism is taken into account. This method is biologically motivated, because a biological neuron is insensitive to stimulus after activation. In an artificial network we define for each (i-th) neuron his potential (for activation) as:

$$p_i^{(k)} = \begin{cases} p_i^{(k)} - \dfrac{1}{c}, & i \ne h, \\ p_i^{(k)} - p_{tr}, & i = h, \end{cases} \tag{4.17}$$

where p_{tr} is the threshold value of potential, and we search the winning neuron among neurons that have potential greater than this value. Typically we set: $0.6 < p_{tr} < 0.8$. Ritter and Schulten (1986) proved that updating weights according to (4.5) give the same result as gradient minimization of the following criteria:

$$E = \frac{1}{2} \sum_k \sum_j N(j, h(k)) \, \| \underline{x}_k - \underline{w}_{h(k)} \|^2, \tag{4.18}$$

where summations are over input vectors (index k) and output neurons (index j). The $h(k)$ denotes the index of winning neuron for k-th input vector.

4.3
Vector quantization and learning vector quantization

In self-organizing networks the input vector is replaced by weight vector of winning neuron. If in criterion (4.18) we use winner-takes-all type of neighborhood function, then we get following criteria function:

$$E = \frac{1}{2} \sum_k \| \underline{x}_k - \underline{w}_{h(k)} \|^2. \tag{4.19}$$

Minimization of these criteria leads to such weight vectors $\underline{w}_i$, which minimize a sum of difference between input vectors and weight vectors of winning neuron. This is a type of approximation of input vectors by means of the so-called codebook (template, reference) vectors. Such an approach is named vector quantization. This method is used for example to the compression of signals and images, for detection of faults and clustering of data. Vector quantization is a frequently used method in communication systems. The transmitted signal is mapped into the nearest codebook vector, and after transmitting the codebook, only proper indexes are transmitted. The codebook is determined to minimizing criteria (4.19). If we denote i-th codebook vector (weight vector) as $\underline{w}_i$, and winning vector index as h then the updating rule has the following form:

$$\underline{w}_i^{(k+1)} = \underline{w}_i^{(k)} + \begin{cases} \eta^{(k)}\,(\underline{x} - \underline{w}_i^{(k)}), & i \neq h, \\ 0, & i = h, \end{cases} \tag{4.20}$$

where k denotes iteration index, and $\eta^{(k)}$ is learning rate decreasing with k.

Vector quantization method uses unlabeled data (without information about belonging to class) to locate codebook vectors. If we add to the vector quantization method supervised learning which utilizes information about belonging to class as second step, we obtain the learning vector quantization method. During this second step codebook vectors are fine-tuned using information about belonging of vectors to classes from the training set. After the first step is completed the output neurons must be initially labeled. Such labeling is done by the so-called voting method. A neuron (weight vector) is labeled to i-th class if majority of input vectors cause the winning of this (i-th) output neuron. After the labeling process input vectors are sequentially presented to the network, and depending on whether input and weight vectors belong to the same class or not we update weight vectors:

$$\underline{w}_i^{(k+1)} = \underline{w}_i^{(k)} + \begin{cases} \eta^{(k)}\,(\underline{x} - \underline{w}_i^{(k)}), & i = h;\ \underline{x}, \underline{w}_h \text{ are from the same class,} \\ -\eta^{(k)}\,(\underline{x} - \underline{w}_i^{(k)}), & i = h,\ \underline{x}, \underline{w}_h \text{ are not from the same class,} \\ 0, & i \neq h. \end{cases} \tag{4.21}$$

The learning rate $\eta^{(k)}$ is initially selected as a small number (typically 0.05) and is reduced linearly to zero after the pre-specified number of iterations. Updating rule (4.21) moves codebook (weight) vectors towards the input vectors of its own class, and away from vectors from other classes. The above described method is signed as LVQ1 (or simply LVQ). There are several modifications of this basic method. For example OLVQ1, where learning rate for the updating of i-th output neuron weight is decreased if the input vector is classified correctly:

$$
\eta_i^{(k+1)} = \begin{cases} \dfrac{\eta_i^{(k)}}{1 - \eta_i^{(k)}}, & \underline{x}, \underline{w}_i \text{ are from the same class}, \\[3mm] \dfrac{\eta_i^{(k)}}{1 + \eta_i^{(k)}}, & \underline{x}, \underline{w}_i \text{ are not from the same class}. \end{cases} \tag{4.22}
$$

In LVQ2.1 the updating is made for two neighbors of input vector. For details see Ripley (1996).

4.4
An overview of clustering methods

The competitive networks described in previous sections perform on-line grouping processes of the input vectors. Similarly, clustering methods divide a set of N observations (input vectors) $\underline{x}_1, \underline{x}_2, ..., \underline{x}_N$ into c groups denoted $\Omega_1, \Omega_2, ..., \Omega_c$ so that members of the same group are more similar than members of other groups. This method usually works in off-line mode. The number of clusters may be pre-specified or it may be decided by the method. In Fig. 4.2 we have an example of seven two-dimensional vectors ($N = 7$). Intuitively, we may choose two clusters ($c = 2$) with a solidly marked curve or three clusters ($c = 3$) bound by a dotted curve. The solution in this case is rather easy, because data are 2-dimensional. Generally, practice data vectors are p-dimensional, and can not be visualized like data in Fig. 4.2. The optimal (in the sense of the used criterion) solution can be theoretically by testing all possible partitions found. However, in practice such an approach is unrealistic, because there is a very large number of possible combinations of data assignment.

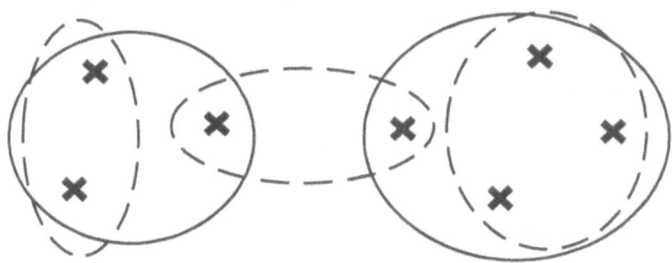

Fig. 4.2. An example of clustering for 7 data vectors.

There are

$$\frac{1}{c!} \sum_{i=1}^{c} \binom{c}{i} (-1)^{(c-i)} \, i^N \tag{4.23}$$

partitions of N vectors into c nonempty subsets (see Feller 1962; Duda and Hart 1973). If $c << N$ then the last term in (4.23) is the most significant, and equal to $c^N/c!$. For example, there are $2.54578 \cdot 10^{347}$ different partitions for 500 data vectors grouped in 5 clusters. For data from Fig. 4.2, where $N = 7$, there are 63 different partitions in 2 clusters and 301 in 3 clusters. Partitions marked in the Figure seem to be the most reasonable. However, in practice clustered vectors are in high-dimensional space, and selection of optimal partitions must be performed automatically. The result of that clustering may be presented as partition matrix U. Dimension of that matrix is $c \times N$, and its elements are:

$$u_{ik} = \begin{cases} 1, & \underline{x}_k \in \Omega_i, \\ 0, & \underline{x}_k \notin \Omega_i. \end{cases} \tag{4.24}$$

where Ω_i stands for i-th cluster.

If we denote the vector space of all real $(c \times N)$-dimensional matrices over R as V_{cN}, then the set of all possible partition matrixes is defined by:

$$M_c = \left\{ U \in V_{cN} \mid 1°, 2°, 3° \right\}, \tag{4.25}$$

where the conditions are:

$1°$ each $\underline{x}_k$ is in or not in i-th cluster:

$$\underset{\substack{1 \le i \le c \\ 1 \le k \le N}}{\forall} u_{ik} \in \{0, 1\}, \tag{4.26}$$

$2°$ each $\underline{x}_k$ is exactly in one of c cluster:

$$\underset{1 \le k \le N}{\forall} \sum_{i=1}^{c} u_{ik} = 1, \tag{4.27}$$

$3°$ no cluster is empty:

$$\underset{1 \le i \le c}{\forall} 0 < \sum_{k=1}^{N} u_{ik} < N. \tag{4.28}$$

The cardinality of set (4.25) is given by (4.23). Generally, clustering methods can be divided into:

- hierarchical,
- graph theoretic,
- by decomposition of density function,
- by minimization of criterion function.

Let us describe these methods more precisely.

4.4.1
Hierarchical clustering

The classical example of hierarchical clustering occurs in biological taxonomic hierarchies, where individuals are grouped into species, species are grouped into genera which are grouped into families, and so on. In other words, we have clusters of clusters. Hierarchical clustering may operate in two directions: in agglomerative way, where clusters are merged, and in divisive way, where clusters are split into a number of clusters. In order to group N data into c clusters, first these data are grouped into N clusters, each data create a cluster. In the next step we find the two clusters with the smallest dissimilarity and merge them, obtaining N-1 clusters. The next step is grouping into N-2 clusters, N-3, and so on until we obtain c clusters. This method can be written in the following steps:

1° $\Omega_i = \{ \underline{x}_i \}$, $i = 1, 2, ..., N$ and $c^* = N$,
2°   find the nearest pair of clusters Ω_k and Ω_j,
3°   merge Ω_k and Ω_j into Ω_k and delete Ω_j, $c^* \to c^* - 1$,
4°   if $c^* > c$ then goto 2°.

The hierarchical clustering method of clustering can be presented graphically by the so-called dendrograms (see any book on pattern recognition, for example Duda and Hart 1973). Similarity (or dissimilarity) between cluster Ω_k and Ω_j can be measured, for example, by distance between single data in clusters (single-link clustering):

$$d_{\min}(\Omega_k, \Omega_j) = \min_{\underline{x} \in \Omega_k, \underline{x}' \in \Omega_j} \| \underline{x} - \underline{x}' \|, \tag{4.29}$$

and

$$d_{\max}(\Omega_k, \Omega_j) = \max_{\underline{x} \in \Omega_k, \underline{x}' \in \Omega_j} \| \underline{x} - \underline{x}' \|, \tag{4.30}$$

or by distance between all data in clusters (complete-link clustering):

$$d_{ave}(\Omega_k, \Omega_j) = \frac{1}{N_k N_j} \sum_{x \in \Omega_k} \sum_{x' \in \Omega_j} \| x - x' \|,$$ (4.31)

or by distance between centers of clusters (group-average clustering):

$$d_{mean}(\Omega_k, \Omega_j) = \| \underline{m}_k - \underline{m}_j \|,$$ (4.32)

where N_i denotes cardinality of i-th cluster, and $\underline{m}_i$ stands for its center (mean).

Frequently, we use distance minimizing sum-of-square-to-center as similarity measure (see Section 4.3 and Subsection 4.4.4):

$$d_e(\Omega_k, \Omega_j) = \sqrt{\frac{N_k N_j}{N_k + N_j}} \, \| \underline{m}_k - \underline{m}_j \|.$$ (4.33)

The use of various definitions of distance between clusters results in various cluster shapes. For example d_{max} increases the diameter of a cluster as little as possible, and in contrast, using d_{min} increases the diameter as much as possible. d_{mean} and d_{ave} are a compromise between the above distances. d_e distance creates clusters with minimal variance of data with respect to the center of cluster.

Divisive methods are less known and less used in practice. For example we may select vector $\underline{x}^*$ whose average similarity to remaining vectors is the smallest, and merging $\underline{x}^*$ to vectors for which similarity is greater than to reminder vectors $\underline{x}$. This method can split a single cluster. The splitting process starts from a cluster with the largest diameter.

4.4.2
Graph theoretic clustering

This method of clustering uses directed tree coming from graph theory. The tree consists of branches and nodes. Each vector becomes an initial node. Each node initiates a branch to another node (representing vector) called predecessor. A chain of branches leading from data vector to final node is called directed path. The end of this path is named the root of the tree, that does not have a predecessor. The cluster is determined by the root of the tree and contains nodes (data vectors) connected to them. An example of graph theoretic clustering is presented in Fig. 4.3. To create directed paths we need an algorithm to find a predecessor for each vector. Usually, we select the predecessor as a data vector along the steepest ascent of density function $p(\underline{x})$. If we define steepness of density function from $\underline{x}_k$ to $\underline{x}_j$ as:

$$s_{jk} = \frac{p(\underline{x}_j) - p(\underline{x}_k)}{\|\underline{x}_j - \underline{x}_k\|}, \tag{4.34}$$

where $p(\underline{x})$ is density function (replaced by its estimate), then predecessor $\underline{x}_k$ is $\underline{x}_p$ for which:

$$s_{pk} = \max_{\underline{x}_j \in \Gamma(\underline{x}_k)} s_{jk}, \tag{4.35}$$

where $\Gamma(\underline{x}_k)$ is ellipsoidal neighborhood of $\underline{x}_k$:

$$\Gamma(\underline{x}_k) = \left\{ \underline{x} \mid d(\underline{x}_k, \underline{x}) \leq d_0 \right\}. \tag{4.36}$$

where d is distance, and d_0 is constant. The estimation of density function can be obtained using nonparametric approach as the Parzen or K-nearest neighbor methods (see Fukunaga 1992). The root is identified when for all indexes j, $s_{jk} \leq 0$. This method has several advantages: its noniterative process, which does not require initial partitioning and this method automatically determines a number of clusters.

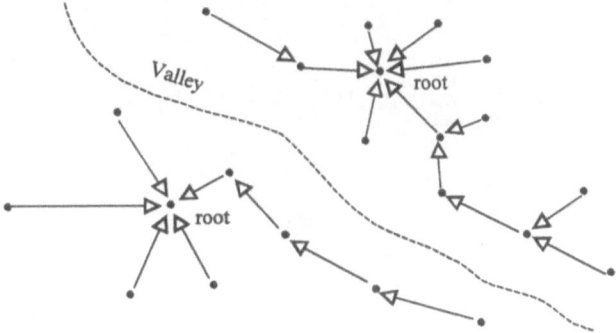

Fig. 4.3. An example of graph theoretic clustering.

4.4.3
Decomposition of density function

Another view to clustering is decomposition of density function which consists of c overlapping distributions:

$$p(\underline{x}) = \sum_{i=1}^{c} P_i \, p_i(\underline{x}), \tag{4.37}$$

where $p_i(\underline{x})$ is the density function of i-th cluster, P_i is the probability that vector $\underline{x}$ belongs to i-th cluster. The problem is estimate $p_i(\underline{x})$, P_i from available data vectors $\underline{x}_1, \underline{x}_2, ..., \underline{x}_N$. The most frequently used method to solve this problem is maximization of likelihood function:

$$J = \sum_{j=1}^{N} \ln p(\underline{x}_j) - \lambda \left(\sum_{j=1}^{c} P_j - 1 \right),$$

(4.38)

where the second term derives from constraint $\Sigma_{i=1}^{c} P_i = 1$, and λ is a Lagrange multiplier. Usually, we consider that $p_i(\underline{x})$ has Gaussian distribution, and we maximize (4.38) with respect to P_i, mean $\underline{\mu}_i$, and covariance matrix Σ_i of Gaussian distribution. It can be proved (see Fukunaga 1992; Duda and Hart 1973) that by maximizing (4.38), we obtain:

$$P_i = \frac{1}{N} \sum_{j=1}^{N} Q_i(\underline{x}_j),$$

(4.39)

and:

$$\underline{\mu}_i = \frac{1}{N_i} \sum_{j=1}^{N} Q_i(\underline{x}_j) \underline{x}_j,$$

(4.40)

and finally:

$$\Sigma_i = \frac{1}{N_i} \sum_{j=1}^{N} Q_i(\underline{x}_j) (\underline{x}_j - \underline{\mu}_i)(\underline{x}_j - \underline{\mu}_i)^T,$$

(4.41)

where:

$$Q_i(\underline{x}_j) = \frac{P_i \, p_i(\underline{x}_j)}{p(\underline{x}_j)}.$$

(4.42)

From above equations we see that it is impossible to obtain a solution explicitly, because Q_is is dependent from estimated P_i, $\underline{\mu}_i$, and Σ_i. These equations can be solved iteratively: first, we choose initial cluster assignment, and calculate P_is, $\underline{\mu}_i$s and Σ_is, next after calculating Q_is, again P_is, $\underline{\mu}_i$s and Σ_is, and so on until Q_is does not change.

To simplify calculations an uncomplicated approximation of Q_is is done. $Q_i(\underline{x}_j)$ can be interpreted as the probability that vector $\underline{x}_j$ comes from i-th cluster. If $\underline{x}_j$ is nearest to $\underline{\mu}_p$ then we approximate $Q_i(\underline{x}_j)$ as:

$$Q_i(\underline{x}_j) = \begin{cases} 1, & i = p, \\ 0, & i \neq p. \end{cases}$$

(4.43)

Additionally, we assume that $\Sigma_i = I$. In this case we obtain a simple and useful algorithm:

    1°   select initial partition of data to c clusters, and compute $\underline{\mu}_i$s using (4.40),

    2°   assign each data vector to cluster with nearest mean,

    3°   compute the means for each cluster by (4.40),

    4°   if any mean changes goto 2°.

4.4.4
Clustering by minimizing criterion function

There are approximately $c^N/c!$ different partitions of N vector set into c clusters. A very popular way of clustering data is to define a criterion function (scalar index) that measures quality of any partition. Then the problem is to find the partition that minimizes (extremizes) the criterion. The simplest and most frequently used criterion is the sum-of-square-error:

$$J_e(U, V) = \sum_{i=1}^{c} \sum_{\underline{x} \in \Omega_i} \| \underline{x} - \underline{v}_i \|^2 = \sum_{i=1}^{c} \sum_{k=1}^{N} u_{ik} \| \underline{x}_k - \underline{v}_i \|^2, \qquad (4.44)$$

where $U = [u_{ik}]$ is partition matrix (4.24), $V = [\underline{v}_1, \underline{v}_2, ..., \underline{v}_c] \in V_{pc}$ is a matrix consisting of cluster's centers defined as:

$$\underset{1 \leq i \leq c}{\forall} \quad \underline{v}_i = \frac{1}{N_i} \sum_{\underline{x} \in \Omega_i} \underline{x} = \frac{\sum_{k=1}^{N} u_{ik} \, \underline{x}_k}{\sum_{k=1}^{N} u_{ik}}. \qquad (4.45)$$

Clustering of this type is called minimum variance partitioning, because it minimizes the sum of squared distances of vectors in a cluster to its center. The clustering problem is replaced by finding such a partition matrix (from class M_c) and matrix of cluster centers (from V_{pc}) that minimizes (4.44):

$$\underset{M_c \times V_{pc}}{\min} \ J_e(U, V) = J_e(U_{opt}, V_{opt}). \qquad (4.46)$$

The most popular algorithm for approximating the minimum of J_e is the iterative process called the hard c-means or ISODATA (Iterative Self-Organizing DATA clustering):

    1°   initialize $U^{(0)} \in M_c$,

    2°   calculate cluster centers $V^{(j)} = [\underline{v}_1^{(j)}, \underline{v}_2^{(j)}, \dots, \underline{v}_c^{(j)}]$ using (4.45) and $U^{(j)}$,

3°   update partition matrix for $(j+1)$-iteration:

$$\underset{\substack{1 \le i \le c \\ 1 \le k \le N}}{\forall} \quad u_{ik}^{(j+1)} = \begin{cases} 1, & \underset{1 \le l \le c}{\min} \| \underline{x}_k - \underline{v}_l^{(j)} \| = \| \underline{x}_k - \underline{v}_i^{(j)} \|, \\ 0, & \text{otherwise}. \end{cases} \tag{4.47}$$

4°   if $\| U^{(j+1)} - U^{(j)} \| > \varepsilon$, then $j \leftarrow j + 1$, goto 2°.

The above described algorithm does not lead to global but only local minimum of criterion function J_e. To avoid that effect we may repeat ISODATA method using different starting partition matrix $U^{(0)}$.

Let us define a hard scatter matrix for i-th cluster as:

$$S_i = \sum_{k=1}^N u_{ik} (\underline{x}_k - \underline{v}_i) (\underline{x}_k - \underline{v}_i)^T, \tag{4.48}$$

a within-cluster scatter matrix as:

$$S_W = \sum_{i=1}^c S_i, \tag{4.49}$$

a between-cluster scatter matrix:

$$S_B = \sum_{i=1}^c N_i (\underline{v}_i - \underline{v}) (\underline{v}_i - \underline{v})^T, \tag{4.50}$$

where $\underline{v}$ is mean over all data vectors, and finally total scatter matrix:

$$S_T = S_W + S_B = \sum_{k=1}^N (\underline{x}_k - \underline{v}) (\underline{x}_k - \underline{v})^T. \tag{4.51}$$

The total scatter matrix is independent of data partitioning into clusters. However, within-cluster and between-cluster scatter matrixes depend on data partitioning. We define optimal partitioning as one that minimizes S_W or maximizes S_B. Because we need a scalar index, the traces (a sum of diagonal elements) or determinants of those matrixes are considered. The trace of S_W is proportional to the sum of variances in the directions of axes. Minimization of this trace leads to criterion (4.44). The same criterion is obtained by maximizing the trace of S_B. The matrix determinant is the product of its eigenvalues. Hence, it is the product of variances in principal directions, determinant it is measure of the square of the hyperellipsoidal scattering volume. It can be proved that determinant criterion leads to the same (4.44) criterion (see Fukunaga 1990).

4.5
Fuzzy clustering methods

Clustering methods described in the previous sections assume that each data vector can belong to one and only one class. This method can be natural for clustering compact and well-separated clusters. However, in practice clusters overlap, and some data vectors can belong partially to several clusters. A natural way to describe this situation results in the fuzzy set theory, and belonging or membership of vector $\underline{x}_k$ to i-th cluster (u_{ik}) is a value from [0, 1] interval. This idea was first introduced by Ruspini (1969). A so-called fuzzy c-partition as a set of all possible fuzzy partitions to c clusters is defined by:

$$M_{fc} = \left\{ U \in V_{cN} \mid 1a°, 2°, 3° \right\},\qquad(4.52)$$

where condition $1a°$ is:

$$\underset{\substack{1 \le i \le c \\ 1 \le k \le N}}{\forall} \quad u_{ik} \in [0, 1],\qquad(4.53)$$

conditions $2°$ and $3°$ are defined previously in (4.27) and (4.28), respectively. From condition $2°$ we see that for each data vector the sum of memberships to c clusters is still the one. Fuzzy cardinality (defined as sum u_{ik} over k) of each cluster is still in $[2, N\text{-}1]$. M_{fc} is superset of M_c and its infinite set whose cardinality is the same as the real number set $\boldsymbol{R}$. Like in Subsection 4.4.4 we use some criterion function to measure quality of any partition. Fuzzy c-means criteria function has the form:

$$J_m(U, V) = \sum_{i=1}^{c} \sum_{k=1}^{N} \left(u_{ik} \right)^m d_{ik}^2,\qquad(4.54)$$

where $U \in M_{fc}$, $V \in V_{pc}$, d_{ik} is any inner product induced norm:

$$d_{ik}^2 = \| \underline{x}_k - \underline{v}_i \|_A^2 = (\underline{x}_k - \underline{v}_i)^T A (\underline{x}_k - \underline{v}_i),\qquad(4.55)$$

where A is positive definite matrix, m is weighting exponent $m \in [1, \infty)$. Optimal partition is a solution of:

$$\underset{M_{fc} \times V_{pc}}{\min} J_m(U, V) = J_m(U_{opt}, V_{opt}).\qquad(4.56)$$

Criteria (4.54) were introduced by Dunn (1973) for $m = 2$. Bezdek generalized (4.54) to the infinite family of fuzzy c-means criterion where $m \in [1, \infty)$. Using Lagrange multipliers the following theorem can be proved (see Bezdek 1982): If we fix parameters m and c, and define sets:

$$\underset{1 \le k \le N}{\forall} \quad \begin{cases} I_k = \{i \mid 1 \le i \le c; \, d_{ik} = 0\}, \\ \tilde{I}_k = \{1, 2, \ldots, c\} \setminus I_k, \end{cases} \tag{4.57}$$

then $(U_{opt}, V_{opt}) \in (M_{fc} \times V_{pc})$ may be globally minimal for $J_m(U, V)$ only if:

$$\underset{\substack{1 \le i \le c \\ 1 \le k \le N}}{\forall} \quad u_{ik} = \begin{cases} \left[\left(\dfrac{1}{d_{ik}} \right)^{\frac{2}{m-1}} \middle/ \left[\sum\limits_{j=1}^{c} \left(\dfrac{1}{d_{jk}} \right)^{\frac{2}{m-1}} \right] \right], & I_k = \varnothing, \\ \forall\ 0, \quad \sum\limits_{i \in I_k} u_{ik} = 1, & I_k \ne \varnothing, \\ i \in \tilde{I}_k \end{cases} \tag{4.58}$$

and

$$\underset{1 \le i \le c}{\forall} \quad \underline{v}_i = \left[\sum_{k=1}^{N} (u_{ik})^m \, \underline{x}_k \right] \middle/ \left[\sum_{k=1}^{N} (u_{ik})^m \right]. \tag{4.59}$$

Optimal partition matrix U_{opt} is a fixed point of (4.58) and (5.59), and the solution is obtained from Pickard algorithm. This solution is called fuzzy ISODATA or fuzzy c-means, and can be described as:

1°   fix c $(1 < c < N)$, $m \in [1, \infty)$. Initialize $U^{(0)} \in M_{fc}$,
2°   calculate fuzzy centers $V^{(j)} = [\underline{v}_1^{(j)}, \underline{v}_2^{(j)}, \ldots, \underline{v}_c^{(j)}]$ using (4.59) and $U^{(j)}$,
3°   update fuzzy partition matrix $U^{(j+1)}$ for $(j+1)$-th iteration using (4.58),
4°   if $\| U^{(j+1)} - U^{(j)} \| > \varepsilon$, then, $j \gets j + 1$, goto 2°.

In this algorithm, parameter m influences the fuzziness of the clusters; the larger is m the fuzzier are the clusters. For $m \to 1^+$, fuzzy c-means solution becomes the hard one, and for $m \to \infty$ the solution is as fuzzy as possible: $u_{ik} = 1/c$, for all i,k. There is no theoretical basis for the selection of m, and usually $m = 2$ is chosen. It can be easily proved that for Euclidean norm $(A = I)$ minimization of criteria function (4.54) is equivalent to minimization of the trace of the fuzzy within-cluster scatter matrix:

$$S_{fW} = \sum_{i=1}^{c} S_{fi}, \tag{4.60}$$

where S_{fi} is fuzzy scatter matrix for i-th cluster:

$$S_{fi} = \sum_{k=1}^{N} (u_{ik})^m \left(\underline{x}_k - \underline{v}_i \right) \left(\underline{x}_k - \underline{v}_i \right)^T, \tag{4.61}$$

where the fuzzy center $\underline{v}_i$ is calculated by (4.59).

Bezdek (1980) introduced the use of Zangwill's theory of convergence to prove that fuzzy c-means converges to the local minimum of criterion function (4.54). This theory has counterexamples and Bezdek et al. (1987) gives the correct theory, i.e., fuzzy c-means iterates to either a local minimum or saddle point of (4.54).

In the above described algorithm we assume that all clusters have the same geometric shape. In this case the used norm (4.55) influences all cluster shapes. Gustafson and Kessel (1979) proposed an interesting modification of the fuzzy c-means algorithm, that allows clusters to have different geometrical shapes. This is realized by using different norms for each cluster. Let us use the following norm for i-th cluster:

$$\underset{\substack{1 \leq k \leq N \\ 1 \leq i \leq c}}{\forall} \quad d_{ik}^2 = \| \underline{x}_k - \underline{v}_i \|_{A_i}^2 = \left(\underline{x}_k - \underline{v}_i \right)^T A_i \left(\underline{x}_k - \underline{v}_i \right). \tag{4.62}$$

If we define $\underline{A} = (A_1, A_2, ..., A_c)$ as a c-tuple, then the modified criterion function has the form:

$$\hat{J}_m(U, V, \underline{A}) = \sum_{i=1}^{c} \sum_{k=1}^{N} \left(u_{ik} \right)^m \| \underline{x}_k - \underline{v}_i \|_{A_i}^2. \tag{4.63}$$

Let us denote c-fold Cartesian product of the symmetric, positive definite matrixes from V_{pp} as PD^c, then we find the following solution:

$$\underset{M_{fc} \times V_{pc} \times PD^c}{\min} \quad \hat{J}_m(U, V, \underline{A}) = \hat{J}_m(U_{opt}, V_{opt}, \underline{A}_{opt}). \tag{4.64}$$

Gustafson and Kassel (1979) proved the following theorem:

If we fix U and V satisfying equations (4.58) and (4.59), and $\det(A_i) = \rho_i$, then $\underline{A}_{opt}$ is the local minimum criterion (4.63) only if:

$$\underset{1 \leq j \leq c}{\forall} \quad A_{j\,opt} = \left[\rho_j \det(C_{fj}) \right]^{\frac{1}{p}} C_{fj}^{-1}, \tag{4.65}$$

where C_{fj} is fuzzy covariance matrix:

$$C_{fj} = \left[\sum_{k=1}^{N} \left(u_{jk} \right)^m (\underline{x}_k - \underline{v}_j)(\underline{x}_k - \underline{v}_j)^T \right] \bigg/ \left[\sum_{k=1}^{N} \left(u_{jk} \right)^m \right]. \tag{4.66}$$

This algorithm searches an optimal cluster shape varying each A_j assuming that its determinant is fixed (volume of cluster proportional to ρ_j). Without constraint to cluster volume, the criterion function (4.63), which is linear with respect to A_js, could be as small as we would by making A_js less positive definite. Because A_j is an inversion of fuzzy covariance matrix, norm (4.62) can be called fuzzy Mahalonobis distance. Clustering with fuzzy covariance matrixes can be summarized as:

1°   fix c $(1 < c < N)$, $m \in [1, \infty)$, and volume constraints $\rho_j \in R^+$. Initialize $U^{(0)} \in M_{fc}$,

2°   calculate fuzzy centers $V^{(j)} = [\underline{v}_1^{(j)}, \underline{v}_2^{(j)}, \ldots, \underline{v}_c^{(j)}]$ using (4.59) and $U^{(j)}$,

3°   calculate fuzzy covariance matrixes C_{fj} using (4.66), calculate their determinants and inverses,

4°   calculate the norm-inducing matrixes A_js using (4.65),

5°   update fuzzy partition matrix $U^{(j+1)}$ for $(j+1)$-th iteration using (4.58), and norm (4.62),

6°   if $\| U^{(j+1)} - U^{(j)} \| > \varepsilon$, then, $j \leftarrow j + 1$, goto 2°.

The fuzzy c-varieties (FCV) introduced by Bezdek is in some sense opposite to the method presented by Gustafson and Kessel. In this method fuzzy centers (point in R^p) are replaced by r-dimensional linear varieties $(0 \leq r < p)$. This type of clusters modeling is useful for a data set which consists of c the same dimensional linear varieties. r-dimensional linear variety through the point $\underline{v} \in R^p$, spanned by the linearly independent vectors $\underline{s}_1, \underline{s}_2, \ldots, \underline{s}_r$ is the set:

$$V_r(\underline{v}, \underline{s}_1, \underline{s}_2, \ldots \underline{s}_r) = \left\{ \underline{y} \in R^p \ \middle| \ \underline{y} = \underline{v} + \sum_{j=1}^r t_j \underline{s}_j, \ t_j \in R \right\}. \tag{4.67}$$

For $r = 0$ we have a point, for $r = 1$ a line, $r = 3$ a plane and for larger r a hyperplane. If vectors $\{\underline{s}_i\}$ are an orthogonal $(\underline{s}_i^T A \ \underline{s}_i = \delta_{ij})$ then the distance from data point (vector) $\underline{x}_k$ to the i-th linear variety is:

$$D(\underline{x}_k, V_{R_i})^2 = \| \underline{x}_k - \underline{v}_i \|_A^2 - \sum_{j=1}^r \left[(\underline{x}_k - \underline{v}_i)^T A \ \underline{s}_{ji} \right]^2 = D_{ik}^2. \tag{4.68}$$

Let us denote the set of c linear varieties as $V_r = (V_{r1}, V_{r2}, \ldots, V_{rc})$. Now criterion function gets the form:

$$J_{mV_r}(U, V, V_r) = \sum_{i=1}^c \sum_{k=1}^N (u_{ik})^m \ D_{ik}^2. \tag{4.69}$$

The following theorem can be proved (see Bezdek 1982): If we fix U, then a local minimum of (4.69) is for varieties given by:

$$\underset{1 \le i \le c}{\forall} \quad \underline{v}_i = \left[\sum_{k=1}^{N} (u_{ik})^m \underline{x}_k \right] \Bigg/ \left[\sum_{k=1}^{N} (u_{ik})^m \right]. \qquad (4.70)$$

and

$$\underline{s}_{ij} = A^{-1/2} \underline{y}_{ij}, \qquad (4.71)$$

where $\underline{y}_{ij}$ is the j-th, generalized unit eigenvector of matrix $A^{1/2} S_{fi} A^{1/2}$ corresponding to its j-th largest eigenvalue.

The fuzzy c-varieties algorithm can be summarized as follows:

1°   fix c $(1 < c < N)$, r $(0 \le r < p)$, $m \in [1, \infty)$. Initialize $U^{(0)} \in M_{fc}$,
2°   calculate fuzzy centers $V^{(j)} = [\underline{v}_1^{(j)}, \underline{v}_2^{(j)}, \ldots, \underline{v}_c^{(j)}]$ using (4.70) and $U^{(j)}$,
3°   calculate the c generalized fuzzy scatter matrixes S_{fi} using (4.61),
4°   calculate r largest eigenvectors $\underline{y}_{ij}$ and $\underline{s}_{ij}$ using (4.71),
5°   update fuzzy partition matrix $U^{(j+1)}$ for $(j+1)$-th iteration using (4.58) with d_{ik} replaced by D_{ik} from (4.68),
6°   if $\| U^{(j+1)} - U^{(j)} \| > \varepsilon$, then, $j \leftarrow j + 1$, goto 2°.

Bezdek also introduced another clustering method for which criterion function is a convex combination of criteria (4.69) with different r_i-dimensional linear varieties. This algorithm is called fuzzy c-elliptotypes (FCE). The main advantage of this method is that it requires each cluster to contain a center $\underline{v}_i$ in or near its convex hull (see Bezdek 1982).

There are many extensions and generalizations of the above described methods to other geometrical shapes. For example Krishnapuram et al. (1995,1995a), Krishnapuram (1992), Davé and Bhaswan (1992) introduced fuzzy c-shell algorithms, which can solve clustering problems for unsegmented, scattered and sparse data vectors using hyper-linear or -quadratic shell clusters model.

At the end of the section let us recall fuzzy c-regression model (FCRM) introduced by Hathaway and Bezdek (1993). Let us have a set of data $\{(\underline{x}_1, y_1), (\underline{x}_2, y_2), \ldots, (\underline{x}_N, y_N)\}$, where each independent vector $\underline{x}_i$ has corresponding y_i value. To model these data we use so-called switching regressions:

$$\underset{1 \le i \le c}{\forall} \quad y_k = f_i(\underline{x}_k, \underline{\theta}_i) + \varepsilon_i, \qquad (4.72)$$

where θ_i is parameter vector, and ε_i is random value with zero mean and variance σ_i^2.

This method produces estimates of $\underline{\theta}_i$ and assigns each data pair to corresponding regression model. Let us interpret u_{ik} as the importance attached to the extent to which the model value $f_i(\underline{x}_k, \underline{\theta}_i)$ matches y_k. This matching is measured by:

$$E_{ik}(\underline{\theta}_i) = [f_i(\underline{x}_k, \underline{\theta}_i) - y_k]^2. \tag{4.73}$$

Functions f_i are obtained as a global minimum of the minimizer properties:

$$\mathop{\forall}_{1 \le i \le c} \quad \psi_i(\underline{\theta}_i) = \sum_{k=1}^{N} (u_{ik})^m E_{ik}(\underline{\theta}_i). \tag{4.74}$$

Criterion function for fuzzy c-regression model is defined as:

$$J_m(U, \{\underline{\theta}_i\}) = \sum_{i=1}^{c} \sum_{k=1}^{N} (u_{ik})^m E_{ik}(\underline{\theta}_i). \tag{4.75}$$

Usually we apply a linear model:

$$f_i(\underline{x}_k, \underline{\theta}_i) = \underline{\theta}_i^T \underline{x}_k. \tag{4.76}$$

For minimization of (4.74) we use the weighted least-squares method in a matrix version:

$$\psi_i(\underline{\theta}_i) = \left[Y - X\underline{\theta}_i \right]^T D_i \left[Y - X\underline{\theta}_i \right], \tag{4.77}$$

where $Y = [y_1, y_2, ..., y_N]^T$, $X = [\underline{x}_1, \underline{x}_2, ..., \underline{x}_N]^T$, and $D_i = \mathrm{diag}[(u_{i1})^m, (u_{i2})^m, ..., (u_{iN})^m]$. Minimization of this criterion yields the weighted least-squares estimator:

$$\underline{\theta}_i = \left[X^T D_i X \right]^{-1} X^T D_i Y. \tag{4.78}$$

For the frequently used recursive version see Section 3.7. The fuzzy c-regression model can be summarized as follows:

1°   fix c $(1 < c < N)$, $m \in [1, \infty)$. Initialize $U^{(0)} \in M_{fc}$,
2°   calculate a set of parameters $\{\underline{\theta}_i^{(j)}\}$ using (4.59) and $U^{(j)}$,
3°   update fuzzy partition matrix $U^{(j+1)}$ for $(j+1)$-th iteration using (4.58) with d_{ik} replaced by $E_{ik}(\underline{\theta}_i^{(j)})$, from (4.73),
4°   if $\| U^{(j+1)} - U^{(j)} \| > \varepsilon$, then, $j \leftarrow j + 1$, goto 2°.

Fuzzy c-medians (FCMED) clustering algorithm is more resistant to outliers version of fuzzy c-means method described by Kersten (1997). In this case computation of cluster centers is replaced by fuzzy median operator.

4.6
A possibilistic approach to clustering

In this approach cluster centers $\underline{v}_i$ represent cluster, and u_{ik} is the degree of compatibility (typicality) of data vector $\underline{x}_k$ with $\underline{v}_i$, or the possibility that $\underline{x}_k$ belonging to i-th cluster. There are two main reasons for the introduction of this method:

(i). Due to constraints, increasing membership to one cluster automatically decreases memberships to other clusters, however, intuitively this membership can depend only on distance from cluster center.

(ii). The performance in the presence of noise data vectors is improved.

This method was introduced by Krishuapuran and Keller (1993). The so-called possibility c-partitioning as a set of all possible partitions to c clusters is defined as:

$$M_{pc} = \left\{ U \in V_{cN} \mid 1a°, 2°, 3a° \right\},\qquad (4.79)$$

where conditions $1a°$, $2°$ are defined by (4.53) and (4.27), respectively, and condition $3a°$ is:

$$\underset{1 \leq k \leq N}{\forall} \quad \sum_{i=1}^{c} u_{ik} \leq 1.\qquad (4.80)$$

The criterion function for possibilistic clustering has the form:

$$J_m(U, V) = \sum_{i=1}^{c} \sum_{k=1}^{N} \left(u_{ik} \right)^m d_{ik}^2 + \sum_{i=1}^{c} \eta_i \sum_{k=1}^{N} (1 - u_{ik})^m,\qquad (4.81)$$

where η_is are positive numbers. The first term is identical to criterion in the fuzzy c-means, and the second term forces the u_{ik}s to be as large as possible avoiding the trivial solution. It is easy to prove the following theorem: U may be a global minimum for (4.81) only if:

$$\underset{\substack{1 \leq i \leq c \\ 1 \leq k \leq N}}{\forall} \quad u_{ik} = \cfrac{1}{1 + \left(\cfrac{d_{ik}^2}{\eta_i} \right)^{\frac{1}{m-1}}},\qquad (4.82)$$

and the necessary condition for the cluster centers is identical to that from the fuzzy c-means. From (4.82) we see that for each iteration u_{ik} depends only on distance of $\underline{x}_k$ from $\underline{v}_i$, which is an intuitively pleasing result. The values of η_is determine the distance at which the membership is equal to 0.5. In practice η_is are proportional to the average fuzzy intracluster distance from $\underline{v_i}$:

$$\forall_{1 \le i \le c} \quad \eta_i = \xi \frac{\sum_{k=1}^{N} \left(u_{ik}\right)^m d_{ik}^2}{\sum_{k=1}^{N} \left(u_{ik}\right)^m}, \qquad (4.83)$$

where ξ is constant usually equal to the one, and u_{ik}s derive from the fuzzy c-means clustering method which is used for initialization.

Pal et al. (1997) proposed a connection of the fuzzy and possibilistic approach to clustering. In this method we use the relative typicality denoted u_{ik} and the absolute typicality denoted t_{ik}. The typicality t_{ik} is a function of $\underline{x_k}$ and $\underline{v_i}$ only, whereas, u_{ik} is a function of $\underline{x_k}$ and all cluster centers. It is reasonable to compute typicality based on all N data vectors, rather than all c clusters. The so-called mixed fuzzy-possibilistic c-means (FPCM) model is based on the minimization of criterion:

$$J_{m,\eta}(U, T, V) = \sum_{i=1}^{c} \sum_{k=1}^{N} \left(u_{ik}^m + t_{ik}^\eta\right) d_{ik}^2, \qquad (4.84)$$

subject to the constraints: $m \in [1, \infty)$, $\eta \in [1, \infty)$, $U \in M_{fc}$ and $[t_{ik}] = T \in M_{tc}$ defined as:

$$M_{tc} = \left\{ T \in V_{cN} \mid 1a°, 2a°, 3b° \right\}, \qquad (4.85)$$

where condition $1a°$ is defined by (4.53) when u_{ik} is replaced by t_{ik}, and $2a°$ as:

$$\forall_{1 \le i \le c} \quad \sum_{k=1}^{N} t_{ik} = 1, \qquad (4.86)$$

and $3b°$ as:

$$\forall_{1 \le k \le N} \quad \sum_{i=1}^{c} t_{ik} > 0. \qquad (4.87)$$

The following theorem gives the necessary conditions for the minimum of criterion (4.84):

if we fix m, η and c, then $(U_{opt}, T_{opt}, V_{opt}) \in M_{fc} \times M_{tc} \times V_{pc}$ may be globally minimal for $J_{m,\eta}(U, T, V)$ only if u_{ik} is given by (4.58) and typicality t_{ik} by:

$$\forall_{\substack{1 \le i \le c \\ 1 \le k \le N}} \quad t_{ik} = \left(\frac{1}{d_{ik}}\right)^{\frac{2}{\eta-1}} \Bigg/ \left[\sum_{j=1}^{N} \left(\frac{1}{d_{ij}}\right)^{\frac{2}{\eta-1}}\right], \qquad (4.88)$$

and cluster centers as:

$$\underset{1 \le i \le c}{\forall} \quad \underline{v}_i = \left[\sum_{k=1}^{N} \left(u_{ik}^m + t_{ik}^\eta \right) \underline{x}_k \right] \Bigg/ \left[\sum_{k=1}^{N} \left(u_{ik}^m + t_{ik}^\eta \right) \right]. \tag{4.89}$$

Another clustering method which does not assume that for each data vector memberships to all c clusters summarize to one is proposed by Karayiannis (1996a). In this case c-partition is defined as:

$$M_{gfc} = \left\{ U \in V_{cN} \mid 1b°, 2b°, 3c° \right\}, \tag{4.90}$$

where condition $1b°$ is $u_{ik} \ge 0$, $2b°$ is:

$$\underset{1 \le k \le N}{\forall} \quad c \underset{i=1}{\overset{c}{\boxplus}}_{(\alpha)} u_{ik} = 1, \tag{4.91}$$

and condition $3c°$ is:

$$\underset{1 \le i \le c}{\forall} \quad 0 < \sum_{k=1}^{N} u_{ik} < \infty. \tag{4.92}$$

If function in (4.91) satisfies the condition:

$$\underset{\substack{\varkappa > 0 \\ 1 \le k \le N}}{\forall} \quad \underset{i=1}{\overset{c}{\boxplus}}_{(\alpha)} \varkappa\, u_{ik} = \varkappa \underset{i=1}{\overset{c}{\boxplus}}_{(\alpha)} u_{ik}, \tag{4.93}$$

then the following theorem can be proved. The necessary conditions for minimization (4.54) under constraints (4.91) are (4.92) and:

$$\underset{\substack{1 \le i \le c \\ 1 \le k \le N}}{\forall} \quad u_{ik} = \left(d_{ik} \right)^{\frac{2}{1-m}} \Bigg/ \left[c \underset{j=1}{\overset{c}{\boxplus}}_{(\alpha)} \left(d_{jk} \right)^{\frac{2}{1-m}} \right]. \tag{4.94}$$

This method is named the generalized fuzzy c-means (GFCM). Generalized mean of cu_{ik} is used as a function in (4.91):

$$\underset{1 \le k \le N}{\forall} \quad \underset{i=1}{\overset{c}{\boxplus}}_{(\alpha)} u_{ik} = \left(\frac{1}{c} \sum_{i=1}^{c} \left(u_{ik} \right)^\alpha \right)^{\frac{1}{\alpha}}, \tag{4.95}$$

and then from (4.94) and (4.95) we get:

$$\underset{\substack{1 \le i \le c \\ 1 \le k \le N}}{\forall} \quad u_{ik} = \frac{1}{c} \left(d_{ik} \right)^{\frac{2}{1-m}} \Bigg/ \left[\frac{1}{c} \sum_{j=1}^{c} \left(d_{jk} \right)^{\frac{2\alpha}{1-m}} \right]^{\frac{1}{\alpha}}, \tag{4.96}$$

where $\alpha \in \mathbf{R}$. For example, for $\alpha = 1$ we obtain the fuzzy c-means method, and for $\alpha \to 0$ geometric fuzzy c-means. Let us denote:

$$\underset{1 \le k \le N}{\forall} \quad \gamma_k = \sum_{i=1}^{c} u_{ik} = \frac{\dfrac{1}{c}\sum_{i=1}^{c}(d_{ik})^{\frac{2}{1-m}}}{\left[\dfrac{1}{c}\sum_{j=1}^{c}(d_{jk})^{\frac{2\alpha}{1-m}}\right]^{\frac{1}{\alpha}}} = \frac{\overset{c}{\underset{j=1}{\biguplus}}_{(1)}(d_{jk})^{\frac{2}{1-m}}}{\overset{c}{\underset{j=1}{\biguplus}}_{(\alpha)}(d_{jk})^{\frac{2}{1-m}}}. \tag{4.97}$$

The following conditions can be proved:

- $\alpha \in (1, \infty) \Rightarrow \gamma_k \le 1$, (with equality for $u_{ik} = 1/c$),
- $\alpha \in (-\infty, 0) \cup (0, 1) \Rightarrow \gamma_k \ge 1$, (with equality for $u_{ik} = 1/c$),
- $\alpha \to 0 \Rightarrow \gamma_k \ge 1$, (with equality for $u_{ik} = 1/c$),
- $\alpha = 1 \Rightarrow \gamma_k = 1$.

If $\alpha = 1$ (FCM) then $\gamma_k = 1$ for all k, but if $\alpha \ne 1$ then γ_ks contains significant information about assignment of data vector $\underline{x}_k$ into c clusters. Value $\gamma_k = 1$ implies that the assignment $\underline{x}_k$ into c clusters is maximally fuzzy, and approximately equal to $1/c$. In other words, data vector $\underline{x}_k$ is equidistant from all clusters, and is usually outlier. This method can be reformulated as minimization criterion function (4.54) under constraint:

$$\left(\sum_{i=1}^{c} u_{ik} = \gamma_k\right) > 0, \tag{4.98}$$

and constraints γ_k are given by (4.97).

In the paper by Karayiannis (1996) the weighted generalized c-means method is proposed. The criterion function takes the form:

$$J_{m,\beta}(U, V) = \sum_{i=1}^{c} \sum_{k=1}^{N} \beta_k (u_{ik})^m d_{ik}^2, \tag{4.99}$$

where constants β_k satisfies the condition: $\sum_{k=1}^{N} \beta_k = 1$. In this method condition (4.91) is replaced by:

$$\underset{1 \le k \le N}{\forall} \quad c \overset{c}{\underset{i=1}{\biguplus}}_{(\alpha,\beta)} u_{ik} = 1, \tag{4.100}$$

and function (4.95) is replaced by weighted generalized mean of cu_{ik}:

$$\overset{c}{\underset{i=1}{\biguplus}}_{(\alpha,\beta)} u_{ik} = \left(\sum_{i=1}^{c} \beta_i (u_{ik})^\alpha\right)^{\frac{1}{\alpha}}. \tag{4.101}$$

The updating rule for u_{ik} takes the form:

$$\underset{\substack{1 \le i \le c \\ 1 \le k \le N}}{\forall} \quad u_{ik} = \frac{1}{c} (d_{ik})^{\frac{2}{1-m}} \Bigg/ \left[\sum_{j=1}^{c} \beta_j (d_{jk})^{\frac{2\alpha}{1-m}} \right]^{\frac{1}{\alpha}}, \qquad (4.102)$$

For β_j equal to $1/c$ (4.102) takes the form of (4.96). Each weight β_j provides a measure of the average distance between cluster center $\underline{v}_i$ and data vectors:

$$\underset{1 \le i \le c}{\forall} \quad \beta_i = \frac{\displaystyle\sum_{k=1}^{N} d_{ik}^2}{\displaystyle\sum_{j=1}^{c} \sum_{k=1}^{N} d_{jk}^2}. \qquad (4.103)$$

Instead of the above approaches the search for solution satisfying constraints (4.91) or (4.100) directly specifying γ_k is proposed by Pedrycz (1998) and (1998a). This method is called conditional fuzzy c-means (CFCM) or context-dependent clustering. In this case data vectors $\underline{x}_k$ are clustered under conditions based on some linguistic terms defined in corresponding data vectors $\underline{y}_k$. These linguistic terms are treated as fuzzy relations, defined by membership functions. Finally, we have a corresponding value $f_k \in [0, 1]$ for each data vector $\underline{x}_k$. In this case c-partitions are defined as:

$$M_{cfc} = \left\{ U \in V_{cN} \mid 1a°, 2c°, 3° \right\}, \qquad (4.104)$$

where conditions $1a°$ and $3°$ are given by (4.53) and (4.28), and $2c°$ is defined by:

$$\underset{1 \le k \le N}{\forall} \quad \sum_{i=1}^{c} u_{ik} = f_k. \qquad (4.105)$$

The necessary conditions for minimization criterion (4.54) under constraints (4.105) are (4.59) for cluster center, and:

$$\underset{\substack{1 \le i \le c \\ 1 \le k \le N}}{\forall} \quad u_{ik} = f_k \Bigg/ \left[\sum_{j=1}^{c} \left(\frac{d_{ik}}{d_{jk}} \right)^{\frac{2}{1-m}} \right]. \qquad (4.106)$$

This method develops clusters using similarity of data vectors $\underline{x}_k$ as well as conditional information from dependent variables.

4.7
New generalized weighted conditional fuzzy c-means

Incorporating additional information to the clustering process by (4.106) is one of the many possibilities. We propose following method based on the weighted generalized mean, described as conditions:

$$\mathop{\forall}_{1 \le k \le N} c \; \mathop{\biguplus}_{i=1}^{c} {}_{(\alpha, \beta)} \, u_{ik} = f_k.$$ (4.107)

If we name this condition as $2d°$, then:

$$M_{gcfc} = \left\{ U \in V_{cN} \mid 1b°, 2d°, 3c° \right\},$$ (4.108)

stands for a new c-partition type. The solution of minimization criterion function J_m given by (4.54) under conditions (4.107) is yielded by theorem: The necessary conditions for solution $(U_{opt}, V_{opt}) \in (M_{gfcf} \times V_{pc})$ of (4.54) with conditions (4.107) are:

$$\mathop{\forall}_{\substack{1 \le i \le c \\ 1 \le k \le N}} u_{ik} = \begin{cases} f_k \left(d_{ik}\right)^{\frac{2}{1-m}} \Big/ \left[c \mathop{\biguplus}_{j=1}^{c} {}_{(\alpha, \beta)} \left(d_{jk}\right)^{\frac{2}{1-m}} \right], & I_k = \varnothing, \\[2ex] \mathop{\forall}_{i \in \bar{I}_k} 0, \quad c \mathop{\biguplus}_{i \in I_k} {}_{(\alpha, \beta)} u_{ik} = f_k, & I_k \ne \varnothing, \end{cases}$$ (4.109)

and:

$$\mathop{\forall}_{1 \le i \le c} \underline{v}_i = \left[\sum_{k=1}^{N} \left(u_{ik}\right)^m \underline{x}_k \right] \Big/ \left[\sum_{k=1}^{N} \left(u_{ik}\right)^m \right].$$ (4.110)

Proof: If we fix $V \in V_{cp}$, then columns of U are independent, and minimization of (4.54) can be done term by term:

$$\mathop{\forall}_{1 \le k \le N} g_k(U) = \sum_{i=1}^{c} \left(u_{ik}\right)^m d_{ik}^2.$$ (4.111)

The Lagrangian of (4.54) is:

$$\mathop{\forall}_{1 \le k \le N} G_k(U, \lambda) = \sum_{i=1}^{c} \left(u_{ik}\right)^m d_{ik}^2 - \lambda \left(c \, F_i(u_{ik}) - f_k \right).$$ (4.112)

where $F_i(u_{ik})$ is abbreviation for function (4.101). Setting the Lagrangian's gradient to zero yields:

$$\underset{1 \leq k \leq N}{\forall} \quad \frac{\partial G_k(U, \lambda)}{\partial \lambda} = \left(c F_i(u_{ik}) - f_k\right) = 0, \tag{4.113}$$

and:

$$\underset{\substack{1 \leq t \leq N \\ 1 \leq s \leq c}}{\forall} \quad \frac{\partial G_t(U, \lambda)}{\partial u_{st}} = m \left(u_{st}\right)^{m-1} d_{st}^2 - \lambda c \, \frac{\partial F_j(u_{jt})}{\partial u_{st}} = 0. \tag{4.114}$$

From (4.114) we get:

$$u_{st} = \left[\frac{\lambda c}{m}\right]^{\frac{1}{m-1}} \left[\frac{1}{d_{st}^2} \frac{\partial F_j(u_{jt})}{\partial u_{st}}\right]^{\frac{1}{m-1}}. \tag{4.115}$$

From (4.113) and (4.115) using condition (4.93) for weighted mean, we get:

$$c \left[\frac{\lambda c}{m}\right]^{\frac{1}{m-1}} F_j \left\{ \left[\frac{1}{d_{jt}^2} \frac{\partial F_j(u_{jt})}{\partial u_{jt}}\right]^{\frac{1}{m-1}} \right\} = f_t. \tag{4.116}$$

Combining (4.115) and (4.116), and using condition (4.93) yields:

$$u_{st} = \left(\left(d_{st}\right)^{\frac{2}{1-m}} f_t\right) \bigg/ \left(c \overset{c}{\underset{j=1}{\boxplus}}_{(\alpha, \beta)} \left(d_{jt}\right)^{\frac{2}{1-m}}\right). \tag{4.117}$$

If $I_k \neq \emptyset$, then choosing u_{ik} as in (4.109) results in minimal value of criterion (4.54), because partition matrix elements are zeros for non-zero distance, and non-zero for zero distances. ∎

If we use weighted generalized mean (4.101) then for $I_k = \emptyset$:

$$\underset{\substack{1 \leq i \leq c \\ 1 \leq k \leq N}}{\forall} \quad u_{ik} = \frac{\dfrac{1}{c} f_k \left(d_{ik}\right)^{\frac{2}{1-m}}}{\left(\sum_{j=1}^{c} \beta_j \left(d_{jk}\right)^{\frac{2\alpha}{1-m}}\right)^{\frac{1}{\alpha}}}. \tag{4.118}$$

For $f_k = 1$, we obtain weighted generalized c-means method, and for β_is equal to $1/c$, and $\alpha=1$ we obtain conditional c-means.

4.8
Fuzzy learning vector quantization

Vector quantization is the method of the representation N unlabeled or labeled (learning vector quantization) data vectors by a codebook, i.e. a set of c prototypes (cluster centers). This method is based on minimization of criterion function:

$$L_m = \frac{1}{N} \sum_{k=1}^{N} \left(\sum_{i=1}^{c} (u_{ik})^m \| x_k - v_i \|^2 \right), \tag{4.119}$$

where $(u_{ik})^m$ plays the role of neighborhood function. Criterion (4.119) can be interpreted as averaging over all data vectors of the loss functions (in brackets). We see that criterion (4.119) is proportional to the criterion used by the fuzzy c-means.

If in criterion (4.119) we place optimal form of u_{ik} from (4.58) then we obtain:

$$R_m(V) = \sum_{k=1}^{N} \left[\sum_{k=1}^{c} (d_{ik})^{\frac{2}{1-m}} \right]^{1-m}, \tag{4.120}$$

reformulated criterion for the fuzzy c-means proposed in Hathaway and Bezdek (1995). In this case we search for $V=[v_1, v_2, ..., v_c]$, that minimizes criterion $R_m(V)$. This can be done using genetic algorithm based technique, or classical gradient method. Using the generalized mean (4.95) we get:

$$R_\alpha(V) = \sum_{k=1}^{N} c^{\frac{1}{\alpha}} \biguplus_{i=1}^{c} {}_{(\alpha)} d_{ik}^2, \tag{4.121}$$

where $\alpha = 1 / (1 - m)$, $\alpha \in R \setminus \{0\}$. By comparison of (4.120) and (4.121) we see that the criterion used in the vector quantization method is obtained by dividing c-means criterion by the number of data vectors (N). Using gradient descent optimization method we get the following updating codebook vectors:

$$\underset{1 \le j \le c}{\forall} \quad v_j \leftarrow v_j - \frac{\alpha_j}{N} \frac{\partial R_\alpha(V)}{\partial v_j}. \tag{4.122}$$

Using (4.121) and (4.122) we have:

$$\underset{1 \le j \le c}{\forall} \quad v_j \leftarrow v_j + \eta_j \sum_{k=1}^{N} \left[\sum_{i=1}^{c} \left(\frac{d_{ik}^2}{d_{jk}^2} \right)^\alpha \right]^{\frac{1-\alpha}{\alpha}} (x_k - v_j), \tag{4.123}$$

where $\eta_j = 2\alpha_j / N$ stands for the learning rate. The fuzzy learning vector quantization (FLVQ) algorithm based on (4.123) is introduced by Tsao et al. (1994). From (4.123) we see that each cluster prototype is updated after presentation of all data vectors (off-line method). All prototypes are modified using distance of data vector to all current prototypes.

In the paper by Karayiannis (1996b) a weighted fuzzy learning vector quantization is introduced. In this case generalized means is replaced by weighted generalized means (4.101) and we get:

$$\underset{1 \leq j \leq c}{\forall} \quad \underline{v}_j \leftarrow \underline{v}_j + \eta_j \sum_{k=1}^{N} f_k \left[c \sum_{i=1}^{c} \beta_i \left(\frac{d_{ik}^2}{d_{jk}^2} \right)^{\alpha} \right]^{\frac{1-\alpha}{\alpha}} \left(\underline{x}_k - \underline{v}_j \right), \tag{4.124}$$

where f_ks are weights connected with data vectors.

At the end of this section let us recall entropy constrained fuzzy clustering (ECFC) described by Karayiannis (1996b). Let us define partition entropy as:

$$H(U) = -\frac{1}{N} \sum_{k=1}^{N} \sum_{i=1}^{c} u_{ik} \ln(u_{ik}), \tag{4.125}$$

which measures the average level of fuzziness or uncertainty in c-partition. The maximal value of entropy is obtained for maximally fuzzy partition $u_{ik} = 1/c$, for all i,k and is equal to $\ln(c)$. Criterion function has the form:

$$I_\mu(U, V) = (1 - \mu) \, \sigma \, L_1(U, V) - \mu \, H(U), \tag{4.126}$$

where $\mu \in (0, 1)$ and σ are constant. Entropy constrained fuzzy clustering method minimizing the above criterion can be viewed as minimization criterion (4.126) for $m=1$ at the specified (controlled by μ) level of fuzziness in c-partition matrix U. Like in deterministic annealing (see Section 3.8) μ is a pseudo-temperature parameter, which slowly decreases during the optimization process. The necessary conditions for solution (U, V) are (4.59) and:

$$\underset{\substack{1 \leq k \leq N \\ 1 \leq i \leq c}}{\forall} \quad u_{ik} = \frac{\exp\left(-\sigma \, \delta \, \|\underline{x}_i - \underline{v}_k\|^2\right)}{\sum_{j=1}^{c} \exp\left(-\sigma \, \delta \, \|\underline{x}_i - \underline{v}_j\|^2\right)}, \tag{4.127}$$

where $\delta = (1 - \mu) / \mu$.

If we denote:

$$\underset{1 \leq i \leq c}{\forall} \quad S_i = \frac{1}{c} \sum_{j=1}^{c} \exp\left(-\sigma \, \delta \, \|\underline{x}_i - \underline{v}_j\|^2\right) \tag{4.128}$$

then criterion (4.126) can be written as:

$$I_\mu(U, V) = -\frac{\sigma(1-\mu)}{N} \sum_{j=1}^{c} \frac{1}{\sigma\delta} \ln(S_j) - \mu \ln(c). \tag{4.129}$$

The last term is independent from partition matrix U, and can be eliminated from criterion (4.129). Considering criterion (4.129) without the last term or criterion from c-means clustering in reformulated form (4.120) Karaiyannis proposed the family of criterion functions, that leads to a variety of learning vector quantization methods:

$$R = \frac{1}{N} \sum_{k=1}^{N} f(S_k), \tag{4.130}$$

where:

$$\underset{1 \le k \le N}{\forall} \quad S_k = \frac{1}{c} \sum_{i=1}^{c} g(\|x_k - v_i\|^2). \tag{4.131}$$

The fuzzy c-means criterion in a reformulated form (4.120) is achieved for: $f(x) = x^{1-m}$, $g(x) = x^{(1/(1-m))}$. The ECFC method is obtained for: $f(x) = -\ln(x)/(\sigma\,\delta)$, $g(x) = \exp(-\sigma\delta x)$. Karayiannis proposed the following general conditions for these functions: $f(x)$ and $g(x)$ are both monotonically decreasing (increasing) functions of $x \in (0, \infty)$, $f(g(x)) = x$, and $f'(g(x))\,g'(x) = 1$, and $g'(x)$ is a monotonically increasing (decreasing) function of $x \in (0, \infty)$. If we use gradient descent optimization method to criterion (4.130) then

$$\underset{1 \le j \le c}{\forall} \quad v_j \leftarrow v_j - \eta_j' \frac{\partial R}{\partial v_j} = \eta_j \sum_{k=1}^{N} \alpha_{jk}\left(x_k - v_j\right), \tag{4.132}$$

where $\eta_j = 2\eta_j'/(Nc)$, and:

$$\underset{\substack{1 \le j \le c \\ 1 \le k \le N}}{\forall} \quad \alpha_{jk} = f'(S_k)\,g'(\|x_k - v_j\|^2). \tag{4.133}$$

Using f' and g' dependency, we finally get:

$$\underset{\substack{1 \le j \le c \\ 1 \le k \le N}}{\forall} \quad \alpha_{jk} = \frac{f'(S_k)}{f'[g(\|x_k - v_j\|^2)]}. \tag{4.134}$$

4.9
Cluster validity

The data clustering task may be realized by various methods described (and not described) in this chapter. Each of these methods can be applied with different parameters, such as: a number of clusters c, exponent weight m, and many others. A question arises which c-partition generated by these methods is the best. We use validity criteria (indexes), which are measures of clustering quality. In other words, independently of the used clustering method and its parameters we can measure quality of any c-partition by validity indexes. There are many validity indexes, and in this section we recall only the important ones. Usually, validity is used to obtain optimal number of clusters, while other parameters are pre-specified. But the validity indexes can be used to find optimal values of other parameters.

The simplest indexes are measures of fuzziness in partition matrix U, i.e. partition coefficient:

$$V_{PC}(U) = -\frac{1}{N}\sum_{i=1}^{c}\sum_{k=1}^{N}\left(u_{ik}\right)^2,$$ (4.135)

and, partition entropy:

$$V_{PE}(U) = -\frac{1}{N}\sum_{i=1}^{c}\sum_{k=1}^{N}u_{ik}\ln(u_{ik}).$$ (4.136)

We find c-partition that minimizes one of the above indexes. The lack of direct connection to a geometrical property of data vectors and monotonic decreasing tendency with a number of clusters c are the main disadvantages of these criterions.

Several indexes operate on crisp (hard) c-partitions (4.25). We can easily obtain a crisp c-partition from the fuzzy c-partition (4.52) by the so-called defuzzification of partition matrix. For example we can use the following simple method:

$$\mathop{\forall}_{\substack{1\le i\le c \\ 1\le k\le N}} u_{ik}^{(c)} = \begin{cases} 1, & \max_{1\le p\le c} u_{pk}^{(f)} = u_{ik}^{(f)}, \\ 0, & \text{otherwise}, \end{cases}$$ (4.137)

where superscript (c) stands for crisp and (f) for fuzzy partition matrix.

For crisp c-partitions the Davies-Bouldin index can be defined as:

$$V_{DB}^{(q,t)}(U) = \frac{1}{c}\sum_{i=1}^{c}\max_{j\ne i}\left\{\frac{S_i^{(q)} + S_j^{(q)}}{d_{ij}^{(t)}}\right\},$$ (4.138)

where $S_i^{(q)}$ is a measure of within-cluster scatter:

$$S_i^{(q)} = \left(\frac{1}{n_i} \sum_{x \in \Omega_i} \| x - v_i \|^q \right)^{\frac{1}{q}}, \tag{4.139}$$

n_i is a fuzzy cardinality of i-th cluster, and $d_{ij}^{(t)} = \| v_i - v_j \|_t$, (Minikovsky norm (4.55)). We want to minimize (4.138) index, that corresponds to minimizing within-cluster scatter and maximizes between cluster distance.

Another criterion to identify clusters that are compact and well-separated is the index introduced by Dunn (1973) and has the form:

$$V_D(U) = \min_{1 \le i \le c} \min_{\substack{1 \le j \le c \\ j \ne i}} \left\{ \frac{\delta(\Omega_i, \Omega_j)}{\max\limits_{1 \le k \le c} \Delta(\Omega_k)} \right\}, \tag{4.140}$$

where $\delta(\Omega_i, \Omega_k)$ is the distance between i-th and j-th clusters, $\Delta(\Omega_k)$ denotes the diameter of k-th cluster. We want to maximize V_D index.

The standard (used by Dunn) definition of δ is:

$$\delta(\Omega_i, \Omega_k) = \min_{\substack{x \in \Omega_i \\ y \in \Omega_j}} d(x, y), \tag{4.141}$$

and Δ is:

$$\Delta(\Omega_k) = \max_{x, y \in \Omega_k} d(x, y). \tag{4.142}$$

The Dunn index is sensitive to noisy data (outliers) in clusters. Some new definitions of indexes for δ, Δ are resistant to outliers proposed by Bezdek and Pal (1998):

$$\delta(\Omega_i, \Omega_k) = \begin{cases} \dfrac{1}{n_i n_j} \sum_{\substack{x \in \Omega_i \\ y \in \Omega_j}} d(x, y), \\ d(v_i, v_j), \\ \dfrac{1}{n_i + n_j} \left(\sum_{x \in \Omega_i} d(x, v_i) + \sum_{x \in \Omega_j} d(x, v_j) \right), \end{cases} \tag{4.143}$$

and:

$$\Delta(\Omega_k) = \begin{cases} \dfrac{1}{n_k(n_k - 1)} \sum_{\substack{x, y \in \Omega_k \\ x \ne y}} d(x, y), \\ \dfrac{2}{n_k} \sum_{x \in \Omega_k} d(x, v_k). \end{cases} \tag{4.144}$$

Computationally more efficient validity criteria which operate on fuzzy c-partition matrix were proposed by Xie and Beni (1991). We recall a more general criterion, i.e. extended Xie-Beni index:

$$V_{XB}^{(m)}(U) = \frac{\sum_{k=1}^{N} \sum_{i=1}^{c} \left(u_{ik}\right)^m d_{ik}^2}{N\left(\min_{i \neq j} \|\underline{v}_i - \underline{v}_j\|^2\right)} = \frac{J_m(U, V)}{N\left(\min_{i \neq j} \|\underline{v}_i - \underline{v}_j\|^2\right)}. \tag{4.145}$$

The original Xie-Beni index is obtained for $m = 2$. This criterion is very easy to calculate, because it includes the fuzzy clustering criterion J_m. The Xie-Beni index also measures compactness (by J_m) and separation by distance between cluster centers. In this case we search for partition which minimizes criterion (4.145).

Another computationally attractive method introduced by Fukuyama and Sugeno (see Pal and Bezdek 1995) can be written in the form:

$$V_{FS}^{(m)} = J_m(U, V) - \sum_{i=1}^{c} \left\{ \left[\sum_{k=1}^{N} \left(u_{ik}\right)^m \right] \|\underline{v}_i - \underline{v}\|^2 \right\}, \tag{4.146}$$

where $\underline{v}$ denotes grand mean over all data vectors. For Fukuyama-Sugeno method we also search partition minimizing (4.146) index.

In the paper by Bensaid et al. (1996) another very useful criterion named partition index was defined:

$$V_{PI}(U) = \sum_{i=1}^{c} \frac{\sum_{k=1}^{N} \left(u_{ik}\right)^m \|\underline{x}_k - \underline{v}_i\|^2}{n_i \sum_{j=1}^{c} \|\underline{v}_i - \underline{v}_j\|^2}. \tag{4.147}$$

The above index is a sum of individual cluster validity measures normalized by the fuzzy cardinality of each cluster. Minimization of this index is used for a very interesting validity-guided (re)clustering algorithm. It is a method to improve c-partition generated by other clustering algorithm (FCM for example), by validity controlled sequence of cluster split and merge operations. Each cluster is considered for splitting into two clusters represented by two centers. For this task also FCM can be used. The split operation is accompanied by merge of either the two closest clusters or the two second-closest clusters. So the number of clusters remains constant. The closest of cluster is measured simply by distance between its centers. The split and merge operations are executed when they improve validity (4.147). This process is repeated until no more decrease of validity index is observed.

In the end of this section let us propose a new index which is mean quotient of dissipation against the cluster center by dissipation of cluster centers against the center of a given cluster. The definition of the index takes account of the cardinality of clusters. The measure of data vectors dissipation against the i-th cluster center is:

$$\zeta_i = \frac{\sum\limits_{k=1}^{N} \left(u_{ik}\right)^m \|\underline{x}_k - \underline{v}_i\|^2}{\sum\limits_{k=1}^{N} \left(u_{ik}\right)^m}, \qquad (4.148)$$

whereas the measure of dissipation cluster centers against the center of i-th cluster with regard to cluster cardinality takes the form:

$$\tau_i = \sum\limits_{j=1}^{c} \frac{n_i + n_j}{N} \|\underline{v}_j - \underline{v}_i\|^2, \qquad (4.149)$$

where n_i is the fuzzy cardinality of i-th cluster. The cluster validity is defined as:

$$V_{VAL} = \sum\limits_{i=1}^{c} \frac{n_i}{N} \frac{\zeta_i}{\tau_i} = \sum\limits_{i=1}^{c} \frac{n_i \sum\limits_{k=1}^{N} \left(u_{ik}\right)^m \|\underline{x}_k - \underline{v}_i\|^2}{\sum\limits_{k=1}^{N} \left(u_{ik}\right)^m \sum\limits_{j=1}^{c} (n_j + n_i) \|\underline{v}_j - \underline{v}_i\|^2}. \qquad (4.150)$$

4.10
Summary

In this chapter we have presented the following:

- self-organizing feature map and basic unsupervised learning methods,
- vector quantization and learning vector quantization,
- classical (non-fuzzy) clustering methods and their division into: hierarchical, graph-theoretic, decomposition of density function and clustering by minimizing criterion function,
- fuzzy clustering methods including: fuzzy c-means (FCM), fuzzy c-means with covariance matrixes, fuzzy c-varieties (FCV), fuzzy c-elliptotypes (FCE) and fuzzy c-regressions model (FCRM),
- possibilistic approach to clustering. Connection with fuzzy method as mixed fuzzy-possibilistic c-means (FPCM),
- generalized fuzzy c-means (GFCM) and weighted generalized fuzzy c-means (WGFVM),

- conditional fuzzy c-means (CFCM) method,
- a new generalized weighted conditional fuzzy c-means (GWCFCM) method,
- fuzzy learning vector quantization and its relationship to fuzzy clustering methods,
- entropy constrained fuzzy clustering (ECFC) method and its relationship to fuzzy learning vector quantization,
- frequently used cluster validity methods as well as a new validity index.

Bibliographical notes

A good source for self-organizing networks is a book by Kohonen (1989). Clustering methods are provided in Duda and Hart (1973), Fukunaga (1990), Ripley (1996), Tou and Gonzalez (1974).

An excellent introduction to fuzzy clustering are books edited by Bezdek and Pal (1992) and Bezdek (1982). The convergence and consistency of fuzzy c-means were analyzed by Sabin (1987). A unified view to robust clustering methods is presented in Davé and Krishnapuram (1997).

Interesting papers about fuzzy learning quantization are: Karayiannis et al. (1996, 1996a), Karayiannis (1996b), Karayiannis and Bezdek (1997). A clustering algorithm based on minimum volume is presented in Krishnapuram and Kim (1996).

Fuzzy criteria for clustering other than those presented in the chapter are to be found in a book by Sato et al. (1997). An axiomatic basis for clustering is introduced in Bezdek and Harris (1978).

An application of clustering methods to data mining are in Chen et al. (1996), Pedrycz (1998a). For a method of identifying influential data in fuzzy clustering see Imai et al. (1998). An application of deterministic annealing to clustering is analyzed in Rose et al. (1992, 1993).

The validity of clustering is dealt with Windham (1982), Pal and Bezdek (1994, 1995), Rhee and Oh (1996).

Clustering based on local geometrical properties is shown in Flores-Sintas (1998, 1999).

Other interesting papers on fuzzy clustering are: Bajcsy and Ahuja (1998), Beni and Liu (1994), Cheng et al. (1998), El-Sonbaty and Ismail (1998), Eltoft and deFigueiredo (1998), Gath and Geva (1989), Li and Mukaidono (1999), Windham (1983), Mitra and Pal (1996).

5 Fuzzy systems

5.1
Introduction

Fuzzy systems meant here as rule-based or knowledge-based systems. These systems consist of a knowledge base and a reasoning mechanism called fuzzy inference engine. A fuzzy rule base consists of a collection of fuzzy if-then rules. A fuzzy inference engine combines these rules into a mapping from the inputs of the system into its output, using fuzzy reasoning methods (see Chapter 2). The fuzzy systems can take either fuzzy sets or crisp values as inputs. In the latter case, we use a fuzzifier at the system input. Fuzzy systems produce a fuzzy set as output. In some applications we need real-valued output. To extract crisp value from the output fuzzy set defuzzification methods are used (see Section 2.9).

The structure of fuzzy systems is illustrated in Fig. 5.1. If crisp inputs and output are used in a fuzzy system, then the system represents nonlinear mapping accompanied by fuzzy if-then rules from the rule-base. Each of these rules describes the local mapping, and antecedent defines a fuzzy region in which the rule operates.

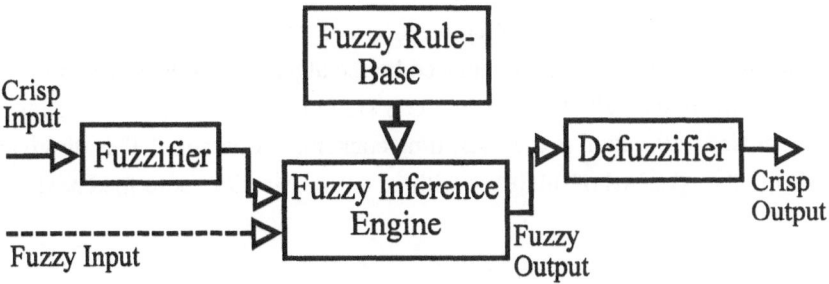

Fig. 5.1. Fuzzy systems structure.

Two methods are used to obtain collection of fuzzy if-then rules in the construction of fuzzy systems:

- from human expert or based on domain knowledge,
- automatic generation or extraction of rules using numerical input-output data of the desired system.

Fuzzy systems have successful applications in a wide variety of fields, as for example: automatic control, pattern recognition, signal processing, expert systems, communications, system identification and time series prediction. In the next section we recall structures of frequently used fuzzy systems. The difference between these systems concentrate on consequences of if-then rules. In accordance with practical requirements we describe systems with crisp inputs, which are equivalent to using fuzzy singletons as inputs. In this case FITA and FATI inference schemes provide the same system output (see Section 2.8).

5.2
The Mamdani fuzzy systems

Historically, the first fuzzy system applied to control by a set of if-then rules obtained from the human operator is called Mamdani fuzzy inference system. In this system we use a set of if-then rules in canonical form (see Section 2.5), the minimum t-norm as both AND connection in premises and conjunctive implication interpretation in if-then rules, the maximum t-conorm as aggregation operation, and finally the center of gravity (COG) defuzzification method. Graphically, Mamdani system for two if-then rules and two inputs is illustrated in Fig.5.2. In this case approximate reasoning is realized by Equ. (2.72) representing conjunctive interpretation of if-then rule. If we use fuzzy sets as inputs, then formula (2.68) can be used. Frequently the minimum operation from AND connection and the conjunctive interpretation of implication in if-then rules are replaced by the algebraic product. This very useful inference method is called the Larsen fuzzy system. In the above described inference methods defuzzification is the most time-consuming operation. This disadvantage leads to other systems of inference without defuzzification, described next.

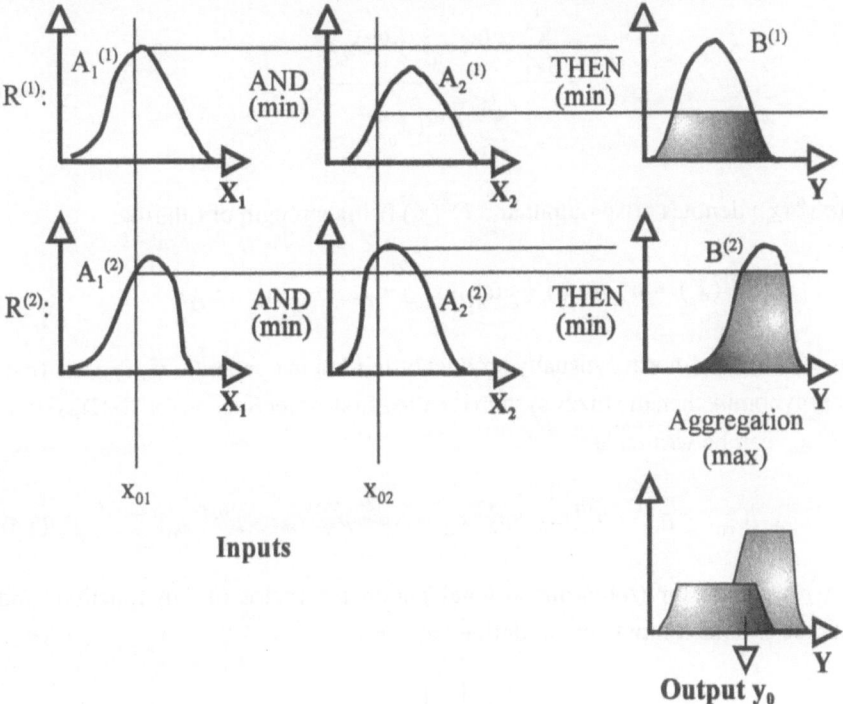

Fig. 5.2. An illustration of the Mamdani fuzzy system.

5.3
The Takagi-Sugeno-Kang fuzzy systems

The Takagi-Sugeno-Kang system was introduced by Takagi and Sugeno (1985), and Sugeno and Kang (1988). The system also known as a TSK fuzzy system, is described by a set of the following if-then rules:

$$R = \left\{ R^{(i)} \right\}_{i=1}^{I} = \left\{ \textbf{IF and} \atop {n=1}^{N} \; x_{n0} \text{ is } A_n^{(i)} \textbf{ THEN } \; y = f_i(\underline{x}_0) \right\}_{i=1}^{I}, \tag{5.1}$$

where x_{n0} denotes fuzzy singletons, $A_n^{(i)}$ stands for linguistic terms in antecedent, while $y = f_i(\underline{x}_0)$ is a crisp function in consequent. Each rule has a crisp output, and the overall output is determined as weighted average of single rules output:

$$y_0 = \frac{\sum_{i=1}^{I} F^{(i)}(\underline{x}_0) \; y^{(i)}(\underline{x}_0)}{\sum_{i=1}^{I} F^{(i)}(\underline{x}_0)}, \tag{5.2}$$

where $y^{(i)}(\underline{x}_0)$ denotes crisp output and $F^{(i)}(\underline{x}_0)$ firing strength of i-th rule:

$$F^{(i)}(\underline{x}_0) = \mu_{A_1^{(i)}}(x_{10}) \star_T \mu_{A_2^{(i)}}(x_{20}) \star_T \dots \star_T \mu_{A_N^{(i)}}(x_{N0}), \tag{5.3}$$

where $\star_T$ denotes t-norm T, usually product or minimum operation. If $f_i(\underline{x}_0)$ is a first-order polynomial then the fuzzy system is called first-order Sugeno (or TSK) system, and $y^{(i)}(\underline{x}_0)$ can be written as:

$$y^{(i)}(\underline{x}_0) = p_0^{(i)} + p_1^{(i)} x_{10} + p_2^{(i)} x_{20} + \dots + p_N^{(i)} x_{N0} = \underline{p}^{(i)T} \underline{x}_0', \tag{5.4}$$

where $\underline{p}^{(i)}$ stands for $(N+1)$-dimensional parameter vector of i-th function, and $\underline{x}_0'$ denotes extended input vector, defined as:

$$\underline{x}_0' = \begin{bmatrix} 1 \\ \underline{x}_0 \end{bmatrix}. \tag{5.5}$$

A low time consumption is an advantage of this system. The Sugeno system is usually used when we operate on numerical (crisp) data. This system can be viewed as switching regression model or mixture of local experts. A collection of simple local linear models (5.4) can represent very complicated nonlinear inputs-output mappings. The region of operation of i-th model (rule) is determined by Cartesian product of sets $A_1^{(i)}(x_{10}) \times A_2^{(i)}(x_{20}) \times \dots \times A_N^{(i)}(x_{N0})$. Overlapping of fuzzy sets from the premise of if-then rules guarantees smooth switching between models from consequents. These consequents can be interpreted as fuzzy singletons, whose localization is determined by local function $f_i(\underline{x}_0)$. The TSK systems can be named as systems with "moving" singletons. The main disadvantage of TSK systems is the inability to use various fuzzy implications and aggregation operations due to singletons in consequents. In other words, approximate reasoning methods introduced in Chapter 2 can not be used in Takagi-Sugeno-Kang fuzzy systems.

5.4
Fuzzy systems with parameterized consequents

In the papers by Łęski and Czogała (1997, 1999) a fuzzy system with fuzzy sets in consequence, whose localization is determined by linear combination of input singletons are presented. This system is called a system with "moving" fuzzy consequents. More generally, some other parameters (like width, weight) of fuzzy sets in consequence may depend on crisp inputs of the system. In case when fuzzy sets are used as inputs consequence may depend on some other parameters of these sets (like center of gravity, height). If these parameters are denoted as $\underline{\theta}$ then the i-th N-input and one-output (MISO) if-then rule can be written as follows:

$$R^{(i)}: \quad \textbf{IF } \underset{n=1}{\overset{N}{\textbf{and}}} \; X_n \text{ is } A_n^{(i)} \textbf{ THEN } Y \text{ is } B^{(i)}(\underline{\theta}), \tag{5.6}$$

or in a pseudo-vector notation:

$$R^{(i)}: \quad \textbf{IF } \underline{X} \text{ is } \underline{A}^{(i)} \textbf{ THEN } Y \text{ is } B^{(i)}(\underline{\theta}), \tag{5.7}$$

where:

$$\underline{X} = \left[X_1 \, X_2 \ldots X_N\right]^T; \quad \underline{A}^{(i)} = \left[A_1^{(i)} \, A_2^{(i)} \ldots A_N^{(i)}\right]^T, \tag{5.8}$$

$X_1, X_2, ..., X_N$ and Y are linguistic variables which may be interpreted as inputs of fuzzy system $(X_1, X_2, ..., X_N)$ and the output of that system (Y). $A_1^{(i)} \, A_2^{(i)} \ldots A_N^{(i)}$ are linguistic values (terms) of the linguistic variables $X_1, X_2, ..., X_N$ and $B^{(i)}(\underline{\theta})$ is a parameterized linguistic value of the linguistic variable Y. A collection of the above written rules for $i=1, 2, ..., I$, creates a rule-base which may be activated (fired) under fuzzy sets (5.6), (5.7) or fuzzy singleton inputs:

$$X_1 \text{ is } x_{10} \textbf{ and } X_2 \text{ is } x_{20} \textbf{ and } \ldots \textbf{ and } X_N \text{ is } x_{N0} \overset{\wedge}{=} \underset{n=1}{\overset{N}{\textbf{and}}} \; X_n \text{ is } x_{n0}, \tag{5.9}$$

or in a pseudo-vector notation:

$$\underline{X} \text{ is } \underline{x}_0. \tag{5.10}$$

In this case i-th if-then rule has the form:

$$R^{(i)}: \quad \textbf{IF } \underline{x}_0 \text{ is } \underline{A}^{(i)} \textbf{ THEN } Y \text{ is } B^{(i)}(\underline{x}_0), \tag{5.11}$$

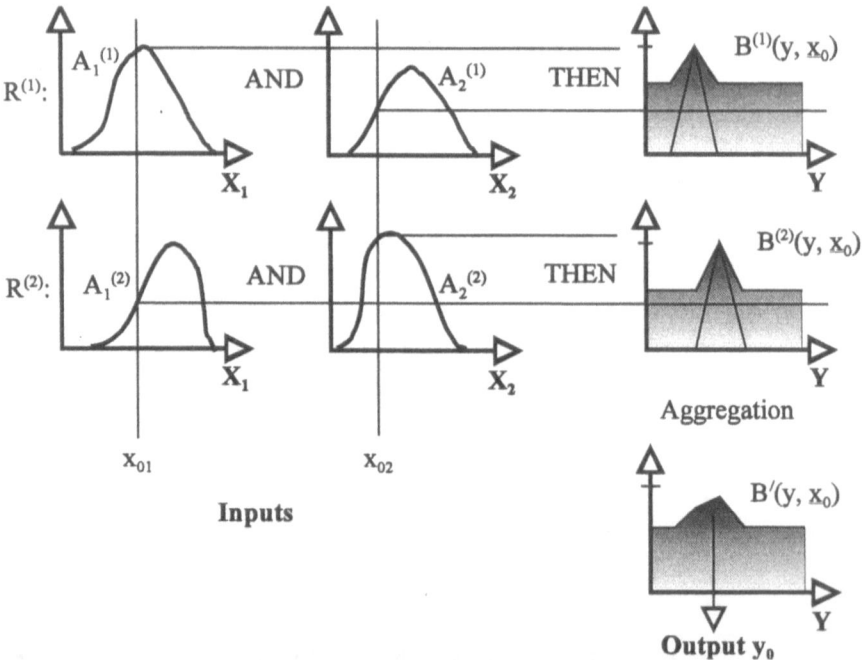

Fig. 5.3. An example of fuzzy system with parameterized consequents.

For logical interpretation of if-then rules the final output (fuzzy set) can be written by (2.73) as:

$$\mu_{B'}(y, \underline{x}_0) = \bigoplus_{i=1}^{I} \mu_{B^{(i)'}}(y) = \bigoplus_{i=1}^{I} \Psi(\mu_{A^{(i)}}(\underline{x}_0), \mu_{B^{(i)}}(y, \underline{x}_0)), \qquad (5.12)$$

where Ψ stands for fuzzy implication $I(\bullet, \bullet)$. For conjunctive interpretation Ψ denotes t-norm T (see (2.72)). To explain the above used symbols see Chapter 2. Graphically, this inference method is presented in Fig. 5.3. In this Figure the Reichenbach fuzzy implication, normalized sum as aggregation are used. The resulting fuzzy set has a non-informative part and according to considerations from Chapter 2, we use MICOG as a defuzzification method. We can get the crisp value of the output from modified indexed center of gravity (MICOG) as defuzzification:

$$MICOG_\alpha[\mu_B(y)] = \frac{\int_{Y_\alpha} y(\mu_B(y) - \alpha) \, dy}{\int_{Y_\alpha} (\mu_B(y) - \alpha) \, dy}, \qquad (5.13)$$

where α is constant. The subtraction of $\alpha \in [0, 1]$ eliminates the non-informative part of the membership function $\mu_B(y)$. For $\alpha=0$ we get the well-known COG defuzzification. The final crisp value of the system output for normalized arithmetic mean as aggregation and MIGOG defuzzification can be evaluated from formula:

$$
y_0 = \frac{\int \frac{y}{I} \sum_{i=1}^{I} \left[\Psi(\mu_{A^{(i)}}(\underline{x}_0), \mu_{B^{(i)}}(y, \underline{x}_0)) - \alpha_i \right] dy}{\int \frac{1}{I} \sum_{i=1}^{I} \left[\Psi(\mu_{A^{(i)}}(\underline{x}_0), \mu_{B^{(i)}}(y, \underline{x}_0)) - \alpha_i \right] dy} = \frac{\sum_{i=1}^{I} \int y \left(\mu_{B^{(i)'}}(y, \underline{x}_0) - \alpha_i \right) dy}{\sum_{i=1}^{I} \int \left(\mu_{B^{(i)'}}(y, \underline{x}_0) - \alpha_i \right) dy}. \tag{5.14}
$$

The $\mu_{B^{(i)'}}(y, \underline{x}_0)$ stands for the resulting conclusion for i-th if-then rule before aggregation. Now we introduce a symbol:

$$
\mu_{B^{(i)\bullet}}(y, \underline{x}_0) = \mu_{B^{(i)'}}(y, \underline{x}_0) - \alpha_i. \tag{5.15}
$$

Membership functions of fuzzy sets $\mu_{B^{(i)\bullet}}(y, \underline{x}_0)$ can be represented by the parameterized functions:

$$
\mu_{B^{(i)\bullet}}(y, \underline{x}_0) \sim f^{(i)} \left[\text{Area}\left(\mu_{B^{(i)\bullet}}(y, \underline{x}_0)\right), y^{(i)}(\underline{x}_0) \right], \tag{5.16}
$$

where $y^{(i)}(\underline{x}_0)$ is the modified indexed center of gravity (MICOG) location on Y axis of the fuzzy set $\mu_{B^{(i)\bullet}}(y, \underline{x}_0)$:

$$
y^{(i)}(\underline{x}_0) = \text{MICOG}_{\alpha_i}\left[\mu_{B^{(i)\bullet}}(y, \underline{x}_0) \right] = \frac{\int y\, \mu_{B^{(i)\bullet}}(y, \underline{x}_0)\, dy}{\int \mu_{B^{(i)\bullet}}(y, \underline{x}_0)\, dy}. \tag{5.17}
$$

If we use Equ. (5.15) in (5.14), multiply and divide the nominator of (5.14) by $\int \mu_{B^{(i)\bullet}}(y, \underline{x}_0)\, dy$ and apply (5.17), we obtain:

$$
y_0 = \frac{\sum_{i=1}^{I} \int \mu_{B^{(i)\bullet}}(y, \underline{x}_0)\, dy \dfrac{\int y\mu_{B^{(i)\bullet}}(y, \underline{x}_0)\, dy}{\int \mu_{B^{(i)\bullet}}(y, \underline{x}_0)\, dy}}{\sum_{i=1}^{I} \int \mu_{B^{(i)\bullet}}(y, \underline{x}_0)\, dy} = \frac{\sum_{i=1}^{I} \text{Area}\left[\mu_{B^{(i)\bullet}}(y, \underline{x}_0) \right] y^{(i)}(\underline{x}_0)}{\sum_{i=1}^{I} \text{Area}\left[\mu_{B^{(i)\bullet}}(y, \underline{x}_0) \right]}. \tag{5.18}
$$

We note that this type of fuzzy systems is effective from the computational point of view. The crisp output value is obtained as a normalized sum of the MICOGs of conclusions from fuzzy if-then rules. The areas of conclusions (after removing the non-informative part) are used as weights. We also note that fuzzy systems with Larsen's product operation as conjunctive "fuzzy implication" of if-then rules and symmetric triangle (isosceles triangle) membership functions for consequence, can be written by means of a formula well known from literature:

$$y_0 = \frac{\sum\limits_{i=1}^{I} \dfrac{w^{(i)}}{2} F^{(i)}(\underline{x}_0)\, y^{(i)}}{\sum\limits_{i=1}^{I} \dfrac{w^{(i)}}{2} F^{(i)}(\underline{x}_0)},$$

(5.19)

where $w^{(i)}$ is the width of the triangle base for i-th rule. It should be noted that the $w^{(i)}/2$ factor may be interpreted as a respective weight of i-th rule or its certainty factor (CF).

In the next considerations we assume that consequents $\mu_{B^{(i)}}(y, \underline{x}_0)$ of the i-th if-then rule have symmetric triangle membership function with the width of the triangle base $w^{(i)}$ and location determined by linear combinations of input singletons $\underline{x}_0$ (see (5.4)). For computing the system output we must calculate an area under the fuzzy set in the consequent of if-then rule after removing its non-informative part. From (5.12) and (5.15) we have:

$$\mu_{B^{(i)*}}(y, \underline{x}_0) = \Psi\Big(F^{(i)}(\underline{x}_0), \mu_{B^{(i)}}(y, \underline{x}_0)\Big) - \alpha_i.$$

(5.20)

For the fuzzy implications that satisfy condition I9 (see Chapter 2) we assume:

$$\alpha_i = 1 - F^{(i)}(\underline{x}_0).$$

(5.21)

For example if we use the Reichenbach fuzzy implication we get:

$$\mathrm{Area}\Big[\mu_{B^{(i)*}}(y, \underline{x}_0)\Big] = 2 \int\limits_{y^{(i)}(\underline{x}_0) - \frac{w^{(i)}}{2}}^{y^{(i)}(\underline{x}_0)} \Big[I(F^{(i)}(\underline{x}_0), \mu_{B^{(i)}}(y, \underline{x}_0)) - \alpha_i\Big] dy$$

$$= 2 \int\limits_{y^{(i)}(\underline{x}_0) - \frac{w^{(i)}}{2}}^{y^{(i)}(\underline{x}_0)} \Big[1 - F^{(i)}(\underline{x}_0) + F^{(i)}(\underline{x}_0)\, \mu_{B^{(i)}}(y, \underline{x}_0) - 1 + F^{(i)}(\underline{x}_0)\Big] dy$$

(5.22)

$$= 2 F^{(i)}(\underline{x}_0) \int\limits_{y^{(i)}(\underline{x}_0) - \frac{w^{(i)}}{2}}^{y^{(i)}(\underline{x}_0)} \Big[\frac{2}{w^{(i)}}(y - y^{(i)}(\underline{x}_0)) - 1\Big] dy = \frac{w^{(i)}}{2} F^{(i)}(\underline{x}_0).$$

This situation is graphically illustrated in Fig. 5.4a for the Reichenbach and in Fig.5.4b for the Łukasiewicz fuzzy implication. From this Fig. and (5.22) we see that the area under i-th rule consequent is a function of firing strength of this rule $F^{(i)}(\underline{x}_0)$ and width $w^{(i)}$ of the base of triangular membership function from consequent:

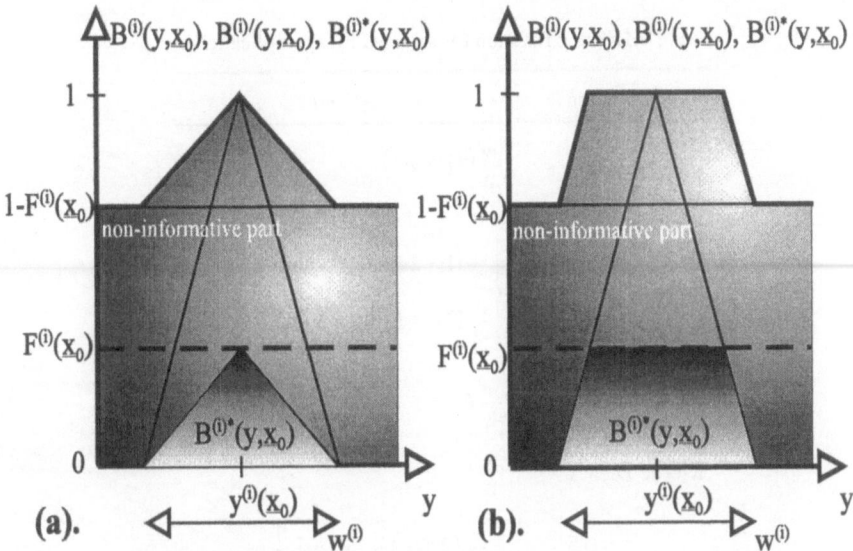

Fig. 5.4. Informative and non-informative parts of conclusion for **(a)** the Reichenbach **(b)** the Łukasiewicz fuzzy implication.

$$\mathrm{Area}\left[\mu_{B^{(i)\cdot}}(y, \underline{x}_0)\right] = g\left(F^{(i)}(\underline{x}_0), w^{(i)}\right).\tag{5.23}$$

Using the above symbols Equ. (5.18) takes the form:

$$y_0 = \frac{\displaystyle\sum_{i=1}^{I} g\left(F^{(i)}(\underline{x}_0), w^{(i)}\right) y^{(i)}(\underline{x}_0)}{\displaystyle\sum_{i=1}^{I} g\left(F^{(i)}(\underline{x}_0), w^{(i)}\right)},\tag{5.24}$$

where function g depends on the used fuzzy implication. The respective formulas for function g for selected implications are shown in Table 5.1. For simplicity the abbreviated forms are used: $F \triangleq F^{(i)}(\underline{x}_0)$ and $w \triangleq w^{(i)}$.

The system described by Equ. (5.24) can be interpreted as mixture of experts model. The response of i-th expert for input data $\underline{x}_0$ is $y^{(i)}(\underline{x}_0)$. The final output of the system is obtained as a weighted average of local expert outputs. The nonnegative weight of association between input data $\underline{x}_0$ and i-th expert is $g(F^{(i)}(\underline{x}_0), w^{(i)})$. These weights in Equ. (5.24) are normalized, so its sum is equal to one. Weight $g(F^{(i)}(\underline{x}_0), w^{(i)})$ depends on firing strength of i-th rule $F^{(i)}(\underline{x}_0)$ and certainty factor of this rule $w^{(i)}$. This dependence on selected fuzzy implications is shown in Table 5.1.

Table 5.1. The g function for selected fuzzy implications.

Implication	$g(F, w)$
Łukasiewicz	$\frac{w}{2}\left(2F - F^2\right)$
Fodor	$\begin{cases} \frac{w}{2}\left(1 - 2F + F^2\right), & \text{if } F \geq \frac{1}{2}, \\ \frac{w}{2}\left(2F - F^2\right), & \text{if } F < \frac{1}{2}. \end{cases}$
Reichenbach	$\frac{w}{2}F$
Kleene-Dienes	$\frac{w}{2}F^2$
Zadeh	$\begin{cases} \frac{w}{2}(2F - 1), & \text{if } F \geq \frac{1}{2}, \\ 0, & \text{if } F < \frac{1}{2}. \end{cases}$
Goguen	$\frac{w}{2}(-2)$
Gödel	$\frac{w}{2}(2F - 2)$
Rescher	$\frac{w}{2}(-2)$

Normalized weights are in [0, 1] interval, and are often interpreted as the probability that x_0 is from i-th model or membership degree of belonging x_0 to i-th model. Each local expert is represented by if-then rule in (5.11) form. The main disadvantage of the system described in this section is the difficulty with obtaining the if-then rule in this form from a human expert. However, this model can be easily used for automatic fuzzy if-then rule (5.11) generation (extraction) directly from numerical data. A particular case of the system presented in this section is Takagi-Sugeno-Kang system when fuzzy singleton is used as consequent (this case excludes using various fuzzy implications). Mamdani system is obtained when the localization of fuzzy consequent is constant.

5.5
Summary

In this chapter we presented the following:

- basic structure of fuzzy systems which consists of a fuzzy rulebase and inference engine,
- Mamdani fuzzy system, i.e. system with fuzzy sets in consequence of fuzzy if-then rules,
- Takagi-Sugeno-Kang fuzzy system, i.e. system with "moving" fuzzy singletons. The localization of these singletons is linearly dependent from inputs of the system,
- a new fuzzy system with parameterized consequents of if-then rules,
- a particular case of parameterized consequents fuzzy sets whose localization is given by linear combination of input singletons,
- Mamdani and Takagi-Sugeno-Kang systems as special cases of a new system with parameterized consequents,
- computationally effective system (with parameterized consequents) based on individual-rule inference (based on logical interpretation of if-then rules), normalized sum as aggregation and modified indexed center of gravity defuzzification,
- the detailed formulas for systems with "moving" triangular membership function in consequents and selected fuzzy implications,
- interpretation of this system as a mixture of experts model.

Bibliographical notes

The following are very good surveys of fuzzy systems: Wang (1994, 1998), Mendel (1995), Takagi and Sugeno (1985), Sugeno and Kang (1988), Pedrycz (1993), Lygeros (1997) and Lee et al. (1995).

Other interesting articles about fuzzy systems are: Chow et al. (1999), Altag et al. (1999), Yam et al. (1999), Shi et al. (1999) and Wang et al. (1998).

Applications of fuzzy logic were presented in Hirota (1993), Chen (1996), Kosko (1997), Berkan and Trubatch (1997), Czogała and Łeski (1996).

6 Neuro-fuzzy systems

6.1
Introduction

There are generally three approaches to building mathematical models:

- white box modeling, where everything is considered to be known from physical laws,
- black box modeling (system identification), where all knowledge derives from measurements,
- gray box modeling, where both physical laws and observed measurements are used to design a model.

The last approach assumes that the structure of the model is given from physical laws as a parameterized function. In the next step the model parameters are obtained using the observed data (measurements) information. In real world a great deal of information is provided by the human expert, e.g. in medicine, biology and control of systems. The human expert does not reason in terms of mathematics and physics. He describes an complicated system by way of a set of imprecise and incomplete statements. Fuzzy logic is an ideal methodology to express uncertainty and incomplete expert knowledge.

The basic problem in fuzzy systems design is obtaining a set of fuzzy if-then rules. Two approaches may be used: first, transforming human expert knowledge and experience, and second, automatic rules generation. Because no standard method exists to utilize expert knowledge, the second method is intensely investigated.

The learning capability of an artificial neural network can be used for automatic fuzzy if-then rules generation. The connection of fuzzy systems with an artificial neural network is called neuro-fuzzy systems. As a result, those systems can utilize linguistic information from the human expert and measurement data. In other words, linguistic prior knowledge from an expert can be incorporated into neuro-fuzzy systems. Sometimes neuro-fuzzy systems utilize only measurement (numerical) information, and expert knowledge can not be used. This method of identification is referred to as automatic rule generation (extraction).

In the literature several methods of automatic fuzzy rule generation from given numerical data have been described. The simplest method of rule generation is based on a clustering algorithm and estimation of proper fuzzy relations from a set of numerical data. Kosko's (1987) fuzzy associative memory (FAM) can store such fuzzy relations and process fuzzy inference simultaneously. This approach, however, causes some difficulties because of conflicts appearing among the generated rules.

Wang and Mendel (1992) proposed a method for generating fuzzy rules from numerical data without conflicting rules. However, they used too many heuristic procedures and a trial-and-error choice of membership functions. Another example of using heuristic method to generate fuzzy if-then rules was presented Nozaki et al. (1997). The main advantage of the method is its simplicity. The method introduced by Abe and Lan (1995) is another example of heuristic rule extraction for a classification task. Ishibuchi et al. (1993) proposes the learning method of a neural network that uses both expert knowledge represented by fuzzy if-then rules, and numerical data. The application of this system for constructing classification and control systems is presented.

Another type of methods which use the learning capability of neural networks and the fact that both fuzzy systems and neural nets are universal approximators, has been successfully applied to various tasks. The problem here is the difficulty in understanding the identified fuzzy rules since they are implicitly acquired into the network itself.

Mitra and Pal (1995) have proposed a fuzzy multilayer perceptron generating fuzzy rules from the connection weights. Several methods of extracting rules from the given data are based on a class of radial basis function networks (RBFNs). The fact that there is a functional equivalence between RBFNs and the fuzzy system has been used by Jang (1992); Jang and Sun (1993) to construct Takagi-Sugeno-Kang type of adaptive neuro fuzzy inference system (ANFIS), which is trained by the back propagation algorithm. More general fuzzy reasoning schemes in ANFIS are employed by Horikawa et al. (1992). Such developed radial basis function based adaptive fuzzy systems have been described by Cho and Wang (1996) and applied to system identification and prediction. TSK systems are a combination of simple submodels (typically linear). Most existing learning methods of these systems are based on minimization overall output error. This method cannot guarantee that the system would have good local performance. Yen et al. (1998) proposes a learning algorithm which uses global and local behavior of the system. This method uses the idea of local weighted regression error minimization (on local models) connected with classical global error minimization (on overall system output). The application of deterministic annealing (see Section 3.8) for such mixture of experts model parameter optimization is introduced by Rose et al. (1998).

Input space partitioning is a method for extraction of if-then rules. Pedrycz (1984) uses c-means clustering to find antecedent variable membership functions and then an identified relational model. Sugeno and Yasukawa (1994) applied c-means to consequent space clustering. An identification method for premise and consequent parameters is determined from the clustering algorithm in succession by Chen et al. (1998). Pedrycz (1998) shows if-then rule generation using a conditional fuzzy clustering method (see Section 4.6). In contrast to another solution that uses c-means clustering, and finds clusters in input space preserving similarity of the clustered input data, the proposed method clusters input space with respect to the system output (in the context determined in the output space). The paper by Kim et al. (1997) presents a fuzzy c-regression model (see Section 4.5) for automatic generation of if-then rules. The suggested algorithm is composed of: coarse tuning by the fuzzy c-regression model (FCRM), and fine tuning realized by gradient descent optimization method. The same authors in another paper (Kim et al. 1998) additionally propose the stage of uncorrelation of input variables using the principal component method. This algorithm partitions the input space more effectively.

In the paper by Pedrycz and Reformat (1997) the rule-based modeling of available nonlinear system input-output relationship is introduced. The distribution and granularity of the linguistic labels of if-then rule premise part are formed using criteria of variability of this relationship, and separability of the linguistic labels. It is well-known that the number of rules increases exponentially with the number of system input variables. Wang (1998a) shows a hierarchical fuzzy system that consists of simple low-dimensional systems connected hierarchically. The number of rules in this system increases linearly with the number of input variables.

The aim of this chapter is to describe theoretically and present the structure of a new artificial neural network based fuzzy inference system (ANNBFIS). The novelty of the system consists in the introduction of the parameterized (moving) fuzzy consequent in if-then rules.

6.2

Artificial neural network based fuzzy inference system

In approximate reasoning realized in fuzzy systems the if-then fuzzy rules or fuzzy conditional statements have played the most important role so far. Often they are also used to capture the human ability to make a decision or control in an uncertain and imprecise environment.

In this section we will use such fuzzy rules to present the important approximate reasoning methods which are basic in future applications. Assume that I numbers of N-input and one-output (MISO) fuzzy implicative rules with parameterized consequent are given:

$$R = \{R^{(i)}\}_{i=1}^{I} = \left\{ \textbf{IF and}_{n=1}^{N} \ x_{n0} \ \text{is} \ A_n^{(i)} \ \textbf{THEN} \ Y \ \text{is} \ B^{(i)}(\underline{x}_0) \right\}_{i=1}^{I}, \qquad (6.1)$$

where $\underline{x}_0$ is the input singleton. From the previous chapter we know that the final crisp value of the system output for arithmetic mean as aggregation, MICOG defuzzification and "moving" (parameterized) fuzzy sets with triangular membership function in consequent can be evaluated from:

$$y_0 = \frac{\sum_{i=1}^{I} g(F^{(i)}(\underline{x}_0), w^{(i)}) \ y^{(i)}(\underline{x}_0)}{\sum_{i=1}^{I} g(F^{(i)}(\underline{x}_0), w^{(i)})}, \qquad (6.2)$$

where function $g(\bullet, \bullet)$ depends on the used fuzzy implication (see Table 5.1), and $y^{(i)}(\underline{x}_0) = p^{(i)T} \underline{x}_0'$. Additionally, we assume that $A_n^{(i)}$ for $n=1,2, ...,N$ and $i=1,2, ...,I$ have a Gaussian membership function:

$$\mu_{A_n^{(i)}}(x_{n0}) = \exp\left\{ -\frac{(x_{n0} - c_n^{(i)})^2}{2\left[s_n^{(i)}\right]^2} \right\}, \qquad (6.3)$$

where $c_n^{(i)}, s_n^{(i)}; i=1,2,...,I$ and $n=1,2,...,N$ are parameters of the membership functions in the premise of if-then rules. The algebraic product (generally t-norm) represents explicit connective (AND) of predicates in (6.1). In this case we have:

$$\mu_{A^{(i)}}(\underline{x}_0) = \prod_{n=1}^{N} \mu_{A_n^{(i)}}(x_{n0}). \qquad (6.4)$$

On the basis of (6.3) we get:

$$F^{(i)}(\underline{x}_0) = \mu_{A^{(i)}}(\underline{x}_0) = \exp\left\{-\frac{1}{2}\sum_{n=1}^{N}\frac{(x_{n0} - c_n^{(i)})^2}{\left[s_n^{(i)}\right]^2}\right\}. \tag{6.5}$$

Additionally, we assume that consequents $B^{(i)}$ of i-th if-then rule have symmetric triangle membership function with the width of the triangle base $w^{(i)}$.

For N inputs and I if-then rules we have to establish the following unknown parameters:

- $c_n^{(i)}, s_n^{(i)}; n=1,2,...,N$ and $i=1,2,...,I$ the parameters of membership function of fuzzy sets from premises of if-then rules,
- $p_n^{(i)}; n=1,2,...,N+1$ and $i=1,2,...,I$ the parameters determining localizations of fuzzy sets from consequents of if-then rules,
- $w^{(i)}; i=1,2,...,I$ the parameters determining the width of fuzzy sets from consequents of if-then rules.

Obviously, the number of if-then rules I is unknown. Let us observe that equations (6.2) and (6.5) describe a radial basis neural network (RBNN) (see Subsection 3.2.2). Graphically this network is presented in Fig.6.1.

We assume that the learning (training) set, i.e. a set of inputs for which the output of system t_0 is known is given by:

$$\left\{\left(\underline{x}_0(k), t_0(k)\right)\right\}_{k=1}^{K} \tag{6.6}$$

The measure of the error of the system output value y_0 may be defined for a single pair from the training set as:

$$E = \frac{1}{2}\left(t_0 - y_0\right)^2, \tag{6.7}$$

where t_0 is the desired (target) value of output. The unknown parameters (except the number of if-then rules) are estimated by means of the steepest descent optimization method. The minimization of error criterion E is made iteratively (for example on parameter α):

$$(\alpha)_{\text{new}} = (\alpha)_{\text{old}} - \eta\left.\frac{\partial E}{\partial \alpha}\right|_{\alpha = (\alpha)_{\text{old}}}, \tag{6.8}$$

where η is the learning rate.

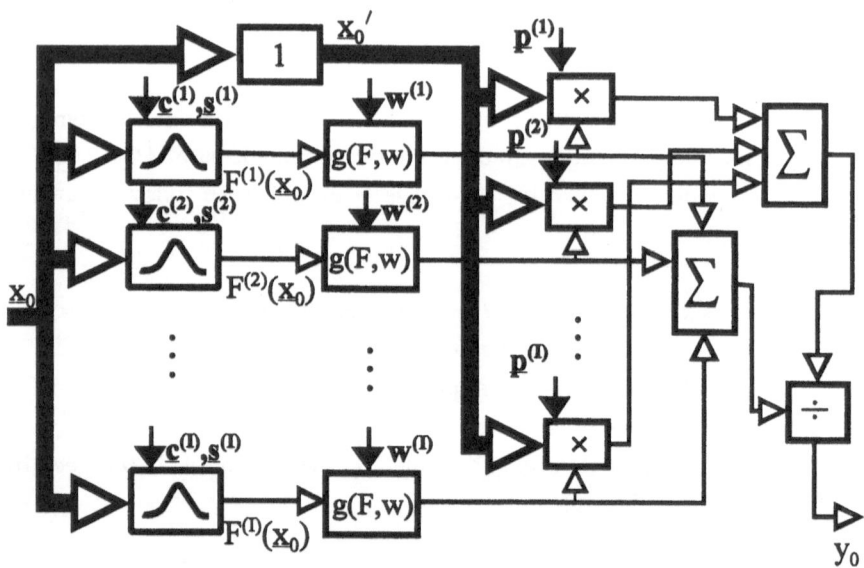

Fig.6.1.   Graphical illustration of artificial neural network based fuzzy inference system.

Now we derive the partial derivatives of error E with respect to unknown parameters:

$$\frac{\partial E}{\partial c_n^{(k)}} = -\left(t_0 - y_0\right) \frac{y^{(k)}(\underline{x}_0) - y_0}{\displaystyle\sum_{i=1}^{I} g(F^{(i)}(\underline{x}_0), w^{(i)})} \frac{\partial g(F^{(k)}(\underline{x}_0), w^{(k)})}{\partial F^{(k)}(\underline{x}_0)} F^{(k)}(\underline{x}_0) \frac{x_{n0} - c_n^{(k)}}{\left[s_n^{(k)}\right]^2}, \quad \textbf{(6.9)}$$

$$\frac{\partial E}{\partial s_n^{(k)}} = -\left(t_0 - y_0\right) \frac{y^{(k)}(\underline{x}_0) - y_0}{\displaystyle\sum_{i=1}^{I} g(F^{(i)}(\underline{x}_0), w^{(i)})} \frac{\partial g(F^{(k)}(\underline{x}_0), w^{(k)})}{\partial F^{(k)}(\underline{x}_0)} F^{(k)}(\underline{x}_0) \frac{x_{n0} - c_n^{(k)}}{\left[s_n^{(k)}\right]^3}, \quad \textbf{(6.10)}$$

$$\underset{j \neq 0}{\forall} \quad \frac{\partial E}{\partial p_j^{(k)}} = -\left(t_0 - y_0\right) \frac{g(F^{(k)}(\underline{x}_0), w^{(k)})}{\displaystyle\sum_{i=1}^{I} g(F^{(i)}(\underline{x}_0), w^{(i)})} x_{j0}, \quad \textbf{(6.11)}$$

$$\frac{\partial E}{\partial p_0^{(k)}} = -\left(t_0 - y_0\right) \frac{g(F^{(k)}(\underline{x}_0), w^{(k)})}{\sum\limits_{i=1}^{I} g(F^{(i)}(\underline{x}_0), w^{(i)})}, \tag{6.12}$$

$$\frac{\partial E}{\partial w^{(k)}} = -\left(t_0 - y_0\right) \frac{y^{(k)}(\underline{x}_0) - y_0}{\sum\limits_{i=1}^{I} g(F^{(i)}(\underline{x}_0), w^{(i)})} \frac{\partial g(F^{(k)}(\underline{x}_0), w^{(k)})}{\partial w^{(k)}}. \tag{6.13}$$

The derivatives of function g with respect to firing strength $F^{(i)}(\underline{x}_0)$ and parameter $w^{(i)}$ are shown in Table 6.1. For simplicity the abbreviated forms are used: $F \triangleq F^{(i)}(\underline{x}_0)$ and $w \triangleq w^{(i)}$.

Table 6.1. Some needed derivatives for selected implications.

Implication	$\dfrac{\partial g(F, w)}{\partial F}$	$\dfrac{\partial g(F, w)}{\partial w}$
Łukasiewicz	$\dfrac{w}{2}(2 - F)$	$\dfrac{1}{2}\left(2F - F^2\right)$
Fodor	$\begin{cases} \dfrac{w}{2}(4F - 2), & \text{if } F \geq \dfrac{1}{2}, \\ \dfrac{w}{2}(2 - 4F), & \text{if } F < \dfrac{1}{2}. \end{cases}$	$\begin{cases} \dfrac{1}{2}\left(1 - 2F + F^2\right), & \text{if } F \geq \dfrac{1}{2}, \\ \dfrac{1}{2}\left(2F - 2F^2\right), & \text{if } F < \dfrac{1}{2}. \end{cases}$
Reichenbach	$\dfrac{w}{2}$	$\dfrac{1}{2}F$
Kleene-Dienes	$\dfrac{w}{2}2F$	$\dfrac{1}{2}F^2$
Zadeh	$\begin{cases} \dfrac{1}{2}F, & \text{if } F \geq \dfrac{1}{2}, \\ 0, & \text{if } F < \dfrac{1}{2}. \end{cases}$	$\begin{cases} \dfrac{1}{2}(2F - 1), & \text{if } F \geq \dfrac{1}{2}, \\ 0, & \text{if } F < \dfrac{1}{2}. \end{cases}$
Goguen	$\dfrac{w}{2}(-1)$	$\dfrac{1}{2}(2 - F)$
Gödel	$\dfrac{w}{2}(2F - 2)$	$\dfrac{1}{2}\left(F^2 - 2F + 2\right)$
Rescher	$\dfrac{w}{2}(-2)$	$\dfrac{1}{2}(2 - 2F)$

The unknown parameters may be modified on the basis of (6.8) after the input of one data collection into the system or after the input of all data collections (cumulative method). Additionally, the following, proposed by Jang et al. (1997), heuristic rules for changes of η parameter have been applied. If in four sequential iterations the mean square error has diminished for the whole learning set, then the learning parameter is increased (multiplied by n_1). If in four sequential iterations the error has been increased and decreased commutatively then the learning parameter is decreased (multiplied by n_D).

Another solution accelerating the convergence of the method is the estimation of parameters $\underline{p}^{(i)}$; $i=1,...,I$ by means of least squares method. The output value y_0 of the system in equation (6.2) may be considered to be a linear combination of unknown parameters $\underline{p}^{(i)}$. If we introduce the following notation:

$$S^{(i)}(\underline{x}_0) = \frac{g(F^{(i)}(\underline{x}_0), w^{(i)})}{\sum_{k=1}^{I} g(F^{(k)}(\underline{x}_0), w^{(k)})}, \tag{6.14}$$

$$\underline{D}(\underline{x}_0) = \left[S^{(1)}(\underline{x}_0)\, \underline{x}_0'^T : S^{(2)}(\underline{x}_0)\, \underline{x}_0'^T : \cdots : S^{(I)}(\underline{x}_0)\, \underline{x}_0'^T \right]^T, \tag{6.15}$$

$$\underline{P} = \left[\underline{p}^{(1)T} : \underline{p}^{(2)T} : \cdots : \underline{p}^{(I)T} \right]^T. \tag{6.16}$$

Equation (6.2) may be written in the form:

$$y_0 = \underline{D}(\underline{x}_0)\, \underline{P}. \tag{6.17}$$

Hence parameters $\underline{P}$ may be estimated by means of the least square method. To eliminate the matrix inverse we use the recurrent method. For $(k+1)$-th step e.g. $((k+1)$-th element from the learning set) we get (see Chapter 3):

$$\hat{\underline{P}}(k+1) = \hat{\underline{P}}(k) + \underline{G}(k)\, \underline{D}\big(\underline{x}_0(k+1)\big) \left[y_0(k+1) - \underline{D}\big(\underline{x}_0(k+1)\big)\, \hat{\underline{P}}(k) \right], \tag{6.18}$$

$$\underline{G}(k+1) = \underline{G}(k) - \underline{G}(k)\, \underline{D}\big(\underline{x}_0(k+1)\big) \times$$
$$\times \left[\underline{D}\big(\underline{x}_0(k+1)\big)^T \underline{G}(k)\, \underline{D}\big(\underline{x}_0(k+1)\big) + 1 \right]^{-1} \underline{D}\big(\underline{x}_0(k+1)\big)^T \underline{G}(k). \tag{6.19}$$

To initialize computation we take:

$$\begin{cases} \hat{\underline{P}}(0) = \underline{0}, \\ \underline{G}(0) = \alpha\, \underline{I}, \end{cases} \tag{6.20}$$

where I is an identity matrix, α is a large positive constant (e.g., 10^6). Finally in each iteration parameters $\underline{p}^{(i)}$; $i=1,...,I$ are estimated on the basis of equations (6.18) and (6.19), whereas the other parameters are estimated by means of a gradient method (6.9), (6.10) and (6.13).

Another problem is the estimation of the number I of if-then rules and initial values of membership functions for premise part. This task is solved by means of preliminary clustering of training data, for which fuzzy c-means method has been used (see Chapter 4). This method assigns each input vector $\underline{x}_0(k)$; $k=1,2,...,K$ to clusters represented by prototypes $\underline{v}_i$; $i=1,2,...,c$ measured by grade of membership $u_{ik} \in [0, 1]$. A $(c \times K)$-dimensional matrix called a partition matrix fulfils the following assumptions:

$$\begin{cases} \underset{1 \le k \le K}{\forall} \quad \sum_{i=1}^{c} u_{ik} = 1, \\ \underset{1 \le i \le c}{\forall} \quad \sum_{k=1}^{K} u_{ik} \in [0, K]. \end{cases} \tag{6.21}$$

The c-means method minimizes the scalar index for parameter $m > 1$:

$$J_m = \sum_{k=1}^{K} \sum_{i=1}^{c} \left(u_{ik}\right)^m D_{ik}^2. \tag{6.22}$$

By defining $D_{ik} = \| \underline{x}_0(k) - \underline{v}_i \|$, where $\|\bullet\|$ is a vector norm (the most frequent Euclidean norm), we get an iterative method of commutative modification of partition matrix and prototypes:

$$\underset{1 \le i \le c}{\forall} \quad \underline{v}_i = \frac{\sum_{k=1}^{K} \left(u_{ik}\right)^m \underline{x}_0(k)}{\sum_{k=1}^{K} \left(u_{ik}\right)^m}, \tag{6.23}$$

$$\underset{\substack{1 \le i \le c \\ 1 \le k \le K}}{\forall} \quad u_{ik} = \left[\sum_{j=1}^{c} \left(\frac{D_{ij}}{D_{jk}} \right)^{\frac{2}{m-1}} \right]^{-1}. \tag{6.24}$$

According to the above written equations the obtained calculations are initialized if we take into account a random partition matrix U which fulfils conditions (6.21). Such a method leads to the local minimum of index (6.22). Therefore the most frequently used solution is multiple repeated calculations in accordance with equations (6.23) and (6.24) for various random realizations of partition matrix initializations. As a termination rule we have applied the execution of the set number of iterations (in our case 500) or when in sequential iterations the change of index value J_m is less than the set value (in our case 0.001) the computation has been completed. Cluster validity is estimated by means of Xie-Beni, Fukujama-Sugeno and proposed in Chapter 5 indexes.

As a result of preliminary clustering the following assumption for ANNBFIS initialization can be made: $\underline{c}^{(i)} = \underline{v}_i$, $i=1,2,...,I$ and:

$$\underset{1 \leq i \leq I}{\forall} \quad \underline{s}^{(i)} = \frac{\sum_{k=1}^{K} \left(u_{ik}\right)^m \left[\underline{x}_0(k) - \underline{v}_i \right]^2}{\sum_{k=1}^{K} \left(u_{ik}\right)^m}. \tag{6.25}$$

Clustering was carried out for 50 various random realizations of partition matrix U. The parameters of the premises are determined on the basis of the above dependencies for a realization for which we obtain the smallest value of the applied cluster validity index.

For calculations presented in the next chapter, the Reichenbach fuzzy implication and the following parameter values: $\eta = 0.01$, $n_I = 1.1$, $n_D = 0.9$, $\alpha = 10^6$, $m = 2$ have been applied. In Appendix A Matlab® m-files implementation of ANNBFIS is presented.

6.3
Classifier based on neuro-fuzzy system

The fuzzy system described in the previous section can be applied to pattern recognition. If patterns from a learning set belong to classes ω_1 and ω_2 then we can build a fuzzy system whose output takes positive values for patterns from class ω_1 and negative values for class ω_2. If we denote a fuzzy system as $y_0 = \Xi_{12}(\underline{x}_0)$, we get:

$$y_0(k) = \Xi_{12}\left[\underline{x}_0(k) \right] \begin{cases} >0, & \text{if } \underline{x}_0(k) \in \omega_1, \\ \leq 0, & \text{if } \underline{x}_0(k) \in \omega_2. \end{cases} \tag{6.26}$$

During the learning process of a classifier we take $t_0(k) = +1$ for pattern $\underline{x}_0(k)$ from class ω_1 and $t_0(k) = -1$ for the pattern from class ω_2. For a bigger number of classes $(\omega_1, \omega_2,...,\omega_p, p > 2)$ we use an extension class-rest or class-class, Tou and Gonzalez (1973). Because of existing common feature regions for which the classifier class-rest does not give the answer which class the classified pattern belongs to the method class-class has been applied. The disadvantage of such a solution is the necessity of constructing a greater number of classifiers. Let us denote a classifier making decision whether a pattern belongs to the i-th or j-th class as:

$$y_0(k) = \Xi_{ij}\left[\underline{x}_0(k)\right] \begin{cases} >0, & \text{if } \underline{x}_0(k) \in \omega_i, \\ \leq 0, & \text{if } \underline{x}_0(k) \in \omega_j. \end{cases} \tag{6.27}$$

Obviously we do not construct the classifier Ξ_{ii} and the information about membership to i-th and j-th classes can be obtained on the basis of Ξ_{ij} or Ξ_{ji} classifiers. Hence we construct $p(p-1)/2$ classifiers Ξ_{ij} for $1 \leq i < p; \ j > i$. The classification condition to i-th class has the form:

$$\left(\underset{j \neq i}{\forall} \ \Xi_{ij}\left[\underline{x}_0(k)\right] > 0 \right) \rightarrow \underline{x}_0(k) \in \omega_i. \tag{6.28}$$

The learning process goes as follows: for each pair of indices ij ($1 \leq i < p; j > i$) we assume $t_0(k) = +1$ for pattern $\underline{x}_0(k)$ belonging to class ω_i and $t_0(k) = -1$ for pattern $\underline{x}_0(k)$ belonging to class ω_j (the patterns belonging to other classes are removed from the training set) and we conduct the learning process of the classifier. The final pattern recognition is conducted on the basis of condition (6.28). Table 6.2 presents the example results of classifier learning for three patterns.

Table 6.2. An example of comparison of classification quality criteria.

k	$t_0(k)$	$y_0(k)$ (Ist case)	$y_0(k)$ (IInd case)
1	+1	+0.9	+0.1
2	-1	-1.1	-0.1
3	-1	+0.1	-0.1
		$E = 1.23$	$E = 2.43$

In case one from that table we may observe the least mean square value of the error, however, in case two we see the lowest number of erroneous classifications. Hence we may infer that the construction of fuzzy system should fulfil the following conditions:

$$\underset{1 \leq k \leq K}{\forall} \ \varphi_k = \begin{cases} +1, & \text{if } \underline{x}_0(k) \in \omega_i, \\ -1, & \text{if } \underline{x}_0(k) \in \omega_j. \end{cases} \tag{6.29}$$

where

$$\underset{1 \le k \le K}{\forall} \quad \varphi_k \, \Xi_{ij}\left[\underline{x}_0(k)\right] > 0.$$

(6.30)

The inequality system (6.30) may be written as:

$$\underset{1 \le k \le K}{\forall} \quad \begin{cases} \varphi_k \, \Xi_{ij}\left[\underline{x}_0(k)\right] = t_0(k), \\ t_0(k) > 0. \end{cases}$$

(6.31)

The question arises how values $t_0(k)$ should be determined. We apply an iterative modification of their values where the following rule is employed: if the output value of the fuzzy system $\varphi_k \, y_0(k)$ is higher than its target value of $t_0(k)$ then we increase $t_0(k)$, otherwise no changes occur. In other words in this method we match the output values of the fuzzy system with the target value in such a way that their values should grow (it assures the fulfilling of the condition $t_0(k) > 0$). After each modification of the system outputs values the learning process is iteratively continued. Let us note:

$$e_k^{(v)} = \varphi_k \, \Xi_{ij}\left[\underline{x}_0(k)\right] - t_0(k)^{(v)},$$

(6.32)

where v stands for iteration index, $t_0(k)^{(v)}$ the target output value of the system for k-th pattern in v-th iteration. The iterative modification of $t_0(k)$ may be written in the form:

$$t_0(k)^{(v)} = t_0(k)^{(v-1)} + \begin{cases} \gamma \, e_k^{(v)}, & \text{if } e_k^{(v)} > 0, \\ 0, & \text{if } e_k^{(v)} \le 0. \end{cases}$$

(6.33)

where γ denotes the convergence coefficient. In appendix B it has been proved that the method is convergent for $0 \le \gamma \le 2$. The iterations may start with arbitrarily chosen values. In further examples we apply $t_0(k)^{(0)} = +1$ for all indexes k. For $\gamma = 0$ we get a method described at the beginning of this section.

6.4
ANNBFIS optimization using deterministic annealing

The hybrid learning method presented in Section 6.2, which is a connection of gradient and least-squares optimization methods may lead to the achievement of local minimum (see Section 3.8). Therefore an application of global optimization technique seems to be reasonable, for example simulated annealing or genetic algorithm. However, such a methods are characterized by a significant cost of computations. An alternative way to solve this problem is the use of deterministic annealing (see Rose 1991). Such a method is based on minimization of a modeled system error energy while its entropy is controlled. The neuro-fuzzy system described in this chapter can be presented as a mixture of local models (experts). Equ. (6.2) can be expressed in the form:

$$y_0 = \sum_{i=1}^{I} \mu_i\left(F^{(i)}(\underline{x}_0), w^{(i)}\right) y^{(i)}(\underline{x}_0), \tag{6.34}$$

where weights μ_is are:

$$\mu_i\left(F^{(i)}(\underline{x}_0), w^{(i)}\right) = \frac{g\left(F^{(i)}(\underline{x}_0), w^{(i)}\right)}{\sum_{j=1}^{I} g\left(F^{(j)}(\underline{x}_0), w^{(j)}\right)}. \tag{6.35}$$

In other words, the neuro-fuzzy system from this chapter can be expressed as a linear combination of simple (linear) models (5.4). The neuro-fuzzy system described in this chapter can be presented as mixture of local models (experts). Deterministic annealing is a method that minimize mean least square criterion E at given level of entropy of the association between the data and local models (see (6.34)). The entropy of this system for training set (6.6) is defined as:

$$S = \sum_{k=1}^{K} \sum_{i=1}^{I} \mu_i\left(F^{(i)}(\underline{x}_0(k)), w^{(i)}\right) \ln\left[\mu_i\left(F^{(i)}(\underline{x}_0(k)), w^{(i)}\right)\right]. \tag{6.36}$$

In deterministic annealing we minimize criterion (6.7) assuming some level of entropy S_0. The constrained optimization problem is therefore:

$$\min E \quad \text{subject to } S = S_0. \tag{6.37}$$

This constrained minimization is equivalent to minimization of the Lagrangian:

$$E' = E - TS. \tag{6.38}$$

Parameter T is the Lagrange multiplier (pseudo-temperature) controls the entropy of the system. On one hand, at high temperature T minimization of Lagrangian (6.38) is equivalent to the maximization of entropy S. On other hand for $T \to 0$ minimization of (6.38) increases importance of criterion E minimization. Using gradient method to minimization a new criterion E' we replace (6.8) by formula:

$$(\alpha)_{new} = (\alpha)_{old} - \eta \left.\frac{\partial E}{\partial \alpha}\right|_{\alpha = (\alpha)_{old}} + T \left.\frac{\partial S}{\partial \alpha}\right|_{\alpha = (\alpha)_{old}}. \tag{6.39}$$

The optimization method consists in iterational determining of the parameters based on (6.38) for fixed parameter T ("temperature"). After the execution of the definite number of iterations parameter T is diminished according to the formula:

$$(T)_{new} = 6\,(T)_{old},\qquad\qquad (6.40)$$

where 6 is the parameter which controls the decreasing of temperature (always near the one). Parameter $\underline{P}$ which linearly depends to system's output are estimated as previously by means of the least square method.

6.5
Further investigations of neuro-fuzzy systems

In our opinion further investigations of neuro-fuzzy systems should concentrate on:

- the application of conditional fuzzy clustering methods (see Section 4.6 and 4.7) to initialize parameters in ANNBFIS system,
- the application of Gaussian membership functions in premises of if-then rules with non-diagonal form, in other words, with non-zero value of elements outside main diagonal of covariance matrix. In this case input space of fuzzy system is linearly transformed,
- the application of genetic algorithms in ANNBFIS learning,
- the application of weighted recurrent least-squares method for optimization of parameters linearly coinciding to ANNBFIS output,
- the examination of ANNBFIS with fuzzy implications from Table 6.1. Compare the results to the system with the Reichanbach fuzzy implication,
- the conjunction of neuro-fuzzy systems with neuro-wavelet systems.

6.6
Summary

In this chapter we demonstrated the following:

- an overview of neuro-fuzzy systems known from literature,
- artificial neural network based on fuzzy inference system (ANNBFIS) with parameterized consequents,
- hybrid method of learning ANNBFIS, which is the combination of the gradient method and least squares method,

- the propositions of a classifier based on ANNBFIS, which minimizes the number of erroneous classifications, method of learning this classifier and proof of its convergence,
- a ready-to-use MATLAB® m-files implementation of ANNBFIS.

Biographical notes

The best source to learn foundations of neuro-fuzzy systems are: Jang et al. (1997), Wang (1998), Kosko (1997). Applications of deterministic annealing to optimization mixture of experts is shown in Rao et al. (1997). Genetic algorithm application to learning in the systems are presented in: Vergara and Moraga (1997), Cordòn and Herrera (1997), Baldi and Brunak (1998), Wang et al. (1998) and Shi et al. (1999).

Other interesting articles about neuro-fuzzy systems are: Babuška and Verbruggen (1997), Delgado et al. (1997), Hollatz (1997), Jang (1994, 1996), Nakoula et al. (1997), Park et al. (1997), Runkler and Bezdek (1999), Su (1997), Yen and Wang (1998). Foundations to wavelet networks are presented in: Zhang and Benveniste (1992), Zhang (1998), Kobayashi (1998).

Appendix A: Artificial neural network based fuzzy inference system - a MATLAB implementation

This appendix presents a MATLAB functions which implements the ANNBFIS system described in this chapter. The main function is named ANNBFIS, whose inputs are: training set (6.6) (DATA) in a $(K \times (N+1))$-dimensional matrix form:

$$\begin{bmatrix} \underline{x}_0(1)^T & t_0(1) \\ \underline{x}_0(2)^T & t_0(2) \\ \vdots & \vdots \\ \underline{x}_0(K)^T & t_0(K) \end{bmatrix}, \tag{A.1}$$

and a number of IF-THEN rules (denoted NRULE). The result of the operation of this function is parameter vector (denoted W), which has the form:

$$\begin{bmatrix} \underline{p}^{(1)} & \underline{p}^{(2)} & \cdots & \underline{p}^{(l)} \\ w^{(1)} & w^{(2)} & \cdots & w^{(l)} \\ \underline{c}^{(1)} & \underline{c}^{(2)} & \cdots & \underline{c}^{(l)} \\ \underline{s}^{(1)} & \underline{s}^{(2)} & \cdots & \underline{s}^{(l)} \end{bmatrix}. \tag{A.2}$$

After training phase the evaluation of the system whose parameters are in matrix (A.2) is made by function ANNBFISE. The input of this function is a set of system inputs (denoted DATA) in the form:

$$\left[\underline{x}_0(1) \ \underline{x}_0(2) \ \cdots \ \underline{x}_0(K_1) \right]^T, \tag{A.3}$$

and parameter matrix (denoted W) in (A.2) format. The result is the output of the system (denoted OUT) in the following format:

$$\left[t_0(1) \ t_0(2) \ \cdots \ t_0(K_1) \right]^T. \tag{A.4}$$

Procedure ANNBFIS uses preliminary clustering, which is implemented in functions CLUSTER and CCLUSTER. The first one realizes the fuzzy c-means clustering, while the second one finds the best c-partition using validity indexes.

```
function w = annbfis(data,nrule)
% W = ANNBFIS(data,nrule);
% data <- training data set matrix
%   (cases in rows; inputs in columns; output in last column),
% nrule <- number of IF-THEN rules,
% w <- learned parameters.

[n1,m1] = size(data);                    % n1 <- # of cases, m1 <- # of inputs + 1
iter = 100;                              % target number of iteration
[c,s,cc] = cclust(data(:,1:m1-1),nrule,nrule,4);
c = c(:,1:m1-1)';                        % premises centers
s = s(:,1:m1-1)';                        % premises sigma-parameters
m = cc;                                  % # of IF-THEN rules
ss = 0.01;                               % initial step-size
a = zeros(m1,m);                         % localization of fuzzy sets in consequence
ww = 2 * ones(1,m);                      % width of fuzzy sets in consequence
co = 0;                                  % used optimization method selector
EEMIN = 1E100;                           % minimal criterion error
lasti = 1;                               % last step-size increasing index
lastd = 1;                               % last step-size decreasing index
EE = zeros(iter,1);                      % criterion error in learning epoch
for l=1:iter,                            % loop under learning epoch
 lst=' ';
 if (co == 0),                           % LMSE method initiallization
  P = 10E6 * eye(m1*m);
  ak = zeros(m1*m,1);
 end;
 if (co == 1),                           % gradient method initialization
  gc = zeros(m1-1,m);
  gs = zeros(m1-1,m);
  gw = zeros(1,m);
 end;
 for n=1:n1,                             % loop under data cases
  d1 = (data(n,1:m1-1)' * ones(1,m)) - c;
  d2 = d1 ./ s;
  d3 = d2 .* d2;
  d4 = -0.5 * sum(d3);
  R = exp(d4);
  mi = (R .* ww) / 2;
  z = ones(1,m) * mi';
  aa = (data(n,1:m1-1) * a(1:m1-1,:)) + a(m1,:);
  y = (aa * mi') / z;
  e = abs(data(n,m1) - y);               % error
  EE(l) = EE(l) + e*e;
  if (co == 0),                          % LMSE method
   mi1 = mi / z;
   M = [data(n,1:m1-1)'; 1] * mi1;
   Rk = M(:);
   P = P - (P*Rk*Rk'*P) / (Rk'*P*Rk+1);
   ak = ak + P*Rk*(data(n,m1) - Rk'*ak);
   if (n == n1), a(:) = ak; end;
  end;
```

```
if (co == 1),                           % gradient method
 ay = ((ones(m1-1,1)*aa) - y) / z;
 gc = gc + (data(n,m1) - y) * ay .* (ones(m1-1,1)*mi) .* (d1 ./ (s .* s));
 gs = gs + (data(n,m1) - y) * ay .* (ones(m1-1,1)*mi) .* ((d1 .* d1) ./ (s .* s .* s));
 gw = gw + (data(n,m1) - y) * ((aa - y)/z) .* R/2;
 end;
end;                                    % loop under data cases
if (co == 1),                           % gradient method
 if (EEMIN > EE(l)),                    % the smallest error in this epoch
 EEMIN = EE(l);
 lst='<--';
 w = [a; ww; c; s];                     % parameters to output
 end;
 if ((l-lasti) > 8),
  if ((EE(l)<EE(l-2))&(EE(l-2)<EE(l-4))&(EE(l-4)<EE(l-6))&(EE(l-6)<EE(l-8))),
  ss=ss*1.1;
  fprintf(1,'Step Increasing: %e\n',ss);
  lasti=l; end; end;
 if ((l-lastd) > 8),
  if ((EE(l)<EE(l-2))&(EE(l-2)>EE(l-4))&(EE(l-4)<EE(l-6))&(EE(l-6)>EE(l-8))),
  ss=ss*0.9;
  fprintf(1,'Step Decreasing: %e\n',ss);
  lastd=l; end; end;
 Sss = ss/sqrt(sum(sum(gc .* gc)) + sum(sum(gs .* gs)) + sum(gw .* gw));
 c = c + Sss * gc;                      % parameters modifications
 s = s + Sss * gs;
 ww = ww + Sss * gw;
 end;
 fprintf(1,'%4d %e %d %d %s\n',l,EE(l)/n1,co,m,lst);
 co = mod(co+1,2);                      % optimization method change
end;                                    % loop under learning epoch
```

```
function out = annbfise(data,w)
% OUT = ANNBFISE(data,w);
% data <- checking data set,
% w <- parameters matrix.

[n1,m1] = size(data);                   % n1 - # of cases, m1 - # of inputs + 1
[q,m] = size(w);                        % m - # of IF-THEN rules
a = w(1:m1,:);
ww = w(m1+1,:);
c = w(m1+2:2*m1,:);
s = w(2*m1+1:q,:);
for n=1:n1,                             % loop under cases
 d1 = (data(n,1:m1-1)' * ones(1,m)) - c;
 d2 = d1 ./ s;
 d3 = d2 .* d2;
 d4 = -0.5 * sum(d3);
 R = exp(d4);
 mi = (R .* ww) / 2;
 z = ones(1,m) * mi';
```

```
  aa = (data(n,1:m1-1) * a(1:m1-1,:)) + a(m1,:);
  out(n) = (aa * mi') / z;
  end;
  out = out';
```

---

function [c,s,cc] = cclust(data,mincl_n,maxcl_n,ni)
```
% [c,s] = cclust(data,mincl_n,maxcl_n,ni) find the best partition.
% DATA <- data matrix,
% MINCL_N <- minimal number of clusters,
% MAXCL_N <- maximal number of clusters,
% NI <- number of iteration,
% C <- cluster centers,
% S <- cluster variability,
% CC <- optimal number of clusters.

wsk = 1E30;
cc = mincl_n;
for i=mincl_n:maxcl_n,
 for j=1:ni,
  [c1,s1,U,XB,FS,SC,VAL] = clust(data,i);
  if (VAL < wsk),
   wsk = VAL;
   c = c1;
   s = s1;
   cc = i;
  end;
 end;
end;
fprintf('Minimal Value of index: %f\n', wsk);
fprintf('Number of Clusters: %f\n', cc);
```

---

function [V,S,U,XB,FS,SC,VAL] = cluster(data,n_clust)
```
% [V,S,U,XB,FS,SC,VAL] = cluster(data,n_clust) fuzzy c-means clustering.
% data <- data set; cases in rows,
% n_clust <- number of clusters,
% V <- cluster centers,
% S <- cluster variability,
% U <- partition matrix,
% XB <- Xie-Beni index,
% FS <- Fukuyama-Sugeno index,
% SC <- Bezdek Partition Index,
% VAL <- Our index.

[n1,n2] = size(data);
m = 2;                        % exponent parameter
iter = 500;                   % # of iterations
Jm_d = 1e-5;                  % criterion decreasing
Jm = zeros(iter,1);
U = rand(n_clust,n1);         % initialization of partition
sum_c = sum(U);
```

```
U = U./sum_c(ones(n_clust,1),:);
for i = 1:iter,                        % loop
 Um = U.^m;
 V = Um*data./((ones(n2,1)*sum(Um'))');
 DD = zeros(n_clust,n1);
 for k = 1:n_clust,
  DD(k,:) = sqrt(sum(((data-ones(n1,1)*V(k,:)).^2)'));
 end
 Jm(i) = sum(sum((DD.^2).*Um));        % criterion function
 U_new = DD.^(-2/(m-1));               % update U
 U = U_new./(ones(n_clust,1)*sum(U_new));
 if i > 1,
  if abs(Jm(i) - Jm(i-1)) < Jm_d, break; end,
 end
end                                    % end of main loop
Um = U.^m;
V2 = Jm(i) / n1;
V1 = 1e23;
for i=1:n_clust-1,
 for j=i+1:n_clust,
  tm = sum(((V(i,:)-V(j,:)).^2)');
  if (tm < V1),
   V1 = tm;
  end;
 end;
end;
XB = V2 / V1;                          % Xie-Beni index,
VG = mean(data);
tm = sum(Um');
FS = Jm(i) - sum(tm .* sum(((V - (ones(n_clust,1)*VG)).^2)'));
                                       % Fukuyama-Sugeno index,
PI = (sum(((DD.^2).*Um)'))./(sum(U'));
for i=1:n_clust,
 SI(i) = sum(sum(((V - (ones(n_clust,1)*V(i,:))).^2)'));
end;
SC = sum(PI./SI);                      % Bezdek index,
PI = (sum(((DD.^2).*Um)'))./(sum(Um'));
PI = PI .* sum(U');
nt = sum(U');
for i=1:n_clust,
 ni = nt + nt(i);
 SI(i) = sum(sum(((V - (ones(n_clust,1)*V(i,:))).^2)') .* ni);
end;
VAL = sum(PI./SI);                     % a new index
fprintf('X-B: %f F-S: %f SC: %f VAL: %f\n', XB, FS, SC, VAL);
S = zeros(n_clust,n2);
for k = 1:n_clust,
 S(k,:) = U(k,:) * ((data - ones(n1,1)*V(k,:)).^2);
 S(k,:) = S(k,:) / sum(U(k,:)');
end;
S = sqrt(S);
```

Appendix B: Proof of classifier learning convergence

For all patterns from the train set equation (6.30) may be written as:

$$\underline{Y} = \underline{E}\,\underline{P},$$ (B.1)

where:

$$\underline{E} = \begin{bmatrix} \varphi_1\,\underline{D}\big(\underline{x}_0(1)\big)^T \\ \varphi_2\,\underline{D}\big(\underline{x}_0(2)\big)^T \\ \vdots \\ \varphi_K\,\underline{D}\big(\underline{x}_0(K)\big)^T \end{bmatrix}; \qquad \underline{Y} = \begin{bmatrix} y_0(1) \\ y_0(2) \\ \vdots \\ y_0(K) \end{bmatrix}.$$ (B.2)

Similarly, we may present in matrix form Equ. (6.32):

$$\underline{E}^{(v)} = \underline{E}\,\underline{P}^{(v)} - \underline{T}^{(v)},$$ (B.3)

where:

$$\underline{T}^{(v)} = \begin{bmatrix} t_0(1)^{(v)} \\ t_0(2)^{(v)} \\ \vdots \\ t_0(K)^{(v)} \end{bmatrix},$$ (B.4)

and $\underline{P}^{(v)}$ is the parameter vector in v-th iteration.

The recurrent least square method applied for estimation of parameter p may be written in the non-recurrent form:

$$\underline{P}^{(v)} = \big(\underline{E}^T\,\underline{E}\big)^{-1}\,\underline{E}^T\,\underline{T}^{(v)} = \underline{E}^{\#}\,\underline{T}^{(v)},$$ (B.5)

where $\underline{E}^{\#}$ is pseudoinverse matrix.

Equation (6.33) takes the form:

$$\underline{T}^{(v+1)} = \underline{T}^{(v)} + \frac{\gamma}{2}\Big[\underline{E}^{(v)} + |\underline{E}^{(v)}|\Big].$$ (B.6)

On the basis of (B.3) and (B.5) we get:

$$\underline{E}^{(v)} = \underline{E}\,\underline{E}^{\#}\,\underline{T}^{(v)} - \underline{T}^{(v)} = \big(\underline{E}\,\underline{E}^{\#} - \underline{I}\big)\underline{T}^{(v)}.$$ (B.7)

If we substitute Equ. (B.7) for (v+1) index to equation (B.6) and denote:

$$\bar{\underline{E}}^{(v)} = \underline{E}^{(v)} + |\underline{E}^{(v)}|,$$ (B.8)

we get:

$$
\begin{aligned}
\underline{E}^{(v+1)} &= \left(\underline{F}\,\underline{F}^{\#} - \mathbb{I} \right) \left(\underline{T}^{(v)} + \frac{\gamma}{2}\,\bar{\underline{E}}^{(v)} \right) = \\
&= \underline{E}^{(v)} + \frac{\gamma}{2}\left(\underline{F}\,\underline{F}^{\#} - \mathbb{I} \right)\bar{\underline{E}}^{(v)}.
\end{aligned}
\tag{B.9}
$$

Next we determine the square of vector $\underline{E}^{(v+1)}$ norm:

$$
\| \underline{E}^{(v+1)} \|^2 = \| \underline{E}^{(v)} \|^2 + \| \frac{\gamma}{2}\left(\underline{F}\,\underline{F}^{\#} - \mathbb{I} \right)\bar{\underline{E}}^{(v)} \|^2 - \gamma \bar{\underline{E}}^{(v)T}\left(\underline{F}\,\underline{F}^{\#} - \mathbb{I} \right)\bar{\underline{E}}^{(v)}.
\tag{B.10}
$$

On the basis of equations (B.5) and (B.7) we get:

$$
\underline{E}^{(v)T}\underline{F}\,\underline{F}^{\#} = \left(\underline{F}\underline{P}^{(v)} - \underline{T}^{(v)} \right)^{T}\underline{F}\,\underline{F}^{\#} = \left(\underline{F}\,\underline{F}^{\#}\underline{T}^{(v)} - \underline{T}^{(v)} \right)\underline{F}\,\underline{F}^{\#} = 0.
\tag{B.11}
$$

Transforming the second component of the right side of equation (B.10) with the use of equation (B.11) we have:

$$
\begin{aligned}
\| \frac{\gamma}{2}\left(\underline{F}\,\underline{F}^{\#} - \mathbb{I} \right)^{T} \bar{\underline{E}}^{(v)} \|^2 &= \frac{\gamma^2}{4}\bar{\underline{E}}^{(v)T}\left(\underline{F}\,\underline{F}^{\#} - \mathbb{I} \right)^{T}\left(\underline{F}\,\underline{F}^{\#} - \mathbb{I} \right)\bar{\underline{E}}^{(v)} = \frac{\gamma^2}{4}\| \bar{\underline{E}}^{(v)} \|^2 \\
&\quad - \frac{\gamma^2}{2}\bar{\underline{E}}^{(v)T}\underline{F}\,\underline{F}^{\#}\bar{\underline{E}}^{(v)} - \frac{\gamma^2}{4}\bar{\underline{E}}^{(v)T}\left(\underline{F}\,\underline{F}^{\#} \right)^{T}\underline{F}\,\underline{F}^{\#}\bar{\underline{E}}^{(v)} \\
&= \frac{\gamma^2}{4}\| \bar{\underline{E}}^{(v)} \|^2 - \frac{\gamma^2}{4}\bar{\underline{E}}^{(v)T}\left(\underline{F}\,\underline{F}^{\#} \right)^{T}\underline{F}\,\underline{F}^{\#}\bar{\underline{E}}^{(v)}.
\end{aligned}
\tag{B.12}
$$

On the basis of (B.10), (B.11) and (B.12) we get:

$$
\| \underline{E}^{(v+1)} \|^2 = \| \underline{E}^{(v)} \|^2 + \frac{\gamma}{2}\left(\frac{\gamma}{2} - 1 \right)\| \bar{\underline{E}}^{(v)} \|^2 - \frac{\gamma^2}{4}\bar{\underline{E}}^{(v)T}\underline{F}\,\underline{F}^{\#}\bar{\underline{E}}^{(v)},
\tag{B.13}
$$

hence for $0 \leq \gamma \leq 2$ the following condition is satisfied:

$$
\underset{v>0}{\forall} \quad \| \underline{E}^{(v+1)} \|^2 \leq \| \underline{E}^{(v)} \|^2.
\tag{B.14}
$$

∎

7 Applications of artificial neural network based fuzzy inference system

7.1
Introduction

In previous chapters we introduced the artificial neural network based fuzzy inference system (ANNBFIS) network structure. The learning methods, clustering of input space, use of different fuzzy implications in inference process and other related topics are shown. In this chapter we will show several applications of ANNBFIS to solving many practical problems, as: time series prediction, signal compression, classifications of patterns, system identifications, control and equalization of digital communication channel. All above applications will be tested on benchmark data sets. These data can be easily obtained via Internet. This approach ensures easy comparison of the proposed system to systems known from literature, and the readers can compare their own systems to the system presented in this book.

7.2
Application to chaotic time series prediction

A chaotic time series (a discrete signal) obtained on the basis of the solution of the Mackey-Glass equation was investigated (see i.e. Schuster 1988):

$$\frac{dx(t)}{dt} = \frac{0.2\ x(t-\tau)}{1 + x(t-\tau)^{10}} - 0.1\ x(t). \tag{7.1}$$

The prediction of a time series generated by means of equation (7.1) was realized by many authors (Jang (1995); Cho and Wang 1996). To make a precise comparison we applied data generated by Jang and obtained via anonymous ftp (ftp://ftp.cs.cmu.edu/ users/ai/areas/fuzzy/systems/anfis). To obtain such a time series Jang applied fourth-order Runge-Kutta method with the following parameters: time step 0.1, $x(0) = 0.1$, $\tau=17$ (Jang 1995).

Table 7.1. Simulation results of Mackey-Glass chaotic time series prediction.

I	$NDEI_{trn}$	$NDEI_{chk}$	Fukujama-Sugeno index	Xie-Beni index	A new index
2	0.0423	0.0420	41.4960	0.2606	0.3715
3	0.0190	0.0190	-4.2745	0.1876	0.1664
4	0.0168	0.0172	-19.3336	0.1467	0.1033
5	0.0165	0.0172	-26.1472	0.1385	0.0757
6	0.0161	0.0170	-31.1737	0.1404	0.0602
7	0.0131	0.0142	-35.3264	0.1359	0.0503
8	0.0121	0.0123	-38.4075	0.1651	0.0441
9	0.0103	0.0112	-39.4041	0.1544	0.0389
10	0.0072	0.0092	-42.0569	0.1599	0.0307
11	0.0070	0.0081	-42.4187	0.1402	0.0302
12	0.0062	0.0077	-43.5931	0.1749	0.0269
13	0.0059	0.0074	-45.2631	0.1744	0.0239
14	0.0053	0.0072	-45.5465	0.1834	0.0219
15	0.0049	0.0061	-46.3363	0.1743	0.0199
16	0.0041	0.0058	-47.2131	0.1540	0.0181

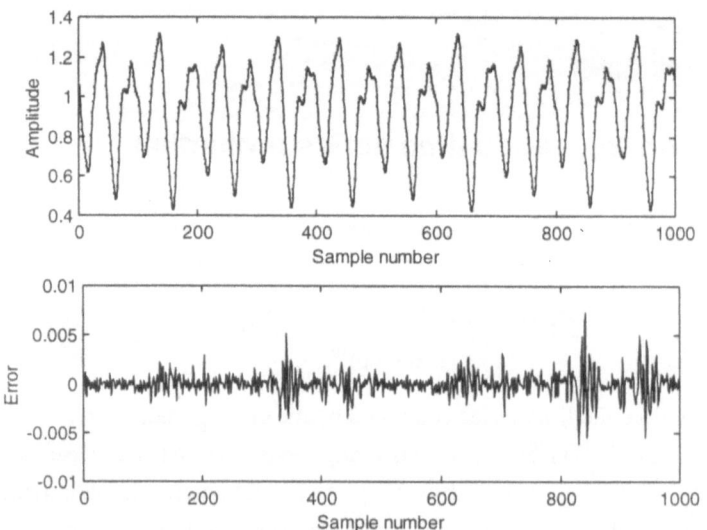

Fig.7.1. Mackey-Glass chaotic time series (continuous line) and predicted values (dotted line) (upper), prediction error (lower).

Such generated data are combined in the embedded vector $[x(n)\ x(n\text{-}6)\ x(n\text{-}12)\ x(n\text{-}18)]^T$.

The goal is the prediction of value $x(n\text{+}6)$ for the embedded vector as input. The data consist of 500 pairs of input-output data of the learning set and 500 pairs of the testing set. 500 iterations were carried out, the number of rules changing from 2 to 16 using ANNBFIS. Prediction quality has been evaluated with non-dimensional error index (NDEI). This index is defined as a root mean square error divided by standard deviation of the target time series. We applied the assessment of the cluster validity by means of Xie-Beni, Fukujama-Sugeno indexes as well as the index presented in Chapter 4. Table 7.1 shows the results.

Taking into account the above mentioned time series and applying 16 if-then rules Jang (1995) obtained the value of non-dimensional error index $NDEI_{trn} = 0.007$ for a training set and $NDEI_{chk} = 0.0066$ for a testing set. Applying 23 if-then rules Cho and Wang (1996) obtained the

values of root mean square error $RMSE_{trn} = 0.0096$ and $RMSE_{chk} = 0.0114$, which corresponds to $NDEI_{trn} = 0.04200$ and $NDEI_{chk} = 0.04987$. Using the ANNBFIS system the results comparable to Jang's results were obtained when 14 if-then rules were applied. However, the results comparable to Wang's results were obtained after only 2 if-then rules (cf, Table 7.1) have been applied. Fig. 7.1 shows the examined chaotic time series (a continuous line), predicted time series (a dotted line) and the prediction error for examined chaotic time series for 16 if-then rules. From that figure

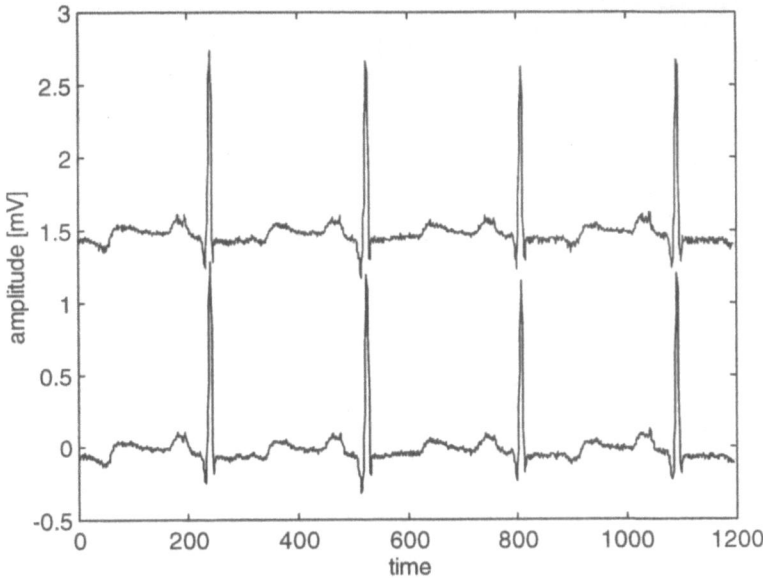

Fig.7.2. Original (lower) and one-step predictor (upper) of ECG signal.

we may observe the same character of error signal for the learning part of data (discrete time 1-500) and testing part of data (discrete time 501-1000). If we examine the obtained values of clustering validity indexes together with non-dimensional error NDEI index, the monotonic dependence between these indexes should be observed.

To sum up the investigations in this section, we can conclude that the system described in previous chapters may be successfully applied to the prediction of time series generated by means of nonlinear differential equations.

7.3
Application to ECG signal compression

On the basis of the ANNBFIS system described in the previous chapter we build a nonlinear one-step predictor:

$$\hat{x}(n) = \Xi\big[x(n-1),\, x(n-2),\, \ldots, x(n-u)\big],\qquad(7.2)$$

where Ξ is a function of u-th order modeled by a fuzzy system. The prediction error is defined:

$$e(n) = \hat{x}(n) - x(n).\qquad(7.3)$$

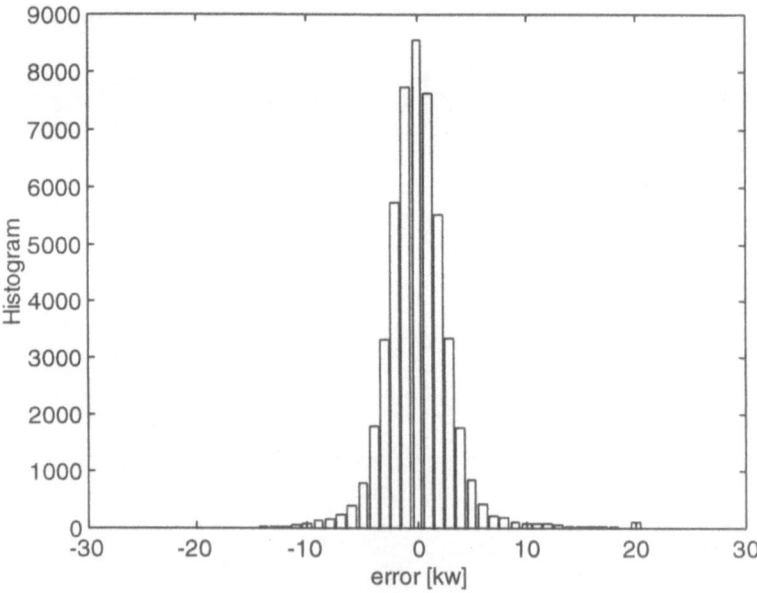

Fig.7.3. Histogram of one-step prediction error.

The compression method is based on the fact that the error signal $e(n)$ is less dynamic than the original signal. Such a method leads to lossless compression. The original values can be obtained on the basis of the predictate and a memorized prediction error. The preliminary investigation has been made for ECG signal from MIT-BIH database numbered 100. The sampling frequency of that signal is equal to 360 Hz and quantization step size is 5 µV. The learning process of the fuzzy system was conducted for the first 500 samples (the learning set). The order of the model and the number of if-then rules varied from 2 to 6. The values of variance (in qu^2) of prediction error after 10 iterations are shown in Table 7.2. For further testing 5-th order of the model and 4 if-then rules were chosen arbitrarily. For 50000 samples such a model have a variance of prediction error 9.39 qu^2 (testing set). A fragment of the original ECG signal with the values of one-step predictor (after adding 300 qu. for better presentation) is shown in Fig. 7.2. Fig. 7.3 presents a histogram of one-step prediction errors for the tested signal. An error signal $e(n)$ is coded by means of a modified Huffman code. A maximal length of the coding symbol is equal to 16 bits. For the tested ECG signal an average data rate 4.247 bits/sample has been obtained.

For the tested ECG signal in Hamilton and Tompkins (1991), after re-sampling with frequency 100 Hz and decreasing the quantization step size to ca 35µV, an average data rate of ca 2 bits/sample was obtained. Taking into account the facts mentioned above the results seem to be promising and the testing of all MIT-BIH database should be made.

Table 7.2   The variance of prediction error for ECG signal.

I	order 2	order 3	order 4	order 5	order 6
2	15.89	11.07	9.92	9.48	8.71
3	11.12	9.41	9.26	9.22	8.71
4	10.49	7.98	7.24	7.01	6.57
5	9.47	8.03	6.66	6.21	5.97
6	8.21	6.15	5.69	5.44	5.16

7.4
Application to Ripley's synthetic two-class data classification

The tests were done for data generated by Ripley (1996) and obtained via anonymous ftp (ftp://markov.stats.ox.ac.uk/pub/PRNN). These data consist of patterns having

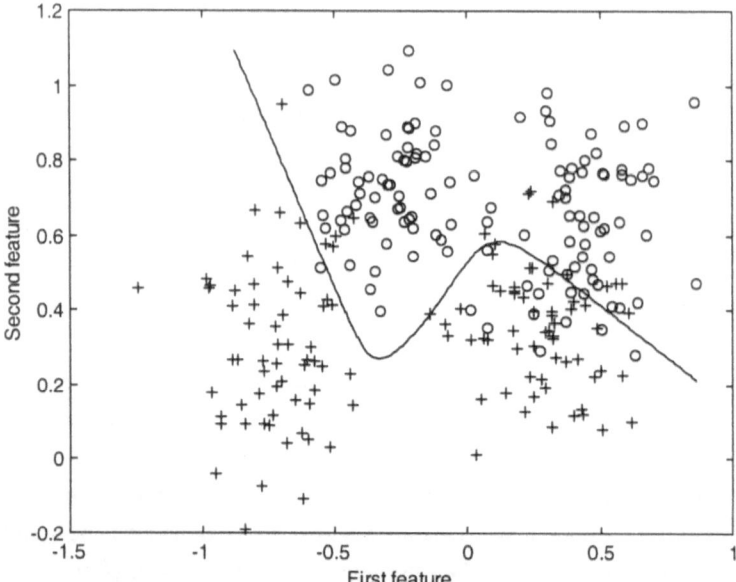

Fig. 7.4. Training set for Ripley two-class problem with classification curve.

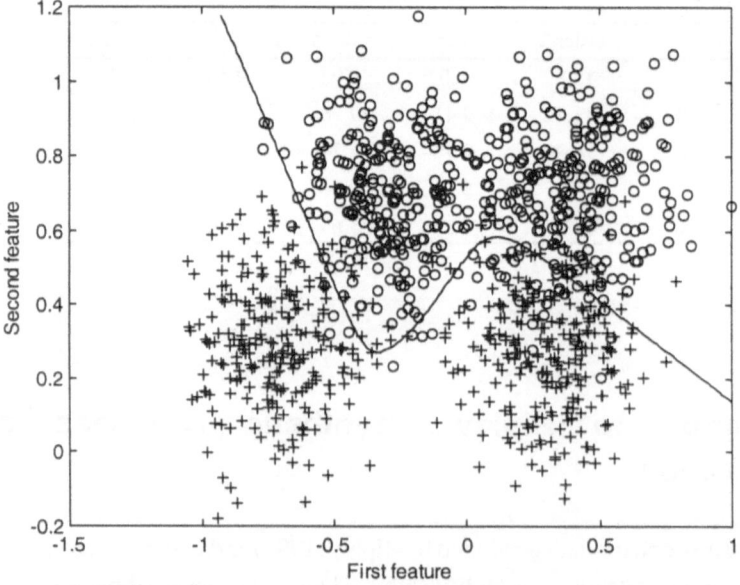

Fig. 7.5. Testing set for Ripley two-class problem with classification curve.

two features and assigned to two classes. Each class has bimodal distribution.

The class distribution was chosen to allow the best-possible error rate of about 8%.The training set consists of 250 patterns (125 patterns belong to each class), and the testing set consists of 1000 patterns (500 patterns belong to each class). Figs. 7.4 and 7.5 present the training set and testing set, respectively. The patterns belonging to the first class are denoted by '+' and to the second class by 'o'. The obtained results after 100 iterations, for a number of if-then rules changing from 2 to 10 are presented in Table 7.3.

Table 7.3. Simulation results for classification of Ripley data.

I	E_{trn} [%]	E_{chk} [%]	Xie-Beni index	Fukuyama-Sugeno index	A new index
2	11.6	8.8	0.1781	31.8546	0.2340
3	10.4	9.7	0.1001	-34.8939	0.0730
4	8.8	11.9	0.0826	-63.3164	0.0295
5	9.2	12.2	0.3688	-62.1861	0.0249
6	8.8	10.3	0.3895	-64.4603	0.0217
7	6.8	14.3	0.3218	-65.9093	0.0192
8	7.1	16.1	0.3440	-68.9501	0.0168
9	5.7	18.2	0.3037	-67.0154	0.0149
10	5.7	19.6	0.2846	-66.6524	0.0134

In that table the values of Xie-Beni, Fukujama-Sugeno and new indexes with percentage of false classification for training and testing sets are presented as well. From the point of view of false classification for a testing set (pessimistic evaluation) the best results are obtained for two if-then rules. Also for two if-then rules the Xie-Beni index takes the minimal value and it suggests appropriateness of this index to the evaluation of rule number in the construction of a classifier. The course of the curve dividing the feature space into two parts representing first class and second class for a training set and for a testing set are presented in Figs. 7.4 and 7.5, respectively.

7.5

Application to the recognition of diabetes in Pima Indians

The data considered in this subsection were obtained via anonymous ftp (see 7.4). The data were collected by US National Institute of Diabetes and Kidney Diseases. According to World Health Organization criteria, a population of women who were at least 21 years old was tested for diabetes. The women are of Pima Indians (living near Phoenix, Arizona). For each women the following personal data were collected:

- number of pregnancies,
- plasma glucose concentrations in an oral glucose tolerance test,
- diastolic blood pressure (mm Hg),
- triceps skin fold thickness (mm),
- body mass index (weight in kg / (height in m)^2),
- diabetes pedigree function,
- age in years.

The training set of data consists of 200 patterns and a testing set of 332. It should be pointed out that about 33% of this population suffers from diabetes. The best classification methods show about 20% of false classifications (Ripley 1996). The result of examination for a number of if-then rules changing from 2 to 6 are shown in Table 7.4. For each number of rules 100 iterations are preformed. The values of the Xie-Beni and Fukujama-Sugeno indexes with percent of false classification for training and testing sets, respectively are shown in Table 7.4 as well. The best results (from the point of view of false classifications for the testing set-pessimistic evaluation) are obtained for 2 if-then rules. Like in Section 7.4, the number of if-then rules is correctly evaluated using the Xie-Beni index.

Table 7.4. Results for classification of Pima Indians diabetes.

I	E_{tm} [%]	E_{chk} [%]	Xie-Beni index	Fukuyama-Sugeno index	A new index
2	23	21	0.1889	67191.78	0.2590
3	16	21.6	0.4135	2107.16	0.2233
4	15	23.1	0.5302	-12194.25	0.1740
5	14	24	0.5627	-22047.62	0.1413
6	12.5	26.5	0.6531	-32377.04	0.1480

7.6
Application to the iris problem

The iris database is perhaps the best known database to be found in the pattern recognition literature. The data set contains 3 classes of 50 instances each, where each class refers to a type of iris plant. The data were collected by Anderson (1935). The vector of features consists of:

    1).sepal length in cm,
    2).sepal width in cm,
    3).petal length in cm,
    4).petal width in cm.

We consider three classes of patterns: Iris Setosa, Iris Versicolour i Iris Virginica. A confusion matrix for 50 learning iterations and two if-then rules has been shown in Table 7.5. The lowest error rate equaling 0% has been obtained for coefficient γ = 1. For the rest of the values of coefficient γ the error rate equals 1.33%. The results were independent of the applied index of cluster validity.

Table 7.5. Simulation results for classification of the famous iris problem.

Confusion Matrix											
$\gamma = 0.0$			$\gamma = 0.5$			$\gamma = 1.0$			$\gamma = 2.0$		
50	0	0	50	0	0	50	0	0	50	0	0
0	50	0	0	49	1	0	50	50	0	49	1
0	2	48	0	1	49	0	0	50	0	1	49

7.7
Application to Monk's problems

The Monk's problem was the basis of a first international comparison of learning algorithms. The result of this comparison is summarized in Thrun et al. (1991). One significant characteristic of this comparison is that it was performed by a collection of researchers, each of whom was an advocate of the technique they tested (often they were the authors of various methods). In this sense, the results are less biased than in comparison with results obtained by a single person advocating a specific learning method, and more accurately reflect the generalization behavior of the learning techniques as applied by knowledgeable users.

There are three Monk's problems. The domains for all Monk's problems are the same. One of the Monk's problems has noise added. For each problem, the domain has been partitioned into a training and testing set. The vector of features for each pattern consists of 7 features which take the following values:

- first feature - 1,2,3,
- second - 1,2,3,
- third - 1,2,
- fourth - 1,2,3,
- fifth - 1,2,3,4,
- sixth - 1,2.

The patterns are classified into two classes. Taken from Thrun et al. (1991), the results of testing for various methods are collected in Table 7.6. The testing results obtained by means of the method described in this paper are presented in Table 7.6 as well. It should be pointed out that methods which gave the highest percentage of correct classification have been selected for coefficient $\gamma = 0.5$.

The number of executed iterations varied from 12 to 6000 depending on the considered problem. Like in the previous case, the results were independent of the applied index of cluster validity.

Table 7.6. Simulation results for classification of MONKS problems.

Method		MONKS-1	MONKS-2	MONKS-3
AQ-15 Genetic		100 %	86.8 %	100 %
Assistant Professional		100 %	81.3 %	100 %
mFOIL		100 %	69.2 %	100 %
ID5R-hat		90.3 %	65.7 %	-
CN2		100 %	69.0 %	89.1 %
PRISM		86.3 %	72.7 %	90.3 %
ECOBWEB leaf prediction		71.8 %	67.4 %	68.2 %
Backprop. with weight decay		100 %	100 %	97.2 %
Cascade Correlation		100 %	100 %	97.2 %
ANNBFIS $l = 3$	$\gamma = 0.0$	100 %	100 %	97.6 %
	$\gamma = 0.5$	100 %	100 %	98.2 %
	$\gamma = 1.0$	100 %	100 %	97.8 %
	$\gamma = 2.0$	100 %	100 %	97.5 %

7.8
Application to system identification

The benchmark data originating from Box and Jenkins (1976) work concerning the identification of a gas oven were included in our examination as well. Air and methane were delivered into the gas oven (gas flow in ft/min - an input signal x) to obtain a mixture of gases containing CO_2 (percentage content - output signal y). The data consisting of 296 pairs of input-output samples in 9 sec. periods are presented in Fig. 7.6. To identify a model the following vectors have been applied as input: $[y(n-1) ...y(n-4) \ x(n) \ x(n-1) ... x(n-6)]^T$ and output $y(n)$. The results of examinations carried out for the numbers of if-then rules changing from 2 to 6 are shown in Table 7.7 after 500 iterations. The calculations were carried out by applying indexes described in chapter 5 in order to evaluate cluster validity. In the original book Box and Jenkins obtained the value of RMSE = 0.4494 for linear methods, which is a worse result than ours obtained for 2 if-then rules. Paper by Kim et al. (1998) presents the comparison of performance of the methods of fuzzy modeling known from literature for the Box-Jenkins data. According to this comparison the best results were obtained for the method proposed in the paper by Kim et al. (1998). In this case RMSE equal to 0.2345 was obtained. The worst result obtained on the basis of modeling presented in chapter 6 amounts to RMSE = 0.1473 (see Table 7.8).

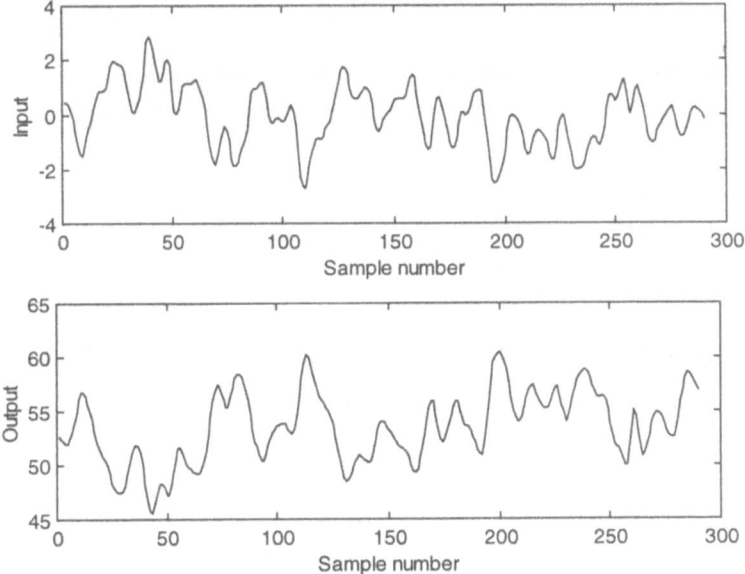

Fig. 7.6. The Box-Jenkins data for system identification.

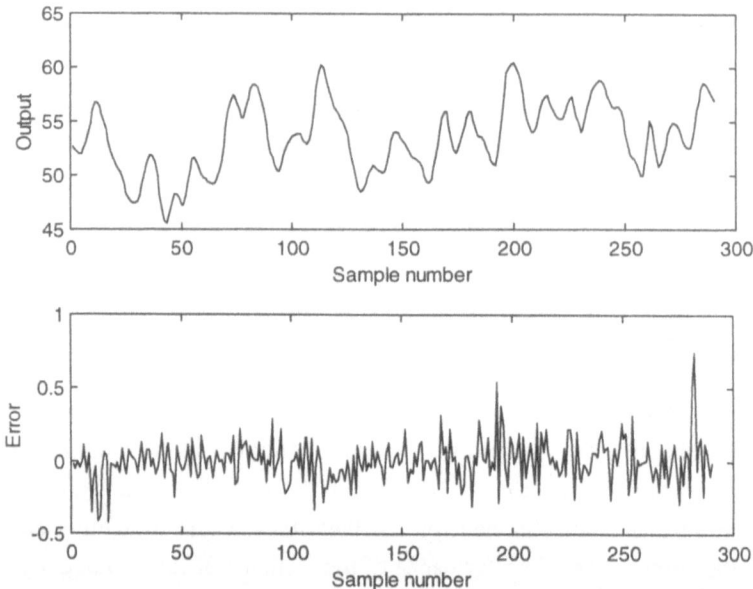

Fig. 7.7. Original (continuous line) and modeled (dotted line) output signal for the Box-Jenkins data(upper), error signal for six if-then rules (lower).

Fig. 7.7 presents an original (a continuous line) and modeled (a dotted line) output signal course and the error signal course, respectively.

Table 7.7. Simulation results for identification of the Box-Jenkins data.

m	RMSE	Fukujama-Sugeno Index	Xie-Beni index	A new index
2	0.21676	1886.85	0.1291	0.1663
3	0.20250	-2893.05	0.1583	0.1089
4	0.16689	-3576.40	0.2327	0.0935
5	0.15518	-4732.48	0.2198	0.0630
6	0.14732	-5509.53	0.3407	0.0571

Table 7.8. Comparison of system identification methods.

Model	Inputs	Rules	Parameters	RMSE
Tong	2	19	-	0.6848
Pedrycz	2	81	-	0.5656
Xu-Lu	2	25	-	0.5727
Box-Jenkins	6	-	10	0.4494
Sugeno-Yasukawa	3	6	96	0.4358
Wang-Langari	6	2	-	0.2569
Sugeno-Tanaka	6	2	17	0.2607
Lin-Cunningham	5	4	354	0.2664
Kim et al.	6	2	110	0.2190
ANNBFIS	10	6	84	0.1473

7.9
Application to control

The main goal in control theory is to design a controller that modifies input of the plant so that it would acquire a certain desired behavior, measured at its output. In this section application of ANNBFIS to the specific method known as inverse learning for designing the controller will be shown. We assume that the plant can be written in discrete time k as:

$$x(k+1) = f[x(k), u(k)],\qquad\qquad(7.4)$$

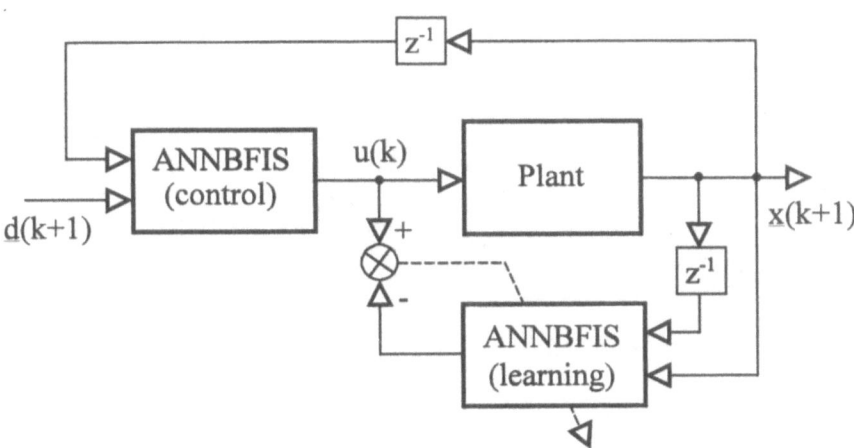

Fig. 7.8. The ANNBFIS in automatic control.

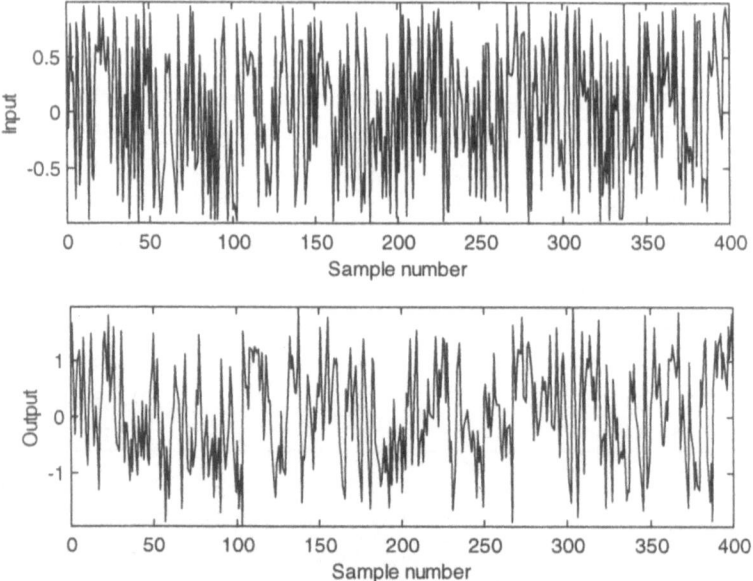

Fig. 7.9. Training data used to learning ANNBFIS.

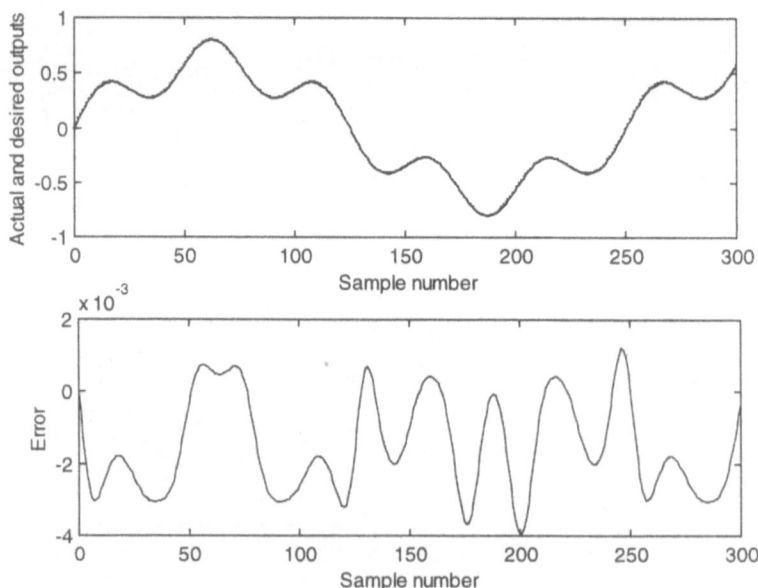

Fig. 7.10. An example of application ANNBFIS to control.

where $\underline{x}$ is state vector and u is the control signal. If we denote $\underline{U}(k) = [u(k), u(k+1), ..., u(k+p-1)]^T$, where p is the order of the plant, then:

$$x(k+p) = F\left[\underline{x}(k), \underline{U}(k)\right], \tag{7.5}$$

Now, we assume that inverse dynamics do exist, and control signal $\underline{U}(k)$ can be expressed as:

$$\underline{U}(k) = \Xi\left[\underline{x}(k+p), \underline{x}(k)\right]. \tag{7.6}$$

In training phase we use ANNBFIS for modeling (7.6). Next, in application phase the desired state of the plant, denoted as $\underline{d}(k+p)$, is obtained using the following control signal:

$$\hat{\underline{U}}(k) = \Xi\left[\underline{d}(k+p), \underline{x}(k)\right]. \tag{7.7}$$

These two phases for $p = 1$ are presented in Fig.7.8.
We assume that the plant is described by:

$$x(k+1) = 0.8 \sin\left[2 x(k)\right] + 1.2\, u(k). \tag{7.8}$$

The training data are obtained by choosing $u(k)$; $k=0, 1, ..., 400$, as uniformly distributed on [-1, 1] interval random numbers, and $x(0) = 0$. Fig 7.9 presents input signal $u(k)$ and output sequence for the plant modeled by (7.8). For these data nine-rule ANNBFIS are trained. The controller is tested after 100 iterations of learning. The desired plant output is specified by:

$$d(k) = 0.6 \sin\left(\frac{2\,\pi\,k}{250}\right) + 0.2 \sin\left(\frac{2\,\pi\,k}{50}\right). \tag{7.9}$$

The actual and desired outputs for plant (7.8) are presented in Fig. 7.10.

7.10
Application to channel equalization

In this section application of ANNBFIS to nonlinear digital channel equalization was investigated. Due to nonperfectness of transmission channel, interference, attenuation and noise received symbols are a nonlinear function of the past values of transmitted symbols. The transmitted data sequence denoted $s(k)$ is assumed as an independent symbols from set {-1, 1}. After transmitting thought channel this sequence is corrupted by an additive noise $e(k)$. The delayed and noisy outputs are used to obtain an estimate of signals transmitted by an equalizer. Graphically, the equalization

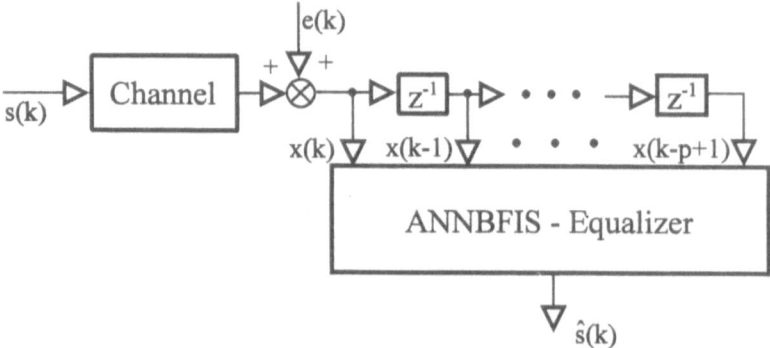

Fig. 7.11. An application of ANNBFIS to channel equalization process.

process is illustrated in Fig. 7.11.

Symbol p denotes the equalizer order. Let us assume that a nonlinear channel has the characteristic:

$$y(k) = s(k) + \frac{1}{2} s(k-1) - 0.9 \left[s(k) + \frac{1}{2} s(k-1) \right]^3, \tag{7.10}$$

and corruption is white Gaussian noise with zero mean and variance $E[e^2(k)]=0.2$. Assuming that symbols -1 and 1 have equal probabilities, 1000 training points are collected. These data are presented in Fig. 7.12.

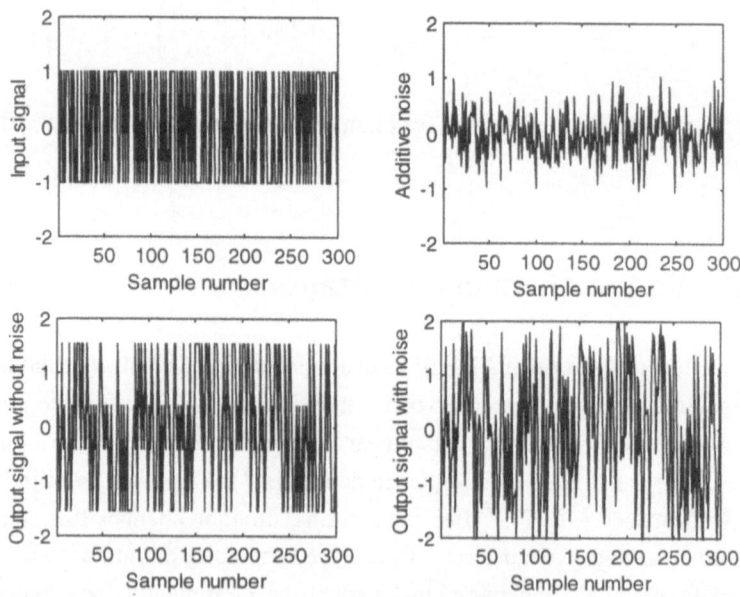

Fig. 7.12. The training sequences used to learning ANNBFIS.

Using these data 100 learning iterations of nine-rule ANNBFIS are performed. Fig. 7.13 presents optimal decision rule (right) obtained from Bayesian decision theory (with channel outputs without noise) and rule obtained by ANNBFIS (with training data).

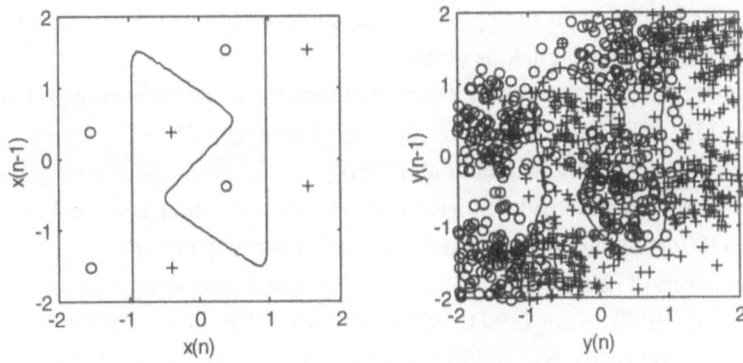

Fig. 7.13. Ideal (left) and actual (right) decision regions for channel equalization.

7.11
Summary

In this chapter we presented the following applications of artificial neural network based on fuzzy inference system (ANNBFIS):

- to chaotic time series prediction,
- to electrocardiographic (ECG) signal compression,
- to classification of Ripley synthetic data and diabetes in Pima Indians,
- a new classifier design method to famous iris and MONK's problems,
- to system identification of Box-Jenkins data,
- to control,
- to digital channel equalization.

Bibliographical notes

A very good introduction to chaotic systems and signals is presented in Schuster (1988). Application of this theory to biomedical signal processing is to be found in Fisher and Akai (1998). To compare results in Mackey-Glass chaotic time series prediction obtained by other authors see: Jang (1993a), Cho and Wang (1996), Wang (1994).

A good foundation to biological signal compression can be found in: Cohen (1986), Hamilton and Tompkins (1991).

For an exposition of classifier design methods the reader may consult Duda and Hart (1973), Tou and Gonzalez (1974), Fukunaga (1990), Ripley (1996), Devroye et al. (1996) and Miller et al. (1996).

The following is an introduction to the system identification: Box-Jenkins (1976), Eykhoff (1974), Söderström and Stoica (1994), Lindskog (1997).

Applications of neuro-fuzzy systems to control and communication are presented in: Jang et al. (1997), Wang (1994, 1998), Haykin and Thomson (1998), Jang (1992), Kim and Kosko (1996), Nie and Linkens (1993), Còrdon et al. (1997).

References

Abe, S., Lan, M.-S. (1995): A method for fuzzy rules extraction directly from numerical data and its application to pattern recognition. IEEE Trans. Fuzzy Systems 3(1), 18-28

Altug, S., Chow, M.-Y., Trussell, H.J. (1999): Heuristic constraints enforcement for training of and knowledge extraction from a fuzzy/neural architecture-Part II: Implementation and application. IEEE Trans. Fuzzy Systems 7(2), 151-159

Amari, S.-I. (1967): A theory of adaptive pattern classifiers. IEEE Trans. Electronic Computers 16, 299-307

Anderson, B.D.O., Moore, J.B. (1979): Optimal filtering. Prentice-Hall, New Jersey

Anderson, E. (1935): The irises of the gaspe peninsula. Bull. Amer. IRIS Soc. 59, 2-5

Babuška, R., Verbruggen, H.B. (1997): Constructing fuzzy models by product space clustering. In: Hellendoorn, H., Driankov, D. (eds.): Fuzzy model identification. Selected approaches. Springer, New York

Bajcsy, P., Ahuja, N. (1998): Location- and density-based hierarchical clustering using similarity analysis. IEEE Trans. Pattern Analysis and Machine Intelligence 20(9), 1011-1015

Baldi, P., Brunak, S. (1998): Bioinformatics. The machine learning approach. The MIT Press, Cambridge

Beni, G., Liu, X. (1994): A least biased fuzzy clustering method. IEEE Trans. Pattern Analysis and Machine Intelligence 16(9), 954-960

Bensaid, A.M., Hall, L.O., Bezdek, J.C., Clarke, L.P., Silbiger, M.L., Arrington, J.A., Murtagh, R.F. (1996): Validity-guided (re)clustering with application to image segmentation. IEEE Trans. Fuzzy Systems 4(2), 112-123

Berkan, R.C., Trubatch, S.L. (1997): Fuzzy systems design principles. Building fuzzy if-then rule bases. IEEE Press, New York

Bezdek, J.C., Harris, J.D. (1978): Fuzzy partitions and relations; An axiomatic basis for clustering. Fuzzy Sets and Systems 1, 111-127

Bezdek, J.C. (1980): A convergence theorem for the fuzzy ISODATA clustering algorithms. IEEE Trans. Pattern Analysis and Machine Intelligence 2(1), 1-8

Bezdek, J.C. (1982): Pattern recognition with fuzzy objective function algorithms. Plenum Press, New York London

Bezdek, J.C., Hathaway, R.J., Sabin, M.J., Tucker, W.T. (1987): Convergence theory for fuzzy c-means: counterexamples and repairs. IEEE Trans. System, Man and Cybernetics 17(5), 873-877

Bezdek, J.C., Pal, S.K. (eds.) (1992): Fuzzy models for pattern recognition. Methods that search for structures in data. IEEE Press, New York

Bezdek, J.C., Li, W.Q., Attikiouzel, Y., Windham, M. (1997): A geometric approach to cluster validity for normal mixtures. Soft Computing 1, 166-179

Bezdek, J.C., Pal, N.R. (1998): Some new indexes of cluster validity. IEEE Trans. System, Man and Cybernetics 28(3), 301-315

Bouchon-Meunier, B. (1991): Inferences with inaccuracy and uncertainty in expert systems. In: Kandel, A. (ed.): Fuzzy Expert Systems. CRC Press, London

Box, G.E.P., Jenkins, G.M. (1976): Time series analysis. Forecasting and control. Holden-Day, San Francisco

Bryson, A.E., Ho, Y.-C. (1969): Applied optimal control. Blaisdell, New York

Buckley, J.J., Hayashi, Y., Czogała, E. (1993): On the equivalence of neural nets and fuzzy expert systems, Fuzzy Sets and Systems 53, 129-134

Chen, C.H. (ed.) (1996): Fuzzy logic and neural network handbook. McGraw-Hill, Inc., New York

Chen, M.-S, Han, J., Yu, P.S. (1996): Data mining: an overview from a database perspective. IEEE Trans. Knowledge and Data Engineering 8(6), 866-883

Chen, J.-Q., Xi, Y.-G., Zhang, Z.-J. (1998): A clustering algorithm for fuzzy model identification. Fuzzy Sets and Systems 98, 319-329

Cheng, T.W.C., Goldgof, D.B., Hall, L.O. (1998): Fast fuzzy clustering. Fuzzy Sets and Systems 93, 49-56

Cho, K.B., Wang, B.H. (1996): Radial basis function based adaptive fuzzy systems and their applications to system identification and prediction. Fuzzy Sets and Systems 83, 325-339

Chow, M.-Y., Altug, S., Trussell, H.J. (1999): Heuristic constraints enforcement for training of and knowledge extraction from a fuzzy/neural architecture-Part I: Foundation. IEEE Trans. Fuzzy Systems 7(2), 143-150

Cohen, A. (1986): Biomedical signal processing, Vol. I: Time and frequency domains analysis, Vol. II: Compression and automatic recognition. CRC Press, Boca Raton

Cordòn, O., Herrera, F. (1997): Identification of linguistic fuzzy models by means of genetic algorithms. In: Hellendoorn, H., Driankov, D. (eds.): Fuzzy model identification. Selected approaches, Springer. New York

Cordòn, O., Herrera, F., Peregrin, A. (1997): Applicability of the fuzzy operators in the design of fuzzy logic controllers. Fuzzy Sets and Systems 86, 15-41

Czogała, E., Mrózek, A., Pawlak, Z. (1995): The idea of a rough fuzzy controller and its application to the stabilization of a pendulum-car system. Fuzzy Sets and Systems 72, 61-73

Czogała, E., Łęski, J. (1996): A new fuzzy inference system with moving consequents in if-then rules. Application to pattern recognition. Bulletin of the Polish Acad. of Science 45(4), 643-655

Czogała, E., Łęski, J. (1999): On equivalence of approximate reasoning results using different interpretations of if-then rules. Fuzzy Sets and Systems, (in print)

Davé, R.N., Bhaswan, K. (1992): Adaptive fuzzy c-shells clustering and detection of ellipses. IEEE Trans. Neural Networks 3(5), 643-662

Davé, R.N., Krishnapuram, R. (1997): Robust clustering methods: a unified view. IEEE Trans. Fuzzy Systems 5(2), 270-293

Delgado, M., Vila, M.A., Gomez-Skarmeta, A.F. (1997): Rapid prototyping of fuzzy models based on hierarchical clustering. In: Hellendoorn, H., Driankov, D. (eds.): Fuzzy model identification. Selected approaches. Springer, New York

Demirli, K., Türksen, I.B. (1994): A review of implications and the generalized modus ponens. Proceedings of the Third IEEE International Conference on Fuzzy Systems. IEEE Press, 1440-1445

Deutsch, R. (1965): Estimation theory. Prentice-Hall, Englewood Cliffs

Devroye, L., Györfi, L., Lugosi, G. (1996): A probabilistic theory of pattern recognition. Springer, New York

Drewniak, J. (1989): Fuzzy relation calculus. The Silesian University Press, Katowice

Drewniak, J. (1995): Equations in classes of fuzzy relations. Fuzzy Sets and Systems 75, 215-228

Dubois, D., Prade, H. (1991): Fuzzy sets in approximate reasoning, Part 1: Inference with possibility distributions. Fuzzy Sets and Systems 40, 143-202

Dubois, D., Lang, J., Prade, H. (1991): Fuzzy sets in approximate reasoning, Part 2: Logical approaches. Fuzzy Sets and Systems 40, 203-244

Dubois, D., Prade, H. (1996): What are fuzzy rules and how to use them. Fuzzy Sets and Systems 84, 169-185

Duda, R.O., Hart, P.E. (1973): Pattern classification and scene analysis. John Wiley & Sons, New York

Dunn, J.C. (1973): A fuzzy relative of the ISODATA process and its use in detecting compact well-separated cluster. Journal Cybernetics 3(3), 32-57

El-Sonbaty, Y., Ismail, M.A. (1998): Fuzzy clustering for symbolic data. IEEE Trans. Fuzzy Systems 6(2), 195-204

Elbert, T.F. (1984): Estimation and control of systems. Van Nostrand Reinhold Company, New York

Eltoft, T., deFigueiredo, R.J.P. (1998): A new neural network for cluster-detection-and-labeling. IEEE Trans. Neural Networks 9(5), 1021-1035

Emami, M.R., Türksen, I.B., Goldenberg, A.A. (1998): Development of a systematic methodology of fuzzy logic modeling. IEEE Trans. Fuzzy Systems 6(3), 346-361

Eykhoff, P. (1974): System identification. Parameter and state estimation. John Wiley & Sons, London

Fahlman, S.E. (1989): Faster learning variations on back-propagation: an empirical study. Proceedings of the 1988 Connectionist Models Summer School. In: Touretzky, D.S., Hinton, G.E., Sejnowski, T. (eds.), Morgan Kaufmann, San Mateo, 38-51

Feller, W. (1959): An introduction to probability theory and its applications. John Wiley, New York

Fisher, R., Akay, M. (1998): Fractal analysis of heart rate variability. In: Akay, M. (ed.): Time frequency and wavelets in biomedical signal processing. IEEE Press, New York

Flores-Sintas, A., Cadenas, J.M., Martin, F. (1998): A local geometrical properties application to fuzzy clustering. Fuzzy Sets and Systems 100, 245-256

Flores-Sintas, A., Cadenas, J.M., Martin, F. (1999): Membership functions in the fuzzy C-means algorithm. Fuzzy Sets and Systems 101, 49-58

Fodor, J.C. (1991): On fuzzy implication operators. Fuzzy Sets and Systems 42, 293-300

Fodor, J.C. (1993): Fuzzy connectives via matrix logic. Fuzzy Sets and Systems 56, 67-77

Fodor, J.C. (1993a): A new look at fuzzy connectives. Fuzzy Sets and Systems 57, 141-148

Fodor, J., Roubens, M. (1994): Fuzzy preference modelling and multicriteria decision support. Kluwer Academic, Dordrecht

Fodor, J.C. (1995): Contrapositive symmetry of fuzzy implications. Fuzzy Sets and Systems 69, 141-156

Fodor, J.C. (1996): Fuzzy implications. Proceedings on International Panel Conference on Soft and Intelligent Computing, Technical University of Budapest, 91-98

Fodor, J.C., Keresztfalvi, T. (1996): Generalized modus ponens and fuzzy connectives. Proceedings on International Panel Conference on Soft and Intelligent Computing, Technical University of Budapest , 99-106

Fukunaga, K. (1990): Introduction to statistical pattern recognition. 2nd edn. Academic Press, San Diego

Gath, I., Geva, A.B. (1989): Unsupervised optimal fuzzy clustering. IEEE Trans. Pattern Analysis and Machine Intelligence 11(7), 773-781

Giles, R (1976): Lukasiewicz logic and fuzzy set theory. International Journal Man-Machine Studies 8, 313-327

Gill, P., Murray, W., Wright, M. (1981): Practical optimization. Academic Press, New York

Goldberg, D.E. (1989): Genetic algorithms in serch, optimization and machine learning. Addison-Wesley, New York

Gustafson, D.E., Kessel, W.C. (1979): Fuzzy clustering with a fuzzy covariance matrix. Proceedings IEEE CDC, San Diego, 761-766

Hamilton, P.S., Tompkins, W.C. (1991): Compression of the ambulatory ECG by average beat subtraction and residual differencing. IEEE Trans. Biomed. Eng. 38, 253-259,

Hathaway, R.J., Bezdek, J.C. (1993): Switching regression models and fuzzy clustering. IEEE Trans. Fuzzy Systems 1(3), 195-204

Hathaway, R.J., Bezdek, J.C. (1995): Optimization of clustering criteria by reformulation. IEEE Trans. Fuzzy Systems 3(2), 241-245

Haykin, S, Thomson, D.J. (1998): Signal detection in a nonstationary environment reformulated as an adaptive pattern classification problem. Proceedings IEEE 86(11), 2325-2344

Haykin, S. (1999): Neural networks. A comprehensive foundation. Prentice Hall Int., Upper Saddle River

Hebb, D.O. (1949): The organization of behavior. Wiley, New York

Hertz, J., Krogh, A., Palmer, R.G. (1991): Introduction to the theory of neural computing. Addison-Wesley, Redwood City

Hinton, G.E. (1986): Learning distributed representations of concepts. Proceedings of the 8th Annual Conference of the Cognitive Science Society. Erlban, Hillsdale, 1-12

Hirota, K. (1993): Industrial applications of fuzzy technology. Springer-Verlag, Tokyo

Hofmann, T., Buhmann, J.M. (1997): Pairwise data clustering by deterministic annealing. IEEE Trans. Pattern Analysis and Machine Intelligence 19(1), 1-14

Holland, J.H. (1975): Adaptation in natural and artificial systems. ANN Arbor, The University of Michigan Press

Hollatz, J. (1997): Fuzzy identification using methods of intelligent data analysis. In: Hellendoorn, H., Driankov, D. (eds.): Fuzzy model identification. Selected approaches. Springer, New York

Horikawa, S., Furuhashi, T., Uchikawa, Y. (1992): On fuzzy modeling using fuzzy neural networks with the back-propagation algorithm. IEEE Trans. Neural Networks 4, 801-806

Imai, H., Tanaka, A., Miyakoshi, M. (1998): A method of identifying influential data in fuzzy clustering. IEEE Trans. Fuzzy Systems 6(1), 90-101

Ishibuchi, H., Fujioka, R., Tanaka, H. (1993): Neural networks that learn from fuzzy if-then rules. IEEE Trans. Fuzzy Systems 1(2), 85-97

Jang, J.-S.R. (1992): Self-learning fuzzy controllers based on temporal back propagation. IEEE Trans. Neural Networks 3(5), 714-723

Jang, J.-S.R., Sun, C.-T. (1993): Functional equivalence between radial basis function networks and fuzzy inference systems. IEEE Trans. Neural Networks 4(1), 156-159

Jang, J.-S.R. (1993a): ANFIS: adaptive-network-based fuzzy inference system. IEEE Trans.Systems, Man and Cybernetics 23(3), 665-685

Jang, J.-S.R. (1994): Structure determination in fuzzy modeling: a fuzzy CART approach. Proceedings of the Third IEEE International Conference on Fuzzy Systems, IEEE Press,

Jang, J.-S.R. (1995): Neuro-fuzzy modeling and control. Proceedings IEEE 83(3), 378-406

Jang, J.-S.R. (1996): Input selection for ANFIS learning. Proceedings on the Fifth IEEE International Conference on Fuzzy Systems, IEEE Press, 1493-1499

Jang, J.-S.R., Sun, C.-T., Mizutani, E. (1997): Neuro-fuzzy and soft computing. A computational approach to learning and machine intelligence. Prentice-Hall, Upper Saddle River

Jenei, S., Fodor, J.C. (1998): On continuous triangular norms. Fuzzy Sets and Systems 100, 273-282

Kacprzyk, J., Iwański, C. (1992): Fuzzy logic with linguistic quantifiers in inductive learning. In: Zadeh, L.A., Kacprzyk, J. (eds.) Fuzzy logic for the management of uncertainty. Wiley, New York

Kalouptsidis, N. (1997): Signal processing systems. Theory and design. John Wiley & Sons Inc., New York

Karayiannis, N.B., Bezdek, J.C., Pal, N.R., Hathaway, R.J., Pai, P.-I. (1996): Repairs to GLVQ: a new family of competitive learning schemes. IEEE Trans. Neural Networks 7(5), 1062-1071

Karayiannis, N.B., Pai, P.-I. (1996): Fuzzy algorithms for learning vector quantization. IEEE Trans. Neural Networks 7(5), 1196-1211

Karayiannis, N.B. (1996): Weighted fuzzy learning vector quantization and weighted generalized fuzzy c-means algorithms. Proceedings of the Fifth IEEE International Conference on Fuzzy System. IEEE Press, 773-779

Karayiannis, N.B. (1996a): Generalized fuzzy c-means algorithm. Proceedings of the Fifth IEEE International Conference on Fuzzy System. IEEE Press, 1036-1042

Karayiannis, N.B. (1996b): Fuzzy and possibilistic clustering algorithms based on generalized reformulation. Proceedings of the Fifth IEEE International Conference on Fuzzy System. IEEE Press, 1393-1399

Karayiannis, N.B., Bezdek, J.C. (1997): An integrated approach to fuzzy learning vector quantization and fuzzy c-means clustering. IEEE Trans. Fuzzy Systems 5(4), 622-628

Kartalopoulos, S.V. (1996): Understanding neural networks and fuzzy logic. Basic concepts and applications. IEEE Press, New York

Keller, J.M., Tahani, H. (1992): Implementation of conjunctive and disjunctive fuzzy logic rules with neural networks. Journal Approximate Reasoning 6, 221-240

Kerre, E.E. (1992): A comparative study of the behavior of some popular fuzzy implication operators on the generalized modus ponens. In: Zadeh, L.A., Kacprzyk, J. (eds.) Fuzzy logic for the management of uncertainty. Wiley, New York

Kersten, P.R. (1997): Implementation issues in the fuzzy c-medians clustering algorithm. Proceedings of the Sixth IEEE International Conference on Fuzzy Systems. IEEE Press, 957-962

Khanna, T. (1990): Foundations of neural network. Addison-Wesley, Reading

Kim, E., Park, M., Ji, S., Park, M. (1997): A new approach to fuzzy modeling. IEEE Trans. Fuzzy Systems 5(3), 328-337

Kim, E., Park, M., Kim, S., Park, M. (1998): A transformed input-domain approach to fuzzy modeling. IEEE Trans. Fuzzy Systems 6(4), 596-604

Kim, H.M., Kosko, B. (1996): Fuzzy prediction and filtering in impulsive noise. Fuzzy Sets and Systems 77, 15-33

Kirkpatrick, S., Gelatt, C., Vecchi, M. (1983): Optimization by simulated annealing. Science 220, 671-680

Klement, E.P., Navara, M. (1999): A survey on different triangular norm-based fuzzy logics. Fuzzy Sets and Systems 101, 241-251

Kobayashi, K. (1998): Self-organizing wavelet-based neural network. In: Akay, M. (ed.): Time frequency and wavelets in biomedical signal processing. IEEE Press, New York

Kóczy, L.T., Hirota, K. (1993): Approximate reasoning by linear rule interpolation and general approximation. International Journal of Approximate Reasoning 9, 197-225

Kohonen, T. (1982): Self-organized formation of topologically correct feature maps. Biological Cybernetics 43, 59-69

Kohonen, T. (1982a): Analysis of a simple self-organizing process. Biological Cybernetics 43, 135-140,

Kohonen, T. (1988): Self-organization and associative memory. Springer-Verlag, New York, 3rd ed.

Kosko, B. (1987): Fuzzy associative memories, in: Kandel. A. (ed.): Fuzzy expert systems. CRC Press, Boca Raton

Kosko, B. (1997): Fuzzy engineering. Prentice-Hall, Upper Saddle River

Krishnapuram, R., Nasraoui, O., Frigui, H. (1992): The fuzzyc spherical shells algotithm: a new approach. IEEE Trans. Neural Networks 3(5), 663-671

Krishnapuram, R., Keller, J.M. (1993): A possibilistic approach to clustering. IEEE Trans. Fuzzy Systems 1(2), 98-110

Krishnapuram, R., Frigui, H., Nasraoui, O. (1995): Fuzzy and possibilistic shell clustering algorithms and their application to boundary detection and surface approximation - Part I. IEEE Trans. Fuzzy Systems 3(1), 29-43

Krishnapuram, R., Frigui, H., Nasraoui, O. (1995a): Fuzzy and possibilistic shell clustering algorithms and their application to boundary detection and surface approximation - Part II. IEEE Trans. Fuzzy Systems 3(1), 44-60

Krishnapuram, R., Kim, J. (1996): A clustering algorithm based on minimum volume, Proceedings of the Fifth IEEE International Conference on Fuzzy System, IEEE Press, 1387-1392

Kundu, S, Chen, J. (1998): Fuzzy logic or Lukasiewicz logic: a clarification. Fuzzy Sets and Systems 95, 369-379

Larminat, P., Thomas, Y. (1977): Automatique des systemes lineaires. Flammarion Sciences, Paris

Lee, P.G., Lee, K.K., Jeon, Gi.J. (1995): An index of applicability for the decomposition method of multivariable fuzzy systems. IEEE Trans. Fuzzy Systems 3(3), 364-369

Li, R.-P., Mukaidono, M. (1999): Gaussian clustering method based on maximum-fuzzy-entropy interpretation. Fuzzy Sets and Systems 102, 253-258

Lindskog, P. (1997): Fuzzy identification from a gray box modeling point of view. In: Hellendoorn, H., Driankov, D. (eds.): Fuzzy model identification. Selected approaches. Springer, New York

Lippmann, R.P. (1987): An introduction to computing with neural nets. IEEE ASSP Mag. 4, 4-22

Lygeros, J. (1997): A formal approach to fuzzy modeling. IEEE Trans. Fuzzy Systems 5(3), 317-325

Łęski, J., Czogała, E. (1997): A new artificial neural network based fuzzy inference system with moving consequents in if-then rules. BUSEFAL 71, 72-81

Łęski, J., Czogała, E. (1999): A new artificial neural network based fuzzy inference system with moving consequents in if-then rules and it's applications. Fuzzy Sets and Systems 108, 289-297

Łukasiewicz, J. (1963): Elements of mathematical logic. Pergamon Press, Oxford. [Polish original: 2nd edn., PWN, Warszawa, 1958]

Maeda, H. (1996): An investigation on the spread of fuzziness in multi-stage approximate reasoning by pictorial representation - Under sup-min composition and triangular type membership function. Fuzzy Sets and Systems 80, 133-148

Maeda, H., Nobusada, Y. (1998): A study on the parallel computability of multi-fold approximate reasoning. Fuzzy Sets and Systems 97, 129-144

Maren, A.J., Harston, C.T., Pap, R.M. (1990): Handbook of neural computing applications. Academic Press, San Diego

Marichal, J.,-L., Mathonet, P. (1999): A characterization of the ordered weighted averaging functions based on the ordered bisymmetry. IEEE Trans. Fuzzy Systems 7(1), 93-96

McCulloch, W.S., Pitts, W. (1943): A logical calculus of the ideas imminent in nervous activity, Bulletin of Math.Biophys. 5, 115-133

Meditch, J.S. (1969): Stochastic optimal linear estimation and control. McGraw-Hill, New York

Mendel, J.M. (1995): Fuzzy logic systems for engineering: a tutorial. Proceedings of IEEE 83(3), 345-377

Metropolis, N., Rosenbluth, A.W., Rosenbluth, N.M., Teller, A.H., Teller, A.H., Teller, E. (1953): Equation of state calculations by fast computing machines. Journal of Chemical Physics 21(6), 1087-1092

Miller, D., Rao, A.V., Rose, K., Gersho, A. (1996): A global optimization technique for statistical classifier design. IEEE Trans. Signal Processing 44(12), 3108-3121

Mitra, S., Pal, S.K. (1995): Fuzzy multi-layer perceptron, inferencing and rule generation. IEEE Trans. Neural Networks 6, 51-63

Mitra, S., Pal, S.K. (1996): Fuzzy self-organization, inferencing and rule generation. IEEE Trans. System, Man and Cybernetics 26(5), 608-619

Mizumoto, M., Zimmermann, H.J. (1982): Comparison of fuzzy reasoning methods. Fuzzy Sets and Systems 8, 253-283

Mouzouris, G.C., Mendel, J.M. (1997): Nonsingleton fuzzy logic systems: theory and application. IEEE Trans. Fuzzy Systems 5(1), 56-71

Nakoula, Y., Galichet, S., Foulloy, L. (1997): Identification of linguistic fuzzy models based on learning. In: Hellendoorn, H., Driankov, D. (eds.): Fuzzy model identification. Selected approaches. Springer, New York

Nie, J., Linkens, D.A. (1993): Learning control using fuzzified self-organizing radial basis function network. IEEE Trans. Fuzzy Systems 1(4), 280-287

Nozaki, K., Ishibuchi, H., Tanaka, H. (1997): A simple but powerful heuristic method for generating fuzzy rules from numerical data. Fuzzy Sets and Systems 86, 251-270

Pal, N.R., Bezdek, J.C. (1994): Measuring fuzzy uncertainty. IEEE Trans. Fuzzy Systems 2(2), 107-118

Pal, N.R., Bezdek, J.C. (1995): On cluster validity for the fuzzy c-means model. IEEE Trans. Fuzzy Systems 3(3), 370-379

Pal, N.R., Pal, K., Bezdek, J.C. (1997): A mixed c-means clustering model. Proceedings of the Sixth IEEE International Conference on Fuzzy Systems, IEEE Press, 11-22

Pao, Y.-H. (1989): Adaptive pattern recognition and neural networks. Addison-Wesley, New York

Park, M.-K., Ji, S.-H., Kim, E.-T., Park, M. (1997): Identification of Takagi-Sugeno fuzzy models via clustering and Hough transform. In: Hellendoorn, H., Driankov, D. (eds.): Fuzzy model identification. Selected approaches. Springer, New York

Pawlak, Z. (1991): Rough sets. Theoretical aspects of reasoning about data. Kluwer, Dordrecht

Pawlak, Z. (1992): Rough sets: a new approach to vagueness. In: Zadeh, L.A., Kacprzyk, J. (eds.) Fuzzy logic for the management of uncertainty. Wiley, New York

Pedrycz, W, (1984): An identification algorithm in fuzzy relational systems. Fuzzy Sets and Systems 13, 153-167

Pedrycz, W. (1993): Fuzzy control and fuzzy systems. 2nd ed. John Wiley & Sons, New York

Pedrycz, W., Reformat, M. (1997): Rule-based modeling of nonlinear relationships. IEEE Trans. Fuzzy Systems 5(2), 256-269

Pedrycz, W. (1998): Conditional fuzzy clustering in the design of radial basis function neural network. IEEE Trans. Neural Networks 9(4), 601-612

Pedrycz, W. (1998a): Fuzzy set technology in knowledge discovery. Fuzzy Sets and Systems 98, 279-290

Pedrycz, W. (1998b): Shadowed sets: Representing and processing fuzzy sets. IEEE Trans. Systems, Man and Cybernetics, B: Cybernetics 28(1), 103-108

Rao, A.V., Miller, D., Rose, K., Gersho, A. (1997): Mixture of experts regression modeling by deterministic annealing. IEEE Trans. Signal Processing 45(11), 2811-2819

Rasiowa, H. (1992): Toward fuzzy logic. In: Zadeh, L.A., Kacprzyk, J. (eds.) Fuzzy logic for the management of uncertainty. Wiley, New York

Rhee, H.-S., Oh, K.-W. (1996): A validity measure for fuzzy clustering and its use in selecting optimal number of clusters. Proceedings of the Fifth IEEE International Conference on Fuzzy System, IEEE Press, 1020-1025

Ripley, B.D. (1996): Pattern recognition and neural network. Cambridge University Press, Cambridge New York Melbourne

Ritter, H., Schulten, K. (1986): On the stationary state of the Kohonen self-organizing sensory mapping. Biological Cybernetics 54, 234-249

Rose, K. (1991): Deterministic annealing, clustering and optimization. Ph.D. Thesis. California Inst. Tech., Pasadena

Rose, K., Gurewitz, E., Fox, G.C. (1992): Vector quantization by deterministic annealing. IEEE Trans. Information Theory 38(4), 1249-1257

Rose, K., Gurewitz, E., Fox, G.C. (1993): Constrained clustering as an optimization method. IEEE Trans. Pattern Analysis and Machine Intelligence 15(8), 785-794

Rose, K. (1998): Deterministic annealing for clustering, compression, classification, regression, and related optimization problems. Proceedings IEEE 86(11), 2210-2239

Rosenblatt, F. (1958): The perceptron: a probabilistic model for information storage and organization in the brain. Psychol. Rev. 65(6), 386-408

Rudin, W. (1976): Principles of mathematical analysis. McGraw-Hill, New York

Rumelhart, D.E., McClelland, J.L. (1986): Parallel distributed processing: exploration in the microstructure of cognition. Volume I. Foundations. The MIT Press, Cambridge

Rumelhart, D.E., Hinton, G.E., Williams, R.J. (1986a): Learning representations by back-propagating errors. Nature 323(9), 533-536

Runkler, T.A., Bezdek, J.C. (1999): Function approximation with polynomial membership functions and alternating cluster estimation. Fuzzy Sets and Systems 101, 207-218

Ruspini, E.H. (1969): A new approach to clustering. Inform. Control 15(1), 22-32

Sabin, M.J. (1987): Convergence and consistency of fuzzy c-means/ISODATA algorithms. IEEE Trans. Pattern Analysis and Machine intelligence 9(5), 661-668

Sato, M., Sato, Y., Jain, L.C. (1997): Fuzzy clustering models and applications. Springer, New York

Scales, L.E. (1985): Introduction to nonlinear optimization. Macmillan, London

Schuster, H.G. (1988): Deterministic chaos. 2nd edn. VCH Verlagsgesellschaft, New York

Shi. Y., Eberhart, R., Chen, Y. (1999): Implementation of evolutionary fuzzy systems. IEEE Trans. Fuzzy Systems 7(2), 109-119

Shukhat, B. (1998): Supervised fuzzy pattern recognition. Fuzzy Sets and Systems 100, 257-265

Söderström, T., Stoica, P. (1994): System identification. Prentice-Hall, New York

Su, M.-C. (1997): Identification of singleton fuzzy models via fuzzy hyperrectangular composite Neural Network. In: Hellendoorn, H., Driankov, D. (eds.): Fuzzy model identification. Selected approaches. Springer, New York

Sugeno, M., Kang, G.T. (1988): Structure identification of fuzzy model. Fuzzy Sets and Systems 28, 15-33

Sugeno, M., Yasukawa, T. (1994): Qualitative modeling based on numerical data and knowledge data and its application to control. In: Zurada, J.M., Marks II, R.J., Robinson, C.J. (eds.), IEEE Press, Piscataway

Szu, H., Hartley, R. (1987): Fast simulated annealing. Physics Letters 122, 157-162

Takagi, T., Sugeno, M. (1985): Fuzzy identification of systems and its application to modeling and control. IEEE Trans. Systems, Man and Cybernetics 15(1), 116-132

Takagi, H., Hayashi, I. (1991): NN-driven fuzzy reasoning. Journal Approximate Reasoning 5(3), 191-212

Thrun, S. B., Bala, J., Bloedorn, E., Bratko, I., Cestnik, B., Cheng, J., De Jong, K., Džeroski, S., Fahlman, S.E., Fisher, D., Hamann, R., Kaufman, K., Keller, S., Kononenko, I., Kreuziger, J., Michalski, R.S., Mitchell, T., Pachowicz, P., Reich, Y., Vafaie, H., Van de Welde, W., Wenzel, W., Wnek, J., Zhang, J. (1991): The MONK's promlems. A performance comparison of different learning algorithms. Scientific Report CMU-CS-91-197, Carnegie Mellon University

Tou, J.T., Gonzalez, R.C. (1974): Pattern recognition principles. Adison-Wesley, London

Tsao, E.C.-K., Bezdek, J.C., Pal, N.R. (1994): Fuzzy Kohonen clustering networks. Pattern Recognition 27(5), 757-764

Türksen, I.B. (1988): An approximate analogical reasoning approach based on similarity measures. IEEE Trans. Systems, Man and Cybernetics 18(6), 1049-1056

Türksen, I.B. (1989): Four methods of approximate reasoning with interval-valued fuzzy sets. International Journal of Approximate Reasoning 3, 121-142

Türksen, I.B., Kreinovich, V., Yager, R.R. (1998): A new class of fuzzy implications. Axioms of fuzzy implication revisited. Fuzzy Sets and Systems 100, 267-272

Vergara, V., Moraga, C. (1997): Optimization of fuzzy models by global numeric optimization. In: Hellendoorn, H., Driankov, D. (eds.): Fuzzy model identification. Selected approaches. Springer, New York

Wang, C.-H., Hong, T.-P., Tseng, S.-S. (1999): Integrating fuzzy knowledge by genetic algorithms. IEEE Trans. Evolutionary Computation 2(4), 138-149

Wang, L.-X, Mendel, J.M. (1992): Genetating fuzzy rules by learning from examples. IEEE Trans. Systems, Man and Cybernetics 22, 1414-1427

Wang, L.-X. (1994): Adaptive fuzzy systems and control. Prentice-Hall, New York

Wang, L.-X. (1998): A course in fuzzy systems and control. Prentice-Hall, New York

Wang, X.L. (1998a): Universal approximation by hierarchical fuzzy systems. Fuzzy Sets and Systems 93, 223-230

Weber, S. (1983): A general concept of fuzzy connectives, negations and implications based on t-norms and t-conorms. Fuzzy Sets and Systems 11, 115-134

Werbos, P.J. (1974): Beyond regression: new tools for prediction and analysis in the behavioural sciences. Ph.D. Thesis, Harvard University

Whalen, T., Schott, B. (1992): Presumption, prejudice, and regularity in fuzzy material implication. In: Zadeh, L.A., Kacprzyk, J. (eds.) Fuzzy logic for the management of uncertainty. Wiley, New York

Widrow, B., Hoff, M.E. (1960): Adaptive switching circuits. IRE WESCON Convention Record 4, 96-104

Windham, M.P. (1982): Cluster validity for the fuzzy c-means clustering algotithm. IEEE Trans. Pattern Analysis and Machine Intelligence 4(4), 357-363

Windham, M.P. (1983): Geometrical fuzzy clustering algorithms. Fuzzy Sets and Systems 10, 271-279

Xie, X.L., Beni, G. (1991): A validity measure for fuzzy clustering. IEEE Trans. Pattern Analysis and Machine Intelligence 13(8), 841-847

Yager, R.R., Larsen, H.L. (1991): On discovering potential inconsistencies in validating uncertain knowledge bases by reflecting on the input. IEEE Trans. Systems, Man and Cybernetics 21(4), 790-801

Yager, R.R. (1996): On the interpretation of fuzzy it then rules. Applied Intelligence 6, 141-151

Yam, Y., Baranyi, P., Yang, C.-T. (1999): Reduction of fuzzy rule base via singular value decomposition. IEEE Trans. Fuzzy Systems 7(2), 120-132

Yen, J., Wang, L. (1998): Application of statistical information criteria for optimal fuzzy model construction. IEEE Trans. Fuzzy Systems 6(3), 362-371

Yen, J., Wang, L., Gillespie, C.W. (1998): Improving the interpretability of TSK fuzzy models by combining global learning and local learning. IEEE Trans. Fuzzy Systems 6(4), 530-537

Zadeh, L.A. (1965): Fuzzy sets. Information and Control 8, 338-353

Zadeh, L.A. (1968): Fuzzy algorithms. Information and Control 12, 94-102

Zadeh, L.A. (1971): Similarity relations and fuzzy orderings. Inform.Sci. 3, 177-200

Zadeh, L.A. (1973): Outline of a new approach to the analysis of complex systems and decision processes. IEEE Trans. Systems, Man and Cybernetics 3(1), 28-44

Zadeh, L.A. (1978): PRUF - a meaning representation language for natural languages. International Journal Man-Machine Studies 10, 395-460

Zadeh, L.A. (1978a): Fuzzy sets as a basis for a theory of possibility. Fuzzy Sets and Systems 1, 3-28

Zadeh, L.A. (1996): Fuzzy logic = computing with words. IEEE Trans. Fuzzy Systems 4(2), 103-111

Zadeh, L.A. (1997): Toward a theory of fuzzy information granulation and its centrality in human reasoning and fuzzy logic. Fuzzy Sets and Systems 90, 25-41

Zimmermann, H.J. (1985): Fuzzy set theory and its application. Kluwer-Nijhoff, Boston

Zhang, Q., Benveniste, A. (1992): Wavelet networks. IEEE Trans. Neural Networks 3(6), 889-898

Zhang, Q. (1998): Single side scaling wavelet frame and neural network. In: Akay, M. (ed.): Time frequency and wavelets in biomedical signal processing. IEEE Press, New York

List of notations and abbreviations

Studies in Fuzziness and Soft Computing